PREACHING LIKE PAUL

PREACHING LIKE PAUL

Homiletical Wisdom for Today

James W. Thompson

Westminster John Knox Press
Louisville, Kentucky

Book design by Sharon Adams
Cover design by Mark Abrams

First edition
Published by Westminster John Knox Press
Louisville, Kentucky

This book is printed on acid-free paper that meets the American National Standards Institute Z39.48 standard. ∞

PRINTED IN THE UNITED STATES OF AMERICA
01 02 03 04 05 06 07 08 09 10 — 10 9 8 7 6 5 4 3 2 1

Library of Congress Cataloging-in-Publication Data
Thompson, James, 1942–
    Preaching like Paul / James W. Thompson.
        p. cm.
    Includes bibliographical references and index.
    ISBN 0-664-22294-3
        1. Preaching. 2. Paul, the Apostle, Saint. 3. Bible. N.T. Epistles of Paul—
Criticism, interpretation, etc. I. Title

BV4211.2.T49 2000
251—dc21   00-034943

For Carolyn

Contents

Preface   ix

Abbreviations   x

Introduction: The Pauline Gospel in a Post-Christian Culture   1

  1. Paul as the Model for Preaching   21

  2. Paul's Evangelistic and Pastoral Preaching   37

  3. The Shape of Paul's Preaching   61

  4. What Is Pastoral Preaching?   85

  5. Explaining Ourselves: Preaching and Theology   107

  6. Preaching as Remembering   127

Conclusion: Reflections on Paul and the Preaching Ministry   143

Appendix: Preaching Paul's Sermons after Him   149

Index of Names   167

Index of Scripture   171

Index of Greek and Latin Sources   177

Preface

The recent literature on homiletics has challenged preachers to re-vision the role of the *sermon* in forming Christian consciousness. In this book I offer reflections on the agenda for the entire *preaching ministry*, engaging in a dialogue between New Testament studies, my own field of research, and the literature on preaching and theology. I am indebted to many people whose insights and assistance with research have helped me complete this project.

I am grateful to my colleagues at the Graduate School of Theology at Abilene Christian University for their encouragement and helpful suggestions. Dr. Timothy Sensing read earlier drafts of this book and offered bibliographic guidance in the literature of preaching. Frederick Aquino was a valued conversation partner who often clarified issues involving the relationship between preaching and systematic theology. I am also grateful for the encouragement that I received from Dr. Charles Siburt and Dr. Jack Reese.

Dr. Carey C. Newman of Westminster John Knox Press patiently read earlier drafts of this book and offered invaluable critique and guidance as he challenged me to strengthen the argument at numerous points. I am indebted to him for his helpful suggestions. Any weaknesses in the presentation are my own.

Graduate assistants at Abilene Christian University helped with the research and proofreading. I am grateful to Hal Runkel, Todd Foster, and Eli Perkins for their assistance with proofreading and research.

I dedicate this book to my wife, Carolyn. She has been a constant source of encouragement, a conversation partner, and a demanding copyeditor.

Abbreviations

AnBib	Analecta Biblica
ANRW	*Aufstieg und Niedergang der römischen Welt*
ATR	*Anglican Theological Review*
AUSS	*Andrews University Seminary Studies*
BTB	*Biblical Theology Bulletin*
CB	Coniectanea Biblica
CBQ	*Catholic Biblical Quarterly*
DNTT	*Dictionary of New Testament Theology*
EDNT	*Exegetical Dictionary of the New Testament*
EKK	Evangelisch-Katholischer Kommentar
ETS	ETS Studies
FRLANT	Forschungen zur Religion und Literatur des Alten und Neuen Testaments
HTR	*Harvard Theological Review*
JAAR	*Journal of the American Academy of Religion*
JBL	*Journal of Biblical Literature*
JSNTSS	Journal for the Study of the New Testament Supplement Series
JSOT	Journal for the Study of the Old Testament
JSOTSup	Journal for the Study of the Old Testament Supplement Series
KEKNT	Kritisch-Exegetischer Kommentar über das Neue Testament
LEC	Library of Early Christianity
NABPR	National Association of Baptist Professors of Religion
NTS	*New Testament Studies*
NovT	*Novum Testamentum*
NovTSup	Novum Testamentum Supplements
SBLDS	Society of Biblical Literature Dissertation Series
SBLSP	*Society of Biblical Literature Seminar Papers*
SbB	Stuttgarter biblische Beiträge
SNTSMS	Society for New Testament Studies Monograph Series

TH	Theologie Historique
TLZ	*Theologische Literaturzeitung*
WBC	Word Biblical Commentary
WUNT	Wissenschaftliche Untersuchungen zum Neuen Testament
ZNW	*Zeitschrift für die neutestamentliche Wissenschaft und die Kunde der älteren Kirche*

The Pauline Gospel
in a Post-Christian Culture

The "new homiletic" is a generation old now. We heard the call for a new approach to preaching almost three decades ago, and we exchanged the "old wineskins" of argumentative preaching for the "new wineskins" of narrative. A revolution in homiletics occurred, meeting scarcely any resistance. Numerous books and articles, with their chorus of voices challenging traditional views of the sermon, became the homiletics textbooks throughout North America, ensuring the impact of the new homiletics on congregations everywhere.

The sermon has been the constant feature in the worship of Judaism and Christianity for more than two millennia. However, as historians of preaching have observed, at strategic moments preaching has responded to changed cultural situations, and new sermon strategies have replaced older forms, revitalizing the preaching ministry. Recognizing that traditional preaching could not communicate effectively with listeners in a Christian culture who had grown bored with the predictability of older sermon forms and with the familiarity of the biblical story, advocates of the new homiletics offered a solution.

Today we preach to the children of those listeners whom we were attempting to address with revitalized sermons a generation ago. These children, however, have grown up in a post-Christian culture that is not familiar with the Bible. Unlike their parents, whose familiarity with the Christian faith produced the boredom the new homiletics sought to overcome, many Christians today do not know the basics of the Christian message. This change in the cultural situation is crucial to recognize, and it creates special challenges for preachers at the beginning of the new millennium. A homiletic that solved the problems of preaching in the final days of

1

a Christian culture is not likely to be the solution to the problems of preaching in a post-Christian culture. Time may ultimately separate the fads from the lasting contributions to homiletic thought, but we who live between the times must proclaim the gospel now with the confidence that we know what we are doing.

New Wine and Old Wineskins for Preaching

The "old wineskins" of homiletics, according to the general consensus, are the sermons built around the "conceptual method" that dominated preaching for the past two centuries. Preaching, according to the view of the "old wineskins," involves the development of an argument in support of a basic idea.[1] The preacher either explores a topic or "distills" from the text a *basic idea* or *proposition*, which becomes the basis for the sermon.[2] The main idea then becomes the basis for an outline consisting of a series of "points" supported by the addition of appropriate illustrations, an introduction, and a conclusion.[3] The sermon becomes a rational exercise whereby the preacher attempts to "get the idea across" to the congregation through explanation, illustration, and application. However, recent homileticians regard this emphasis on rational persuasion as an alien intrusion into a preaching tradition that once looked and sounded very different from the one that we have inherited.

The tradition of rational persuasion may be the result of several factors. Some have suggested that it is the offspring of the linear mind-set that accompanied the culture of the printing press; rational persuasion is meant for the eye rather than the ear.[4] David Buttrick has suggested that it is distinctively modern—that its insistence on transmitting a fixed truth fits well with the mentality of the

---

1. David M. Greenhaw, "As One with Authority," in *Intersections: Post-Critical Studies in Preaching*, ed. Richard Eslinger (Grand Rapids: Eerdmans, 1994), 106.

2. See David Buttrick, *A Captive Voice* (Louisville, Ky.: Westminster John Knox, 1994), 81.

3. See John Broadus, *On the Preparation and Delivery of Sermons*, 4th ed. (New York: Harper & Row, 1979), 78–198. Cf. Ilion T. Jones, *Principles and Practice of Preaching* (New York: Abingdon, 1956), 87–102.

4. See Clyde Fant, *Preaching for Today*, rev. ed. (San Francisco: Harper & Row, 1987), 159–64; Richard Jensen, *Telling the Story* (Minneapolis: Augsburg, 1980), 26ff.; Richard Jensen, *Thinking in Story: Preaching in a Post-literate Age* (Lima, Ohio: CSS, 1993).

Enlightenment.[5] The homiletic literature also identifies Aristotelian rhetoric as a primary source of this turn to rational persuasion.[6] Indeed, contemporary homileticians commonly attribute much that is wrong with traditional preaching to Aristotelian rhetoric. According to this view, in the golden age of first-century Christianity, narrative was the dominant mode of preaching. It was then corrupted in the second century by Aristotelian rhetoric when the church moved onto Hellenistic soil.[7] From the time of Augustine, preachers turned to the Bible for the *content* of preaching and to Aristotle for the *form* and *style* of the sermon, entering into a marriage that was doomed to fail.[8]

Whereas in the "old wineskins" of preaching in the Aristotelian tradition the task of the preacher was to "get an idea across" through rational persuasion, in the "new wineskins" of homiletic thought the preacher's task is to lead the congregation to "experience" the dynamic of the text—including its aesthetic and affective dimensions.[9] This focus on the listener's experience of the text requires that preachers give special attention to two aspects of the communication process. In the first place, if the listener is to "experience" the text, preachers must pay special attention to the actual phenomenon of the sermon as it is experienced by their congregations.[10] They will not regard congregations as passive recipients of the sermon, but invite them to participate in the preacher's journey and draw their own conclusions. The sermon will proceed by identifying with the concrete realities in the lives of the hearers. Preachers also adapt the form of the message to an audience shaped by an educational experience that has conditioned listeners to resist authoritative pronouncements. Consequently, preaching that is

---

5. Buttrick, *A Captive Voice*, 81.

6. Thomas Troeger, *Imagining a Sermon* (Nashville: Abingdon, 1990), 29; Paul Scott Wilson, *The Practice of Preaching* (Nashville: Abingdon, 1995), 205; Fred Craddock, *As One without Authority* (Nashville: Abingdon, 1971), 54.

7. Don M. Wardlaw, "The Need for New Shapes," in *Preaching Biblically*, ed. Don M. Wardlaw (Philadelphia: Westminster, 1983), 11.

8. Thomas Long, "And How Shall They Hear?" in *Listening to the Word*, Fs. Fred B. Craddock, ed. Gail R. O'Day and Thomas G. Long (Nashville: Abingdon, 1993), 173.

9. See Fred B. Craddock, *As One without Authority*, 52. For the roots of the "new homiletic" in the new hermeneutic, see Wilson, *The Practice of Preaching*, 24. See also Richard Eslinger, *Narrative and Imagination* (Minneapolis: Fortress, 1995), 7.

10. Troeger, "A Poetics of the Pulpit for Post-Modern Times," in *Intersections*, ed. Richard L. Eslinger (Grand Rapids: Eerdmans, 1994), 52.

"democratic" rather than authoritative is "fundamental to the American way of life."[11]

In the second place, preachers will recognize the importance of biblical genres, acknowledging that the genres are not merely empty receptacles into which biblical writers poured *ideas* that became sermon texts. Advocates of the new homiletics insist that the *what* and the *how* of the biblical texts cannot be separated. Paul Ricoeur forcefully argues that the literary genres are not merely a "rhetorical facade" that one can pull down in order to reveal the ideas behind the genres; they are, in fact, theologically significant as modes of revelation.[12] Consequently, preachers who bring their listeners to experience the text will not reduce poetry, parables, or narratives to basic ideas, but will attempt to "do what the text does."[13]

Because one cannot "do what the text does" within the older homiletic tradition of arguing a case with supporting points, the new homiletic has given special attention to an alternative shape of the sermon that is both sensitive to the listeners and consistent with the biblical genres. Eugene Lowry describes the "revolution" in sermonic shape that began with the publication of Fred Craddock's *As One without Authority* in 1971 and continues in the contemporary literature.[14] This "revolution" has focused on induction and the narrative quality of the sermon, taking a special interest in the preaching of narrative texts. Although Craddock was not the first to challenge the traditional shape of the sermon,[15] his proposal was, as Lowry indicated, "revolutionary."

---

11. Craddock, *As One without Authority*, 58.

12. Paul Ricoeur, "Toward a Hermeneutic of the Idea of Revelation," in *Essays on Biblical Interpretation*, ed. Lewis S. Mudge (Philadelphia: Fortress, 1980), 91. See also Mark I. Wallace, *The Second Naiveté*, Studies in American Biblical Hermeneutics 6 (Macon, Ga.: Mercer Univ. Press, 1990), 36.

13. See Amos Wilder, *The Language of the Gospel: Early Christian Rhetoric* (New York: Harper & Row, 1964), 13: "The character of the early Christian speech forms should have much to say to us with regard to our understanding of Christianity and its communication today." Wilder argues that one cannot distinguish between the form and content of scripture in our preaching as if we could extract the one from the other. "We can learn much from our observations as to the appropriate strategies and vehicles of Christian speech and then adapt these to our own situation."

14. Eugene L. Lowry, "The Revolution in Sermonic Shape," in *Listening to the Word*, 93–112. See also Eugene L. Lowry, *The Sermon: Dancing the Edge of Mystery* (Nashville: Abingdon, 1997), 11.

15. See H. Grady Davis, *Design for Preaching* (Philadelphia: Fortress, 1958), 15. Davis gave considerable attention to the form of the sermon, suggesting that it should be an organic whole and comparing it to a tree with its root system and limbs.

Craddock argued that the older homiletics, with its Aristotelian basis and its authoritative tone, failed to reach the contemporary audience. He indicated that, while the older homiletic functioned within Christendom, it could not survive the decline of that culture.[16] He recommended induction because it is less authoritarian and reflects a more natural form of communication for contemporary listeners. According to Craddock, induction gives a narrative quality to the sermon as preachers retrace with their congregations the steps that they have already taken in the study, allowing the listeners to draw their own conclusion to the sermon. The sermon is more descriptive than hortatory. This form of the sermon, according to Craddock, provides unity to the sermon, sustains interest, and allows the preacher to identify with the audience in a common quest.[17]

Eugene Lowry developed Craddock's argument further, indicating that preaching in the form of the text involves treating the sermon as a plot.[18] Thus the form of the sermon can be developed with the analogy of the dramatic presentation. According to Lowry, the sermon is a plot that moves from the homiletical bind when "something is in the air" toward some form of resolution. Between the homiletical bind in the beginning and the resolution at the end, the sermon goes through predictable stages in its development. Storytelling is thus the alternative to the traditional discursive sermon.[19]

David Buttrick's *Homiletic* is a major textbook covering many aspects of preaching theory. Thus his interests cover a wide range of homiletic issues and are not limited to sermonic shape. However, he is a major contributor to the discussion of the shape of the sermon, and he shares the criticism of the older homiletics expressed by Craddock and Lowry. He also develops his homiletic theory with a concern for both the listener and the genre of the text. In a homiletic method that he describes as "phenomenological," he seeks to demonstrate how language forms in

---

16. Craddock, *As One without Authority*, 14.
17. Ibid., 53–58.
18. Eugene Lowry, *The Homiletical Plot* (Atlanta: John Knox, 1980), 15.
19. Ibid. In *The Sermon: Dancing the Edge of Mystery*, 22–28, Lowry lists six identifiable types of models: the inductive sermon, the story sermon, the narrative sermon, the transconscious African American sermon, the phenomenological sermon, and the conversational-episodal sermon. I assume that these are the available options for preaching from all literary genres.

consciousness.[20] Buttrick shares the interest in sermonic movement that has characterized the new generation of preaching. In contrast to the older homiletic emphasis on "points," Buttrick describes the sermon as a series of moves that are logically connected and shaped by the preacher's awareness of how meaning forms in the consciousness of the listeners.

The recent emphasis on genre and narrative movement is the consequence of two developments in the contemporary theological and cultural climate. In the first place, one may observe a renewed attention to the listener. The focus has moved from the ideas to be communicated to the experience of the hearers. Narrative appeals to the listening audience, especially in a postliterate society.[21] We find narrative texts easier to preach than sermons from prophecy, apocalyptic,[22] or epistles because we assume they are more likely to sustain listener interest than the more direct and authoritative means of communication. In the second place, the popularity of narrative preaching also reflects theological developments in our rediscovery of the narrative dimension of revelation,[23] according to which we acknowledge the "strange new world within the Bible" described by Karl Barth[24] and attempt to conform our world to the biblical story. A rational homiletic designed for the presentation of distilled "truths" and "teachings" from historical texts simply is not suitable to the emerging new forms of biblical criticism.[25] According to Hans Frei, in centuries of theological reflection, "Interpretation was a matter of fitting the biblical story into

---

20. David Buttrick, *Homiletic* (Philadelphia: Fortress, 1987), xii.

21. On the return to the listener in homiletic theory, see Beverly Zink-Sawyer, " 'The Word Purely Preached and Heard': The Listeners and the Homiletic Endeavor," *Interpretation* 51 (1997): 342–57.

22. For a useful resource on preaching from apocalyptic literature, see David Schnasa Jacobsen, *Preaching in the New Creation: The Promise of New Testament Apocalyptic Texts* (Louisville, Ky.: Westminster John Knox, 1999).

23. Hans Frei, "Apologetics, Criticism, and the Loss of Narrative Interpretation," in Stanley Hauerwas and L. Gregory Jones, *Why Narrative?* (Grand Rapids: Eerdmans, 1989), 50.

24. See Karl Barth's classic essay by that title in *The Word of God and the Word of Man* (reprint, New York: Harper & Row, 1957).

25. David Buttrick, "On Doing Homiletics Today," in *Intersections*, 90. For the relationship between biblical studies and preaching, see also Stephen Farris, "Limping Away with a Blessing: Biblical Studies and Preaching at the End of the Second Millennium," *Interpretation* 51 (1997): 358–70.

another world with another story rather than incorporating that world into the biblical story."[26] In what Frei calls the "great reversal," theologians and preachers mined narrative literature to determine its referential dimensions. The meaning of narrative was found in its ability to inform us about past events or to offer propositional truths. Narrative theologians argue that the new focus is a rediscovery of narrative as the primary mode of biblical revelation. Rather than look for propositional truths or the realia of history in narrative, theologians acknowledge that revelation occurs within the narrative itself. We recognize the narrative quality of existence and discover the truth of our existence through the medium of story.[27]

If the traditional homiletic fits comfortably within the *modern* era, the new homiletic fits comfortably within the *postmodern* era.[28] Although Craddock never describes his own work as postmodern,[29] his proposal for inductive preaching is the natural consequence of the changed climate in biblical interpretation, which has called into question the legitimacy of searching behind the text and distilling a message from it.[30] Preaching that is indirect and "without authority" acknowledges the loss of authority that is characteristic of the postmodern ethos. The focus on the listener's response rather than the truth to be distilled also fits comfortably within this era. The focus on narrative, as I have suggested above, is the outgrowth of the postcritical approach

---

26. Frei, "Apologetics, Criticism, and the Loss of Narrative Interpretation," 50.

27. On the significance of narrative in contemporary thought in answering the fundamental worldview and moral questions, see J. Richard Middleton and Brian J. Walsh, *Truth Is Stranger Than It Used to Be* (Downers Grove, Ill.: InterVarsity, 1995), 63–66.

28. Ronald Allen speaks of the "homiletical smorgasbord in the postmodern ethos" in Ronald J. Allen, Barbara Shires Blaisdell, and Scott Black Johnston, *Theology for Preaching: Authority, Truth and Knowledge of God in a Postmodern Ethos* (Nashville: Abingdon Press, 1997), 169. See Troeger, "A Poetics of the Pulpit for Post-Modern Times," 42–64.

29. See Scott Black Johnston's perspective in *Theology for Preaching*, 52: "Although Craddock's work encouraged a shift in authority toward the listener, it would be inaccurate to conclude that *As One without Authority* represents a postmodern homiletic. For Craddock based his prescription for the health of preaching on a sweeping understanding of anthropology (that is, all people listen inductively). Postmodern scholars tend to reject such universal claims, and call presumed similarities between 'all people' into question."

30. David Buttrick, "On Doing Homiletics Today," in *Intersections*, 90.

to the reading of texts. While the traditional homiletic worked well in the modern period, when interpreters were confident that they could discover the single meaning of the text, a more postmodern hermeneutic focuses on the experience generated by the text.

The "new wineskins" of homiletics have undoubtedly made a lasting impact on the preaching tradition, offering directions for preachers who wish to communicate in a postmodern cultural situation. In the rediscovery of the listener, the recognition of the revelatory quality of biblical genres, and the focus on narrative movement, the new homiletic has offered an appropriate alternative to a preaching tradition that spoke effectively to a previous generation. Preachers who had struggled with their congregations' boredom at the predictable sermon form found new life in the sermon when they attempted to "do what the text does" rather than distill the idea from the text. Thus scarcely any of us who have read Craddock, Lowry, Buttrick, and the other advocates of the new homiletic will wish to remain comfortably within the "old wineskins" of the homiletic of the last two centuries. Few of us will want to return to a sermonic form that consists of a proposition to be argued or lists of points that we wish to transmit—at least on a regular basis, nor will we confuse Christian proclamation with argumentation. The new homileticians have reminded us, *in the first place*, of the primary place of narrative as a mode of revelation. As Averil Cameron observes, "Christianity was a religion with a story," and the stories in scripture set in motion a discourse distinguished by its stories.[31] They have taught us, *in the second place*, the value of movement and anticipation as a medium for our own communication. They have convinced us, *in the third place*, that form actually shapes the listener's faith and that the Bible is a source not only for what we preach, but also for how we preach. Sensitivity to the genre of the text is necessary in order to "preach the Bible biblically."[32] *Finally*, the new homiletic, with its insistence on the experience of the text, ensures that preaching is rooted in scripture.

---

31. Averil Cameron, *Christianity and the Rhetoric of Empire* (Berkeley, Calif.: Univ. of California Press, 1991), 89.
32. See Leander Keck, *The Bible in the Pulpit* (Nashville: Abingdon, 1978), 105–24.

Reflections a Generation Later

The new homiletic was a needed corrective to a preaching tradition that had turned the sermon into an academic lecture and the
worship service into an arena for debate. When I first read the new
homileticians, beginning shortly after the publication of Fred
Craddock's *Overhearing the Gospel* and *As One without Authority*, I
greeted their proposals with enthusiasm, recognizing that narrative
could give life to the sermon. However, with the passage of time, I
am convinced that, to rescue preaching, something more is needed
than the rediscovery of the narrative form. Although I have learned
very much from the "new wineskins" of preaching, my earlier
enthusiasm for the contributions of the past generation is now
tempered by both unanswered questions and reservations about
this approach. The time has come, I believe, to incorporate the
gains of the past generation, recognize the weaknesses of the new
approaches, and develop a homiletic that will sustain churches in
the future. I begin with the shortcomings of the new homiletic.

1. *Inductive preaching functions best in a Christian culture in which
listeners are well informed of the Christian heritage.* Our initial enthusiasm for the indirect approach grew out of our conviction that we
were already immersed in the Christian tradition and needed
something new to give life to Christian proclamation. Craddock
argued in *Overhearing the Gospel* that induction helps people appropriate the message that is already known.[33] The move toward
inductive preaching was a 1960s response to the world of the
1950s, when preachers faced congregations that were well
instructed in the Christian faith. Answers that were addressed to
the issues of the 1950s are scarcely adequate for the issues that face
the church in the new millennium. Now people have little knowledge of biblical content. The present culture is increasingly post-
Christian and unacquainted with Christian proclamation. We
preach to congregations that are largely shaped by the values of a

---

33. Fred Craddock, *Overhearing the Gospel* (Nashville: Abingdon, 1978), 91. See the
excellent discussion by Charles L. Campbell, in *Preaching Jesus: New Directions for
Homiletics in Hans Frei's Postliberal Theology* (Grand Rapids: Eerdmans, 1997), 127–28.
Campbell notes that Craddock expressed the view that Christendom is dead in *As One
without Authority* (14–15) and in his recent Sprunt Lectures at Union Theological
Seminary. Here he insists that Christendom is dead, but nevertheless argues for indirection as the appropriate response to biblical illiteracy.

new pagan culture.[34] They hear multiple stories that have more influence on shaping their identities than does the Christian story. The metanarrative of *Seinfeld*, which will live for many years in syndicated form, will continue to communicate a generation's commitment to the satisfaction of the self.[35]

The biblical image of "exile" accurately describes the place of the church in a culture that is characterized by consumer capitalism, moral relativism, and narcissism.[36] The loss of the Christian society presents a special problem to the preacher, who must recognize that the current generation did not grow up in a world that was determined by a Christian ethos that provided common understandings of Christian morality. In the contemporary culture, the preacher faces the prospect of upholding a moral vision to a generation that has heard the competing moral vision, according to which moral judgments are only personal preferences.[37] Narrative preaching by itself cannot bear the burden of shaping a communal moral vision in this climate. We must learn once more how to proclaim the gospel to those who have not heard and to initiate them into the Christian faith. Consequently, preaching will be both evangelistic and pastoral. It will announce the good news, shape the corporate memory, and teach communities how to live faithfully in a non-Christian culture. I suggest that preaching in a post-Christian culture has much to learn from the preaching of a pre-Christian culture.

---

34. See N. T. Wright, *What Saint Paul Really Said* (Grand Rapids: Eerdmans, 1997), 94.

35. See Robert Bellah et al., *Habits of the Heart* (Berkeley: Univ. of California Press, 1985). The group chronicles the American drive for individual freedom, choice, and the pursuit of personal happiness. This pursuit overshadows the importance of moral claims or the discussion of the common good.

36. For the image of exile, see Walter Brueggemann, *Cadences of Home: Preaching among Exiles* (Louisville, Ky.: Westminster John Knox, 1997). See also James Thompson, *The Church in Exile* (Abilene, Tex.: Abilene Christian Univ. Press, 1990); and Christopher Lasch, *The Culture of Narcissism* (New York: W. W. Norton & Co., 1979).

37. Bellah et al., *Habits of the Heart*, 6: "Even the deepest ethical virtues are justified as matters of personal preference. Indeed, the ultimate ethical rule is simply that individuals should be able to pursue whatever they find rewarding, constrained only by the requirement that they not interfere with the 'value systems' of others." See also James Davison Hunter, *Culture Wars: The Struggle to Define America* (New York: Basic Books, 1991), 107–32, for the competing moral visions of our culture.

2. *Homileticians have focused on technique to the neglect of a clear understanding of the aims of preaching.* Discussion of the *form* of the sermon dominates the new homiletic. What is missing here, as with the tradition of homiletics as a whole, is an interest in the larger theological agenda of preaching. The sermon is treated as a discrete entity, as if it could be separated from the succession of sermons that make up the preaching ministry. Where each sermon is treated as a plot that moves from the dilemma to the solution, the entire preaching ministry takes on the characteristics of a television series. Just as the television drama begins each week with "something in the air" and moves toward resolution, each sermon becomes one plot within a series of plots. It is an episodic serial rather than a miniseries. One wonders, given this view of sermon, if the preacher envisions a larger plot in which each unit plays a role. Those of us who watch the television series regularly may fail to watch successive programs without really missing anything inasmuch as each episode is an independent entity in which the same plot unfolds each week. One observes no sense of progression in the well-designed television serial because the producers stay with a formula until it loses audience interest. This lack of progression may work well for the television series, but it has serious limitations for the preacher whose work extends into the indefinite future and aims at something larger than the entertainment of the audience each week.[38]

Edmund Steimle once offered a helpful analogy to the preaching ministry when he said that the sermon is a piece within a mosaic pattern. If preaching forms the mosaic pattern, one must still ask what mosaic we are ultimately forming. We must look beyond the "experience" of the sermon to ask the goals and strategies of the entire preaching ministry. Although the recent literature speaks of the goals of the sermon, it offers little to give us direction on the larger agenda of preaching.

3. *Much of the literature of the new homiletics treats narrative as the primary, if not the only, mode of discourse for preaching, in practice ignoring the revelatory significance of other biblical genres.* One may legitimately argue that narrative is the genre that provides the

---

38. See Thomas Long, "When the Preacher Is a Teacher," *Journal for Preachers* 16 (1992): 24.

context for our understanding of the other biblical genres, which provide commentary on the narrative.[39] However, the move toward "preaching in the form of the text" actually becomes "preaching narrative," which then becomes the preaching of parables.[40] Because the parables are models of induction, preachers present them as models for preaching. This equation of narrative and parable is most evident in Eugene Lowry's *How to Preach a Parable*, in which only one of the sermons is actually based on a parable.[41]

In addition to emphasizing the narrative texts, preachers also look for ways to cast other genres into narrative sermons. Thus although one finds in the homiletic literature an appreciation of all of the biblical genres and an emphasis on preaching in the form of the text, in the new "great reversal" all texts are reshaped into narrative for the preaching. Fred Craddock's sermon "Praying through Clenched Teeth," based on Galatians 1:11–24, is an example of the use of the narrative form to preach an epistolary text. This "one size fits all" way of constructing sermons from a variety of genres replaced one kind of one-dimensional preaching with another. Thus the exclusive reliance on story results "in a reduced or distorted rendering of human life and divine revelation."[42]

4. *Listeners shaped only by narrative preaching will have no grasp of the reflective dimensions of faith.* Because faith seeks understanding, the sermon has always been the occasion for deeper instruction in the faith. Stories, symbols, and metaphors are evocative, but ultimately they require reflection. Stories may shape communal identity, but ultimately the cohesiveness of the community requires the interpretation of the communal story.[43] In his work on Galatians,

---

39. See Mark Ellingsen, *The Integrity of Biblical Narrative* (Minneapolis: Fortress, 1990), 29.

40. Campbell, *Preaching Jesus*, 174.

41. Eugene Lowry, ed., *How to Preach a Parable* (Nashville: Abingdon, 1989). Campbell (*Preaching Jesus*, 174–75) notes that the new hermeneutic, which profoundly influenced developments in homiletics, has focused its work on the parables. The new hermeneutic's focus on parables as "existential, experiential events" has influenced contemporary homiletic theory.

42. Richard Lischer, "The Limits of Story," *Interpretation* 38 (1984): 26.

43. See Arthur Van Seters, "Dilemmas in Preaching Doctrine: Theology's Public Voice," *Journal for Preachers* 20 (1997): 34. See also Alister E. McGrath, *The Genesis of Doctrine: A Study of Doctrinal Criticism* (Oxford: Blackwell, 1990), 7–11, for the view that narrative is primary, but doctrine is the secondary interpretation; cited in Van Seters, 34.

Richard Hays appealed to Northrop Frye's numerous works in literary criticism to argue for the continuity between story and nonnarrative explication of the story. Hays argues that the story of Jesus Christ is the narrative, or *mythos*, to which Paul appeals in Galatians, which is actually a reflection on the story of Jesus.[44] Philippians is obviously a reflection on the story that Paul tells in 2:6–11.[45] I suggest that Paul's epistles contain constant allusions to the foundational story of God's vindication of his people through the Christ-event.[46] As Paul Ricoeur argued in *The Symbolism of Evil*, "the symbol gives rise to thought."[47] The shape of the canon suggests that, while narrative stands at the center of biblical faith, it requires conceptualization in the other literary genres.[48] Stories can entertain and engender audience involvement, but ultimately they require interpretation and commentary.

5. *Narrative preaching is reluctant to speak with authority or to make concrete demands for change in the listeners' lives.* The gospel cannot be preached without authority because the gospel makes claims on our lives. Even the narratives are interwoven with the claim on the lives of the listeners. The tradition of narrative in the Bible is the basis for a call to respond to the story with obedience. The narrative of God's mighty acts at the exodus is the basis for the decalogue.

---

44. Richard B. Hays, *The Faith of Jesus Christ*, SBLDS 56 (Chico, Calif.: Scholars Press, 1983), 20–23. Cf. Richard Hays, "ΠΙΣΤΙΣ and Pauline Christology," in E. Elizabeth Johnson and David M. Hay, ed., *Pauline Theology* (Atlanta: Scholars Press, 1997), 4.37. See also Northrop Frye, *Fables of Identity: Studies in Poetic Mythology* (New York: Harcourt, Brace & World, 1963).

45. See Pheme Perkins, "Philippians: Theology for the Heavenly Politeuma," in J. Bassler, *Pauline Theology* (Minneapolis: Fortress, 1991), 1.95–98. Perkins speaks of the hymn as the "governing metaphor of Philippians."

46. See Daniel Patte, *Preaching Paul* (Philadelphia: Fortress, 1984), 32. See also Richard Hays, "Crucified with Christ," in *Pauline Theology*, 1.234. Hays outlines six events in the Pauline story line: (1) God chose Abraham to bless all nations (Gal. 3:6–9); (2) God sent his Son to liberate the people (Gal. 4:1–7); (3) Jesus achieved God's purpose through his death on the cross (Gal. 3:1); (4) Jesus was raised from the dead (1 Thess. 1:10; 4:14); (5) those who belong to Christ Jesus find themselves at the turn of the ages (cf. Gal. 6:14–15); (6) The community's hope rests on the return of Christ. See also Norman Petersen, *Rediscovering Paul: Philemon and the Sociology of Paul's Narrative World* (Philadelphia: Fortress, 1985), 43; N. T. Wright, *The New Testament and the People of God* (Minneapolis: Fortress, 1992), 403–10.

47. Paul Ricoeur, *The Symbolism of Evil* (Boston: Beacon Press, 1967), 347–57. See David M. Greenhaw, "As One with Authority," in *Intersections*, 114–15.

48. See Ricoeur, "Toward a Hermeneutic of the Idea of Revelation," 73–95.

Jesus' announcement of the kingdom is the basis for the call to repent (Mark 1:15). In the letters of Paul, the story of the gospel implies a claim on the lives of the communities.

6. *The exclusive reliance on inductive preaching will not build and sustain communities of faith.* Craddock suggests that inductive preaching allows the readers to draw their own conclusions.[49] Although one may argue that stories form communal identity, the focus of inductive preaching has been on the experience of the individual.[50] Such preaching treats the listeners as a collection of individuals who participate in the same events.[51] The advocates of the new homiletic have said little about how this kind of preaching will create a communal identity with its own ethical norms and mission.

7. *Preaching as rational persuasion is not an alien intrusion into a mode of communication that was originally narrative in nature.* Nor does it function only within the culture of the Enlightenment or of the printed page. The New Testament attests to the presence of both narrative and rational persuasion. Even the narrative portions of the New Testament have subgenres of argumentative discourse. Despite Paul's disclaimers (1 Cor. 2:1–5), his listeners would have noticed elements of Aristotelian rhetoric in his own preaching, as I shall argue in a subsequent chapter. If Aristotelian rhetoric is as old as the New Testament, it can scarcely be peeled away from authentic Christian communication.

The Missing Dimension: Paul and His Letters

To suggest that Paul's preaching in a pagan context of the first century is a model for preaching in the twenty-first century is to invite incredulity and resistance from most contemporary preachers. Robert Jewett recalls the discovery during his recent sabbatical of the pervasive avoidance of Paul. When he had the occasion to visit numerous churches and observe what theological and biblical resources were most useful, he was amazed at the paucity of sermons from Pauline texts.[52] In a kind of "Marcionism-

---

49. Craddock, *As One without Authority*, 67.
50. Campbell, *Preaching Jesus*, 140.
51. Ibid.
52. Robert Jewett, *Paul: The Apostle to America* (Louisville, Ky.: Westminster John Knox, 1994), 14.

in-reverse,"[53] Paul was relegated to the periphery of the preaching canon, reserved for Reformation Sunday, weddings (1 Cor. 13), and funerals (1 Cor. 15).

Undoubtedly, preachers in the new homiletic tradition have avoided Paul for a reason. Pauline texts do not fit easily with the postmodern fascination with story. Paul speaks as one *with* an authority that makes both preacher and congregation uncomfortable. He sometimes communicates in dense theological arguments. The issues that confronted congregations in Galatia and Corinth appear to be so remote from contemporary congregations that they do not recognize the relevance of those epistles for their own situation. They can more readily connect with the healing of blind Bartimaeus than with Paul's arguments about the destiny of Israel (Rom. 9–11). Paul speaks directly, offering concrete instructions for his communities, many of which are unsettling to contemporary listeners because they challenge the assumptions of our own culture. Consequently, despite Paul's overwhelming presence in the New Testament as the creator of a new genre of Christian communication, many will regard Paul's preaching in a pre-Christian culture as an unlikely model for the post-Christian culture.[54]

Despite the common resistance to Paul, I shall argue in this book that his epistles provide the dimension that is lacking in narrative preaching. Twenty-one of the twenty-seven books of the New Testament are not in narrative form, but are epistles that are addressed to Christian communities in a pagan culture. Because Paul's letters played a dominant role in Christian communication, David Bartlett correctly argues, "In the legitimate enthusiasm for narrative preaching, we sometimes undervalue Paul. In some ways his letters are more immediate than even the liveliest biblical narratives."[55] Moreover, if the form of the sermon influences faith, Paul's preaching is a reminder of the importance of direct speech

---

53. Cf. Charles Cousar, "Preaching on Paul," *Journal for Preachers* 18 (1995): 9.

54. A few sources have examined Paul's role as preacher. See Raymond Bailey, *Paul the Preacher* (Nashville: Broadman, 1991); Jerome Murphy-O'Connor, *Paul on Preaching* (New York: Sheed & Ward, 1963); Fred Craddock, "Preaching to Corinthians," *Interpretation* 44 (1990): 158–68.

55. David Bartlett, "Texts Shaping Sermons," in *Listening to the Word*, 160.

and argumentative discourse in the formation of Christian consciousness. If the various biblical genres are themselves revelatory, as Ricoeur has forcefully argued, one can scarcely fail to consider the importance of Paul's letters as a model for preaching. The time has come to recognize Paul as a legitimate model for our own preaching ministry.

I do not suggest that Paul is the only model for the preaching ministry. We have much to learn from those who demonstrate the importance of narrative, law, prophecy, apocalyptic, and the psalms for our preaching. However, as the one who built lasting communities around the Mediterranean basin, he remains an important teacher for the contemporary church. Because we can observe his preaching ministry in a wide variety of situations, we can observe significant models for the preaching ministry. Inasmuch as he formed Christian communities in pagan cultures through the clarity and power of his preaching, he provides a needed model for preachers who face anew the prospect of forming Christian congregations in the context of the new paganism.

Although I affirm the importance of preaching in the form of the text, this study moves beyond the mechanics of describing how to employ the epistolary genre and its subgenres to construct the sermon, to ask about the theological agenda that governs the entire preaching ministry. What is the agenda for preaching in this post-Christian climate? How do we address communities that know little of the Christian story or the demands of the gospel? How do we form genuine communities of faith among listeners who have come to church only as consumers to have their individual needs met? These problems are far too complex to be solved by discussions of sermonic technique and form. Consequently, I wish to ask not only about the impact of the Sunday sermon, but also about the cumulative impact of all of our sermons and the theological agenda that governs our ministry of proclamation.

In chapter 1, I shall examine the epistles of Paul to determine the extent to which they offer a model for preaching. Did he write the way he spoke? Modern readers, who are accustomed to the silent and individual reading of Scripture, easily forget that their ancient counterparts rarely read these letters in a private setting. From the moment that Paul dictated the letters to the moment that they were read in church, the epistles had the immediacy of oral discourse. Although written works are never the exact representations of the spoken word, Paul's letters present strong echoes of his actual preaching. Furthermore, the fact that we have multiple epistles allows us to see the larger picture of the aims of his preaching ministry. The range of letters, from the simplicity of 1 Thessalonians to the complexity of Romans, permits us to see the larger agenda of his preaching. We shall observe that in his earliest epistle his aim is to provide catechetical information that will lay the foundation for the church's continued existence, while in later epistles he responds to issues in the life of the church. This observation of the epistles as oral communication provides insights into the larger agenda of preaching.

In chapter 2, I shall observe the preaching ministry of Paul in order to demonstrate that the epistles describe a preaching ministry that consists not only of the announcement of the gospel, but of the shaping of communities through *paraklesis*. The Pauline model, therefore, involves both *kerygma* and *didache*, and neither the Pauline epistles nor the book of Acts knows a distinction between the two forms of communication. One observes here the larger agenda of Paul's preaching: that it shapes communities through both narrative and exhortation.

In chapter 3, I shall discuss the shape of Paul's preaching in order to determine his relationship with argumentative discourse in general and Aristotelian rhetoric in particular. The question is important in determining the extent to which the aversion to argumentative discourse is rooted in the earliest Christian tradition. Inasmuch as the focus of contemporary homiletics has been on sermonic shape, an analysis of the shape of Paul's preaching should tell us much about the options in early Christian views of the style and arrangement of the sermon. An analysis of the shape of Paul's preaching will also provide insights into our own questions about the relationship between Christian preaching and the rhetorics of any given culture.

The weakness of the new homiletics, as I indicated above, is its inability to shape communities toward a common identity and its limitation in providing pastoral care in the pulpit. In chapter 4, I shall show that Paul provides a useful model for the pastoral preaching that shapes and builds communities. I shall examine his initial efforts at pastoral preaching in 1 Thessalonians, a letter to a church that faced no special crisis, and I shall compare Paul's

understanding of pastoral preaching with contemporary understandings of the preacher's pastoral task. Whereas narrative
preaching speaks with indirection to individuals, Paul's speech
forms community consciousness. He speaks not only to offer
acceptance to broken people; he also offers instructions for the
moral conduct of the whole community.

In chapter 5, I shall examine the role that theological reflection
plays in Paul's preaching. Whereas 1 Thessalonians is an example
of pastoral preaching as catechesis, 1 and 2 Corinthians provide an
example of Paul's response to contingent situations. Paul's original
preaching required clarification. Objections and misunderstandings undoubtedly called for continued conversation. The dense
argumentation by Paul is a model for the reflective form of the sermon in contexts in which the Christian story becomes a battle-
ground between conflicting understandings. For Paul, theological
preaching is the natural development of pastoral preaching.
Whereas pastoral preaching aims at catechesis and the establishment of community identity and vocabulary, in theological preaching Paul responds to contingent situations, leading the church in
the process of reflection on its story. Paul's preaching is, therefore,
a useful reminder that circumstances in the life of the church
require a process of reflection.

Paul's epistles demonstrate that his preaching consists of
reminding communities of what they already know—or should
know. In chapter 6, I shall examine the role that repetition plays in
the preaching of Paul. His use of repetition was vital to ensure that
first-generation communities, who lived in a non-Christian society, would know their story and the expectations of community
life. Whereas narrative preaching presupposes that one can speak
indirectly because "there is no lack of information in a Christian
land," preaching that offers constant reminders of the Christian
story is suitable in a post-Christian society. Paul is a model for the
preacher's appeal to the community's memory in the midst of
changing circumstances.

I do not suggest that the challenge of preaching in a postmodern climate will be resolved with the discovery of an alternative sermonic shape or design. Nor do I wish to retreat from what we have
learned from the "new wineskins" of preaching to the preaching of
the previous generation. In this book I shall argue that Paul is a
forgotten mentor in our understanding of preaching. His preach-

ing in a pre-Christian age has much to tell preachers who live in a post-Christian age. From him we learn that the ultimate effectiveness of preaching rests on the power of the gospel, the preacher's captivity to God's word, and the preacher's knowledge of the larger agenda of the preaching ministry.

Chapter One

Paul as the Model for Preaching

Anyone who attempts to write a history of oral communication faces a problem: all that we know of speakers before the invention of the tape recorder and the video recorder comes from written texts. Consequently, we face special difficulties in reconstructing the dynamics of the spoken word from the documents at our disposal. Written records are either summarized and filtered through third parties, or they are derived from the manuscripts of the speakers themselves. Even where we have transcripts of the speeches, as in the case of Lincoln's Gettysburg Address, the words on the page do not tell the entire story.

The Living Voice and the Written Word:
The Limitations of Our Knowledge

The limitations of the written evidence present a special problem for the central thesis of this book—that Paul is a model for the preaching ministry today. I must concede that we are at a considerable distance from the actual living voice of Paul. We have no transcripts or video recordings of his sermons. What we have is some, but not all, of the letters that he wrote to his congregations. Even if the letters were the actual transcripts of Paul's sermons—and they are not—they would offer something less than the actual voice of Paul. Therefore, the limitations in our knowledge demand that we exercise caution, recognizing the obstacles to our full knowledge of the preaching ministry of Paul. The difficulties can be outlined as follows:

In the first place, we know surprisingly little about early Christian worship and preaching. Many of our reconstructions of early Christian preaching reflect our own ecclesiastical practice more than that of the ancient church. Although the Bible offers abundant examples of the ministry of preaching, it provides scarcely any examples of the dimension I wish to explore in this book: the regular sermon to a Christian audience. Form critics a generation ago *assumed* considerable knowledge about the role of preaching in the early church in preserving the memory of Jesus' words and deeds. Martin Dibelius devotes the opening chapter of *From Tradition to Gospel* to the place of the sermon as the medium for recalling these stories. Such a claim rests on Dibelius's assumption that behind the stories one could locate the echo of the sermons of the early Christian communities. More recently, the advocates of narrative preaching have assumed that they know what forms preaching took before it was "corrupted" by Aristotelian rhetoric. However, if we define the sermon as an address in the context of a worship service, we do not have a single sermon in the entire New Testament. The sermons of Acts are, as C. H. Dodd indicates, missionary sermons, not regular addresses to the believing community.[1] Moreover, although we identify the epistle to the Hebrews and other smaller units as "homilies," we remain uncertain about the form of the homily in the early church or in Judaism of the first two centuries.[2] The New Testament says very little about the structure of corporate worship in the early church and even less about the ministry of the word. We know nothing about the sermon as a regular part of the worship service until Justin Martyr's detailed report in the second century.[3] Indeed, the term *sermon* has no equivalent in the New

---

1. C. H. Dodd, *The Apostolic Preaching and Its Developments* (New York: Harper & Row, 1964).

2. K. Donfried, *The Setting of Second Clement in Early Christianity* (Leiden: E. J. Brill, 1974), 26: "The term 'homily' is so vague and ambiguous that it should be withdrawn until its literary generic legitimacy has been demonstrated. The crux of the problem lies in the definition of the term 'homily.' It has been employed to describe various types of Greek literature, Jewish midrash, the NT book of Hebrews, parts of the pseudo-Clementine literature and Melito's tract on the Pascha. Perhaps the greatest ambiguity in the current usage is when it is used to describe both a certain class of Hellenistic Jewish literature influenced by the Greek diatribe form, on the one hand, and when it is used to define certain typically Jewish midrashic patterns, on the other hand. These are not necessarily exclusive definitions, but they are sufficiently different to warrant greater precision."

3. Justin, *Apol.* 1.67.

Testament.[4] We have no stenographic records of sermons before Origen.[5] A fundamentally oral culture has left large gaps in our knowledge of the models of early Christian preaching.

In the second place, the written word is never precisely the same as the spoken word. Preachers recognize this distinction when they decide whether to work from a manuscript or speak extemporaneously. Some choose not to work from a manuscript, recognizing that the spoken word has an immediacy that is missing in the written word. Other preachers work from a manuscript, but "write for the ear" rather than the eye, attempting to maintain the effects of the spoken word. Preachers and congregations may preserve written sermons, but printed sermons will not produce the same effects as the original sermons.

Ancient writers had a special awareness of the distinction between the written and the spoken word. Plato subjected the written word to a thorough critique, arguing for the superior value of the spoken word.[6] In the *Phaedrus* (276a) Socrates labeled writing a poor substitute for the spoken word of "one who knows." Plato sought knowledge in the individual's mind, not in the external abstractions of the written word.[7] For this reason he criticized the

---

4. F. Siegert, *Drei hellenistisch-jüdische Predigten* (Tübingen: J. C. B. Mohr, 1992), 3. Klaus Berger ("Hellenistische Gattungen im Neuen Testament," *ANRW* 2.25.1363) speaks of the "mythologized concept of the sermon" that was initiated by Luther and continued in the works of Martin Dibelius and Rudolf Bultmann. Without giving a clear definition of the sermon, both Dibelius and Bultmann frequently suggested that it was the setting for the preservation and growth of tradition.

5. See the discussion of Origen's homilies in Éric Junod, "Wodurch unterscheiden sich die Homilien des Origenes von seinen Kommentaren?" in H. Muhlenberg and J. van Oort, *Predigt in der alten Kirche* (Kampen: Pharos, 1994), 50–81. Beginning with Origen's homilies, we have the first examples of oral addresses to Christian communities as they were recorded by stenographers. Origen passed on the model of the sermon as verse-by-verse exposition, a model that was appropriated in the early church. Later Christian preachers found their models for preaching in the Greek rhetorical tradition. Preachers trained in rhetoric then shaped the Christian sermon. See also Hughes Oliphant Old, *The Reading and Preaching of the Scriptures in the Worship of the Christian Church* (Grand Rapids: Eerdmans, 1998), 1.252.

6. *Phaedr.* 248–76. See Dorothea Frede, "Mündlichkeit und Schriftlichkeit: von Platon zu Plotin," in *Logos und Buchstabe: Mündlichkeit und Schriftlichkeit im Judentum und Christentum der Antike,* ed. Gerhard Sellin and François Vouga (Tübingen: Francke, 1997), 33.

7. Tony Lentz, *Orality and Literacy in Hellenic Greece* (Carbondale, Ill.: Southern Illinois Univ. Press, 1989), 15.

work of the poets. Either they were not present with the "pilot of their soul" to explain their ideas when others quoted their words, or they had no knowledge of the things they described.[8] The important point was that the creative intelligence of the maker was not present and the particular meaning at issue could not be clarified by asking questions. In the *Republic*, Plato wrote that the imitations of the poets are "about the third place from truth" (602b–c).[9] Plato preferred the dialogue, which allowed for a genuine exchange between the speaker and the listener. Nevertheless, despite these criticisms of written texts, Plato wrote very much. We face the paradoxical situation that we know his critique of writing only through written texts.

One of the basic criticisms of writing was that the written word could not reply to questions and, therefore, could not explain the intended meanings of its words. Papyrus, in short, did not possess the knowledge of the living mind, or "pilot." Isocrates wrote to Dionysius, saying that, if he were younger, he would not write a letter but would come in person and speak with him, for it is easier to reveal one's thoughts in conversation than in letters (*Ep.* 1,1–2). One may compare the words of John the elder: "Although I have much to write to you, I would rather not use paper and ink; instead I hope to come to you and talk with you face to face, so that our joy may be complete" (2 John 12). Speaking takes precedence because it is, in contrast to written words, living. The written word is regarded as secondary, as the depository of the spoken word, but something less than the spoken word.[10]

We face the same paradoxical situation throughout the Bible. Paul is the heir of a tradition that distinguishes sharply between speaking and writing. The preference for speaking is apparent everywhere. The biblical faith, according to Amos Wilder, is "a matter of hearing rather than of seeing."[11] At Sinai, Israel's experience is auditory: the community hears God's voice. Israel's great

---

8. Ibid.
9. Ibid.
10. Peter Müller, "Der Glaube aus dem Hören: Über das gesprochene und das geschriebene Wort bei Paulus," in *Religious Propaganda and Missionary Competition in the New Testament World*, Fs. Dieter Georgi, ed. Lukas Bormann, Kelly Del Tredici, and Angela Standhartinger, NovTSup 14 (Leiden: E. J. Brill, 1994), 407.
11. Amos Wilder, *The Language of the Gospel: Early Christian Rhetoric* (New York: Harper & Row, 1964), 18.

leaders—Moses, Joshua, and the prophets—are messengers who speak for God in the immediacy of the spoken word, and they summon Israel to listen. The "word of God" in the Old Testament is not reduced to written texts.[12] Similarly, Jesus "came preaching" (Mark 1:14), apparently preferring the spoken word to the written text.

Despite the fact that Paul, through the medium of his letters, introduces a new literary genre into Christian discourse, he too prefers the immediacy of the spoken word. Paul knows that God has called him to preach rather than to write. He describes his mission on numerous occasions as one of preaching. "Christ did not send me to baptize but to proclaim the gospel," he tells the Corinthians (1 Cor. 1:17). The "power of God for salvation" (Rom. 1:16) is the gospel that Paul preaches. Like other writers of antiquity—and many preachers today—Paul prefers the spoken word and considers the written word only a substitute for oral communication. Indeed, he emphasizes the auditory aspect of preaching when he describes his preaching as the "word of hearing," thus indicating that his words were God's own word (1 Thess. 2:13, my translation). He insists that "faith comes from what is heard" (Rom. 10:17), and he describes his preaching as the "hearing with faith" (Gal. 3:2, RSV). In the heat of controversy with the Galatians, he recognizes that the written word is only a substitute for his presence: "I wish I were present with you now and could change my tone, for I am perplexed about you" (4:20).[13] Galatians, therefore, is not merely a substitute for Paul's speech. As a written communication, it is removed from the actual voice of the apostle.[14] Although Paul would prefer to convince the Galatians in person, his letter is a substitute for his preaching.

The issues that stand at the center of Paul's debate with the Corinthians also suggest that both he and this community recognized the

---

12. See Ina Willi-Plein, "Spuren der Unterscheidung von mündlichem und schriftlichem Wort im Alten Testament," in *Logos und Buchstabe,* 77. Willi-Plein describes the story of Baruch's transcription of Jeremiah's words in Jer. 36 as the "first explicit and intrabiblical reference to the use of the written word to record the prophetic word."
13. Peter Müller, "Der Glaube," 421.
14. Ibid., 435.

difference between the written and spoken word. Duane Litfin has argued persuasively that Paul's communication with the Corinthians indicates that neither he nor his opponents equated the written letter with the actual voice of Paul.[15] Paul's statement in 2 Corinthians 1:13 that "we write you nothing other than what you can read and also understand" probably reflects this distinction between his letter writing and his preaching.[16] Moreover, the opponents' charge that "[h]is letters are weighty and strong, but his bodily presence is weak, and his speech contemptible" (2 Cor. 10:10–11) indicates the distinction between Paul's writing and his speaking in the public mind.

In the third place, Paul's letters offer only a small portion of his communication with the churches. We do not have all of his correspondence with the churches (see 1 Cor. 5:9; 2 Cor. 2:1–4). Furthermore, as I shall argue in chapter 2, his evangelistic preaching was followed by an extensive pastoral ministry. His letters were preceded by periods of instruction. In Thessalonica, for example, he was present long enough to engage in an extended teaching program, as his numerous references to his previous instruction demonstrate (1 Thess. 3:4; 4:1–2, 6, 9; 5:1). He also sent Timothy to continue this program of teaching. He spent eighteen months in Corinth, and he remained somewhat longer in Ephesus.[17] Because we have only the letters as the record of Paul's communication with his churches, we easily overestimate their significance in Paul's total communication with his churches, which involved conversation and instruction at the work place (see 1 Thess. 2:9), meetings in private homes, and preaching to the house churches. Even a brief visit of a few weeks has an incomparably greater weight than an impressive letter.

Paul's letters, therefore, are a secondary form of speech, not to be equated with the living voice of the apostle. They comprise one portion of Paul's communication with his churches. Neither he nor his churches equated his letters with his actual preaching. David Bartlett has correctly said, "Paul is a preacher who takes pride in

---

15. Duane Litfin, *St. Paul's Theology of Proclamation*, SNTSMS 70 (Cambridge: Cambridge Univ. Press, 1994), 257.
16. Ibid.
17. Reinhold Reck, *Kommunikation und Gemeindeaufbau*, SbB (Stuttgart: Katholisches Bibelwerk, 1991), 203.

his preaching, but what we have in the canon are not his sermons. . . . What we have in the canon are his letters."[18]

From the Oral to the Written Word:
The Epistles as the Window to Paul's Preaching

These differences between oral and written communications
present formidable obstacles to our presentation of Paul as the
model of preaching. However, despite the differences between the
spoken word and written communication, we consistently recognize the continuity between the two modes of communication. I
observe this continuity frequently when I read the books and articles of those whom I know personally or whose speeches I have
heard regularly. As I read the words, I recognize the distinctive
speech patterns that I have heard in their oral presentations.
Sometimes what I read is the repetition of words that I first heard
in an oral presentation. On many occasions, as I read the words, it
is as if I were hearing the actual voice of the writer. The printed
page may not offer the actual living voice of the speakers, but it
offers a strong echo of their voice. We recognize this continuity
whenever we study the speeches of the great orators who lived
before the audio recording. Although we know the differences
between the effects of the written and the spoken word, we also
recognize sufficient continuity between the two modes of communication to believe that the written speeches of Demosthenes,
Isocrates, and Cicero tell us much about the distinctive characteristics of their work as orators. Quintilian declared that "it is in
writing that eloquence has its roots and foundations, it is writing
that provides that holy of holies where the wealth of oratory is
stored, and whence it is produced to meet the demands of sudden
emergencies."[19] *I suggest that Paul's epistles present a very strong echo
of his actual preaching ministry inasmuch as an important relationship
existed between his living voice and the letter that followed.*[20] In the

---

18. David Bartlett, "Texts Shaping Sermons," in *Listening to the Word*, Fs. Fred
Craddock, ed. Gail R. O'Day and Thomas G. Long (Nashville: Abingdon, 1993), 157.
19. Quintilian, *Inst.* 10.3.3. Cited in Casey Wayne Davis, *Oral Biblical Criticism: The
Influence of the Principles of Orality on the Literary Structure of Paul's Epistle to the
Philippians*, JSNTSS 172 (Sheffield: JSOT, 1999), 28.
20. Peter Müller, "Der Glaube," 422.

epistles of Paul, we come close to the actual voice of Paul as he addresses his communities. Thus, although actual texts of his sermons have not been preserved, his letters provide an indirect witness to his preaching.

Several factors indicate that Paul's letters provide a strong echo of his actual preaching. *In the first place, the close relationship between Paul's oral address and his letters is suggested by the fact that he, like other writers of antiquity, dictated his letters to an amanuensis.*[21] Therefore, the letters were the results of an oral event, and Paul's communication was meant for the ear, not the eye.[22]

As he dictated his letters, he undoubtedly envisioned the community of listeners before him. Like preachers who prepare their sermons as they envision concrete situations and personalities, Paul prepared his letters with specific listeners and situations in mind. The process of dictation allowed Paul to speak to the gathered community at a distance. One may assume that the arrangement of his thoughts approximated his normal mode of presentation. His torrential style, passion, and involved sentences bear the mark of the spoken rather than of the written word.[23] E. P. Sanders portrays the writing process as part of a ferocious debate in which the harassed and distraught apostle paced the floor,

---

21. See E. Randolph Richards, *The Secretary in the Letters of Paul*, WUNT 42 (Tübingen: J. C. B. Mohr, 1991), 169–87. See also Gordon J. Bahr, "Paul and Letter Writing in the First Century," *CBQ* 28 (1966): 465–77. Rom. 16:22 indicates that Paul dictates his letter to the Roman church. Paul's comments in 1 Cor. 16:21, Gal. 6:11, and Philemon 19 suggest that his other letters were dictated as well and that Paul added a final note. See also Paul Achtemeier, "*Omne verbum sonat:* The New Testament and the Oral Environment of Late Western Antiquity," *JBL* 109 (1990): 12–15. Achtemeier observes (15), "The important point for our purposes, however, is the fact that the oral environment was so pervasive that no writing occurred that was not vocalized." See also John D. Harvey, *Listening to the Text: Oral Patterning in Paul's Letters*, ETG Studies (Grand Rapids: Baker, 1998), 52.

22. Harvey, *Listening to the Text*, 18.

23. William Barclay, "A Comparison of Paul's Missionary Preaching and Preaching to the Church," in *Apostolic History and the Gospel*, ed. W. Ward Gasque and R. P. Martin (Exeter: Paternoster, 1970), 170: "Paul's letters are sermons far more than they are theological treatises. It is with immediate situations that they deal. They are sermons even in the sense that they were spoken rather than written. They were not carefully written out by someone sitting at a desk; they were poured out by someone striding up and down a room as he dictated, seeing all the time in his mind's eye the people to whom they were to be sent."

"dictating, sometimes pleading, sometimes grumbling, but often yelling."[24]

In the second place, letters were an ideal substitute for Paul's presence and communicated his apostolic self-understanding. Indeed, as Robert Funk observed, the letters were the means by which Paul established his presence with the churches.[25] The letter was widely regarded as a means of extending friendship and establishing the writer's presence. Paul's statement in 1 Corinthians 5:3 that he is "absent in body" but "present in spirit" suggests that the letter is a means of his presence and a medium of his apostolic authority.[26] The Corinthian charge that his "letters are weighty and strong" (2 Cor. 10:10) reflects the authority communicated by the reading of Paul's letters. Paul clearly communicates his power through his letters, which function as the surrogates for his personal presence. The letter, therefore, partakes of his apostolic authority: It is the unique word he is speaking to that church although he is separated from them.[27] This fact suggests the continuity between Paul's personal presence and his presence through the letters.

In the third place, the fact that Paul called for the public reading of his letters reflects the oral nature of his communication with his churches. Pieter Botha correctly indicates that most of Paul's audience probably never even saw the text.[28] Paul requests that his letter be read in the assembly at Thessalonica: "I solemnly command you by the Lord that this letter be read to all of them" (1 Thess. 5:27). Although this request appears only in 1 Thessalonians, we may assume that Paul expected that all of his letters would be read orally for the benefit of the community gathered for worship[29] inasmuch as all writing was meant for vocalization.[30]

---

24. E. P. Sanders, *Paul* (Oxford: Oxford Univ. Press, 1991), 54.
25. Robert Funk, "The Apostolic Parousia: Form and Significance," in *Christian History and Interpretation*, Fs. John Knox, ed. W. R. Farmer, C. F. D. Moule, and R. R. Niebuhr (Cambridge: Cambridge Univ. Press, 1967), 249.
26. Funk, "Parousia," 264.
27. David Bartlett, "Texts Shaping Sermons," 157.
28. Pieter Botha, "The Verbal Art of the Pauline Letters," in *Rhetoric and the New Testament*, ed. Thomas H. Olbricht and Stanley Porter, JSNTSS 90 (Sheffield: JSOT, 1992), 413.
29. Raymond F. Collins, "1 Thes and the Liturgy of the Early Church," *BTB* 10 (1979): 51.
30. Walter Ong, *Orality and Literacy: The Technologizing of the Word* (New York and London: Routledge, 1982), 115: "In western classical antiquity, it was taken for granted

The role of the letter carrier or public reader was decisive for the communication of the Pauline letter, especially in a culture that placed great significance on the oral performance of texts.[31] In a culture where people preferred the "living voice" over the written text, the oral performance provided the means by which written texts became the living voice. Quintilian's *Institutio oratoria* demonstrates the care that was involved in providing an appropriate oral interpretation.[32] His extensive comments on the voice, inflection, and posture of the reciter indicate the high expectations that were placed on recitation.[33] Besides dictating their letters, the letter writers often briefed the emissary on the contents of the letters and gave supplementary information to the emissary, who could transmit the additional information to the listeners.[34] According to Richard Ward, texts (such as written gospels or letters) recited or orally composed in Christian worship suggested the

---

that a written text of any worth was meant to be and deserved to be read aloud, and the practice of reading texts aloud continued, quite commonly and with many variations, through the nineteenth century. This practice strongly influenced literary style from antiquity until rather recent times."

31. Claude Cox, "The Reading of the Personal Letter as the Background for the Reading of the Scriptures in the Early Church," in *The Early Church in Its Context: Essays in Honor of Everett Ferguson*, ed. Abraham J. Malherbe, Frederick W. Norris, and James W. Thompson, NovTSup 90 (Leiden: E. J. Brill, 1998), 82.

32. Cf. Martin Cobin, "An Oral Interpreter's Index to Quintilian," *Quarterly Journal of Speech* 44 (1958): 61–66. Quintilian applies his extensive instructions on delivery to the reading of texts. He indicates that readers must be thoroughly acquainted with his text. "Our actor will also be required to show how a narrative should be delivered, and to indicate the authoritative tone that should mark the rise of anger, and the change of tone that is characteristic of pathos" (*Inst.* 1.11.12). Quintilian says elsewhere, "The case with which the speech selected for reading is concerned should then be explained, for if this be done they will have a clearer understanding of what is to be read. When the reading is commenced, no important point should be allowed to pass unnoticed either as regards the resourcefulness or the style shown in the treatment of the subject." Quintilian proceeds to show how readers should understand the exordium and the division of the speech into different headings: "How subtle and frequent are the thrusts of argument, what vigour marks the stirrings and what charm the soothing passage, how fierce is the invective and how full of wit the jests, and in conclusion how the orator establishes his sway over the emotions of his audience, forces his way into their very hearts and brings the feelings of the jury into perfect sympathy with his words" (*Inst.* 2.5.8).

33. See Quintilian, *Inst.* 1.11.2–14.

34. Martin McGuire, "Letters and Letter Carriers in Ancient Antiquity," *Classical World* 53 (1960): 148, cited in Richard Ward, "Pauline Voice and Presence as Strategic Communication," *SBLSP* 29 (1990): 289.

immediacy of oral discourse. Sending an emissary to read a letter was an effective means of establishing the writer's presence. Letters served orality and were thus returned to oral space by way of the public reader.[35] The reader embodied the emotional values of the letter and sought to allow those values to shape the presentation.[36] Ward suggests that Paul chose his emissaries with care, expecting them to establish his apostolic presence through the oral delivery. In fact, oral delivery was the second "act" in creating "Paul-in-the-letter."[37] Botha has suggested that Paul coached the reader in anticipation of the actual event.[38] He expected his reader not only to recite the contents of his letters, but to "interpret" the contents.[39] In his statement that Timothy will "remind you of my ways" (1 Cor. 4:17), Paul indicates the importance of his emissary as the interpreter of the letter. One may compare the comments at the conclusion of Ephesians (6:21): "So that you also may know how I am and what I am doing, Tychicus will tell you everything." We may assume, therefore, that Paul sent a handwritten, travel-worn manuscript with someone he trusted in order that the emissary might present his intentions and symbols verbally and bodily to others. "The written words had to be mouthed aloud, in their full being, restored to and made alive in the oral cavities in which they came into existence."[40]

In the fourth place, we may note that the letters actually repeat what Paul has said to the community already. In numerous instances he indicates that his letters repeat what he has already said in his personal address to his readers. At the beginning of Galatians, Paul says (1:9), "As we have said before, so now I repeat." This statement evidently refers to Paul's earlier preaching among the Galatians. In the concluding section he refers to a list of vices and says, "I am warning you, as I warned you before: those who do such things will

---

35. Ward, "Pauline Voice and Presence," 289.
36. Ibid., 290.
37. Ibid.
38. Botha, *The Verbal Art of the Pauline Letters*, 417. "Paul's dictation of his letter was, in all probability, also coaching of the letter carrier and eventual reader. The carrier of the letter would most likely have seen to it that it be read like Paul wanted it to be read."
39. Ward, "Pauline Voice and Presence," 289.
40. Ong, "*Maranatha*: Death and Life in the Text of the Book," *JAAR* 45 (1977): 437, cited in Botha, 418.

not inherit the kingdom of God" (Gal. 5:21). Here Paul refers
either to his prebaptismal or postbaptismal instruction of his new
converts.[41] Paul wrote the letter in anticipation of the aural event
when the messenger read the letter to the congregation. The letter
was his opportunity to "re-preach" his gospel in the context of the
opposition that faced him.[42] In 1 Thessalonians 3:4 he says of the
community's experience of suffering, "We told you repeatedly[43]
that we would endure such things" (my translation). One may also
compare 2 Corinthians 7:3, where Paul says, "I said before that
you are in our hearts, to die together and to live together." In
2 Corinthians 13:2 he apparently refers to the words of a prior visit
when he says, "I warned those who sinned previously and all the
others, and I warn them now while absent . . . that if I come again,
I will not be lenient." In introducing the practical plan for raising
the relief fund, he wrote to the Corinthians, "[A]s I directed the
churches of Galatia, so you also are to do" (1 Cor. 16:1, RSV). On a
doctrinal subject he wrote, "Now I would remind you, brethren, in
what terms I preached to you the gospel" (1 Cor. 15:1, RSV).
Similarly, in his statements about the Parousia, he writes to the
Thessalonians, "Do you not remember that when I was still with
you I told you this?" (2 Thess. 2:5, RSV).[44] From these statements
we see the continuity between Paul's preaching activity and his letters. Paul's oral communication to his churches includes catechetical instruction for the Christian life, repetition of his original
preaching, and instruction about the implications of his previous
instruction in the Christian life and faith. Although the letters cannot be equated precisely with Paul's oral preaching, they resume
the earlier conversations and repeat what Paul has said before.[45]
Thus they offer major insights into his preaching ministry.

---

41. Richard Longenecker, *Galatians*, WBC (Dallas: Word, 1990), 258.

42. J. Louis Martyn, "Events in Galatia," *Pauline Theology*, ed. Jouette M. Bassler
(Minneapolis: Fortress, 1991), 1.161, 179.

43. Note the imperfect tense of προελέγομεν, which indicates repeated action. See
Traugott Holtz, *Der erste Brief an die Thessalonicher*, EKK (Neukirchen: Benziger,
1998), 128.

44. M. Luther Stirewalt Jr., "Paul's Evaluation of Letter-Writing," in *Search the
Scriptures*, Fs. Raymond T. Stamm, ed. J. M. Myers, O. Reimherr, and H. N. Bream
(Leiden: E. J. Brill, 1969), 192.

45. Leander Keck, "Toward a Theology of Rhetoric/Preaching," *Practical Theology*,
ed. Don Browning (San Francisco: Harper & Row, 1983), 130.

In the fifth place, the oral/aural dimension of Paul's preaching undoubtedly determined both his style and his arrangement[46] *in the letters, inasmuch as they, of all written communication, may come closest to oral communication.* Rudolf Bultmann argued that the epistles record how Paul "always expressed himself, whether by letter or by mouth."[47] Letter writing allowed Paul to "stay in near-oral touch with his addressees."[48] Walter Ong notes that this oral character "even in its epistolary sections is overwhelming."[49] Phrases such as "brethren," "I say," "you know yourselves" are numerous in the Pauline epistles. Indeed, he prefers the verb *to say* over the verb *to write* when he refers to his own composition. He uses "to write" (γράφειν) in this way more than twenty times. At least forty times he uses "to say."[50] John D. Harvey has examined the patterns of oral speech in the undisputed letters of Paul, demonstrating that Paul consistently employs the distinctive features of oral communication. His frequent use of chiasm, repetition, refrain, ring composition, and inclusion reflects the common pattern of speech of an oral culture.[51] Moreover, his dialogical style, reflecting his awareness of his relationship to the audience, indicates the oral quality of the address. His use of vocatives, rhetorical questions, and disclosure formulas ("I want you to know") demonstrates the dialogic quality of his discourse.[52] The stylistic character of the epistles demonstrates that Paul imagined himself speaking to the collective audience and not writing to individual readers.[53]

Walter Ong has suggested that the failure to recognize the orality of the Bible "has interfered with our understanding of the

---

46. Raymond Bailey, *Paul the Preacher* (Nashville: Broadman, 1991), 18.

47. R. Bultmann, *Der Stil der paulinischen Predigt und die kynisch-stoische Diatribe*, FRLANT 13 (Göttingen: Vandenhoeck & Ruprecht, 1910), 3.

48. Werner Kelber, *The Oral and Written Gospel: The Hermeneutics of Speaking and Writing in the Synoptic Tradition, Mark, Paul, and Q* (Philadelphia: Fortress, 1983), 168.

49. Ong, *Orality and Literacy*, 75.

50. Stirewalt, "Paul's Evaluation of Letter-Writing," 192.

51. Harvey, *Listening to the Text*, 97–118.

52. See Davis, *Oral Biblical Criticism*, 64. I shall treat the dialogical character of Paul's discourse further in chapters 2 and 4.

53. See R. Dean Anderson Jr., *Ancient Rhetorical Theory and Paul*, rev. ed. (Leuven: Peeters, 1999), 119. Cf. Hans Hübner, "Der Galaterbrief und das Verhältnis von antiker Rhetorik und Epistolographie," *TLZ* 109 (1984): 245; Bo Reicke, "A Synopsis of Early Christian Preaching," in *The Root of the Vine*, ed. A. Fridrichsen (Westminster: Dacre Press, 1953).

nature of the Bible, with its massive oral underpinnings."[54] In their examination of Paul's letters, for example, biblical scholars observe the signals that reflect the writer's organizational arrangement. Writers trained in Western culture naturally look for visual signals of the author's organizing principles. Where the visual signals are nonexistent or confusing, scholars commonly interpret this fact either as a sign of the composite nature of the work or as an indication of the author's use of sources. Such a reading is, according to Paul Achtemeier, highly anachronistic, inasmuch as it assumes the organizing principles of a "print" culture and ignores the organizing principles of an oral culture,[55] in which speakers used a variety of means to assist the hearer in keeping up with the argument and to mark the change of topics.[56]

The letter provided a medium for oral communication because, prior to Paul, the letter had long functioned as a substitute for oral discourse. Letter writing was well established in the first century and was frequently defined as one half of a dialogue.[57] As a substitute for one's presence, a letter was expected to contain what one would have said had one been present and to say it in a style appropriate to the occasion.[58] In the ancient world written letters and oral discourse (conversations, speeches) were closely related. Ignatius describes one of his letters as a conversation (*Eph.* 9:2), and another as an address (*Mag.* 1:1).[59]

In the sixth place, the close relationship of letter writing and oratory also suggests that Paul's letters reflect the spoken word. According to George Kennedy, there has always been a close formal connection between the oration and the epistle.[60] Although ancient theorists

---

54. Walter Ong, *The Presence of the Word* (New Haven: Yale Univ. Press, 1967), 21.

55. Achtemeier, "*Omne verbum sonat,*" 27.

56. Ibid., 26. Because the flow of the argument in 2 Corinthians and Philippians is difficult to follow, the solution most commonly available is that the epistles are composite works. Achtemeier suggests that Philippians may be an example of a communication over a range of topics that are clearly demarcated at 3:1 and 4:1 for the benefit of the listener. On the rhetorical unity of Philippians, see also Duane Watson, "A Rhetorical Analysis of Philippians and Its Implications for the Unity Question," *NovT* 30 (1988). Cf. Davis, *Oral Biblical Criticism*, 141–61.

57. Abraham J. Malherbe, *Paul and the Thessalonians* (Philadelphia: Fortress, 1987), 69.

58. Ibid.

59. David E. Aune, *The New Testament in Its Literary Environment* (Philadelphia: Westminster, 1987), 197.

60. George Kennedy, *New Testament Interpretation through Rhetorical Criticism* (Chapel Hill: Univ. of North Carolina Press, 1984), 86–87.

distinguished clearly between the letter and the epistle,[61] in actual practice the two modes of communication held much in common. Stanley Stowers has pointed out that many letter types could fit into one of the three types of rhetoric (forensic, deliberative, and epideictic).[62] This close relationship between the letter and the oration may be seen also in the fact that some letters in antiquity were essentially rhetorical writings in an epistolary frame.[63] The first four letters of Demosthenes, for example, are written from exile and addressed to the assembly in Athens. Demosthenes states that he would make his case in person if he were present at the assembly, but because of his situation he must express his thoughts in a letter.[64] Although the rhetorical rules and precepts were developed for oral discourses, it is also probable that rhetorical principles were used either directly or indirectly in the composition of letters.[65] The Greek "orator" Isocrates was too nervous to speak in public and wrote out his speeches for publication or for sending to an addressee as an open letter.[66]

Conclusion

Although Paul and others in antiquity distinguished between the written and the spoken word and preferred the latter, we can nevertheless conclude that Paul's letters provided the occasion for *hearing*. This collection of letters, written as a substitute for his presence and read orally in the assembly, provides an insight into the scope of his preaching ministry. If the letters contain what Paul would have said if he had been present, they offer insights into the

---

61. See J. Classen, "St. Paul's Epistles and Ancient Greek and Roman Rhetoric," in *Rhetoric and the New Testament*, ed. Stanley E. Porter and Thomas H. Olbricht, JSNTSS 90 (Sheffield: JSOT Press, 1993); Anderson, *Ancient Rhetorical Theory and Paul*, 118.

62. Stanley Stowers, *Letter Writing in Greco-Roman Antiquity*, LEC (Philadelphia: Westminster, 1986), 23. See also Jeffrey T. Reed, "The Epistle," in *Handbook of Classical Rhetoric in the Hellenistic Period*, ed. Stanley Porter (Leiden: E. J. Brill, 1997), 174–75. Reed argues that the overlap between the species of rhetoric and the classifications of letters may indicate only the presence of culturally shared means of argumentation rather than a dependence of writers on the rhetorical handbooks.

63. Anderson, *Ancient Rhetorical Theory and Paul*, 121.

64. *Ep.* 3.35, cited in Anderson, *Ancient Rhetorical Theory and Paul*, 123.

65. Frank W. Hughes, *Early Christian Rhetoric and 2 Thessalonians*, JSOTSup 30 (Sheffield: JSOT, 1989), 47.

66. Kennedy, *New Testament Interpretation*, 87.

principles of arrangement, modes of argumentation, and stylistic features of the Pauline sermon. Because the letters address many different communities on different occasions, they provide insight into Paul's preaching in a variety of situations. They indicate both the themes common to all of Paul's sermons and his capacity to adapt to new situations. With the variety in the kinds of letters that Paul wrote, we are able to see what J. Christiaan Beker calls the "coherence" and "contingency" in Paul's thought.[67] In 1 Thessalonians, for example, we find Paul's standard catechetical sermon to a community that was doing well. This epistle is useful, as I shall demonstrate in chapter 4, for our understanding of his agenda for pastoral preaching. In the other epistles, we observe his response to contingent situations. In Paul's response to this variety of situations, we find an appropriate model for the continued ministry of the word in our own time. Paul is both an evangelistic and a pastoral preacher who provides insights into the relationship between the two forms of preaching. He preaches to communities that are living up to his expectations for them, and he preaches in moments of crisis. He preaches to communities that share a long history with him, and he preaches to communities that are not familiar with him. In this preaching ministry that lasted more than a decade, Paul offers the modern preacher a model for the entire preaching ministry.

Although Paul's letters are neither the transcripts of his sermons nor his preferred mode of communication with his churches, they offer our only records of his preaching ministry. If we look through this small window into Paul's work, we can ascertain very much about Paul's evangelistic and pastoral work among his churches. As I shall demonstrate in chapter 2, we can observe the progression from Paul's original encounter with his listeners to his ongoing conversation with them through the letters. His preaching resulted in the formation of communities, which he then sustained, first by oral instruction and then through his letters. His letters, therefore, stood in a close relationship to his preaching. As is the case with all ancient speakers, we know him only through written words.

---

67. J. Christiaan Beker, *Paul the Apostle: The Triumph of God in Life and Thought* (Philadelphia: Fortress, 1980), 23–93.

Chapter Two

Paul's Evangelistic and Pastoral Preaching

For more than a century, biblical scholars have noted two distinctive portraits of Paul in the New Testament. On the one hand, we know the Paul of the popular imagination portrayed in Acts. He is a traveler and missionary who preaches evangelistic sermons with equal eloquence before Jewish synagogue leaders and Athenian philosophers. His role as a spokesman is so significant that the people of Lystra call him Hermes, the messenger for the gods (Acts 14:12). Educated in both Tarsus and Jerusalem (Acts 22:3), he addresses crowds in either Greek or Aramaic, and he is an equally capable speaker before the Sanhedrin in Jerusalem and before Roman magistrates.

On the other hand, we also have a portrait of Paul from the letters. Whereas Acts presents Paul as a spokesperson and never mentions him as a letter writer, in the epistles both he and his opponents agree that he is one who is "untrained in speech" (2 Cor. 11:6). Paul does not deny the opponents' charge that "[h]is letters are weighty and strong, but his bodily presence is weak, and his speech contemptible" (2 Cor. 10:10).

Although both Acts and the letters present Paul as a preacher whose ambition is "to proclaim the good news, not where Christ has already been named" (Rom. 15:20), they appear to provide two different portraits of the nature of Paul's preaching ministry. In Acts Paul is primarily an itinerant missionary preacher who speaks so effectively to non-Christian audiences that his preaching results in conversions wherever he travels. In the epistles Paul nurtures churches, speaking only to the congregations that were formed as a result of his evangelistic preaching.

These alternative portraits of the preaching ministry of Paul have provided the basis for the radical distinction in our own time between evangelistic and pastoral preaching. C. H. Dodd's influential book *The Apostolic Preaching and Its Developments* has also contributed to this sharp distinction between a Paul who in Acts preaches to a non-Christian audience and the one who in his epistles gives pastoral instruction to the believing community.[1] On the basis of his examination of the terms *kerygma* and *didache*, Dodd defines preaching "as the public proclamation of Christianity to the non-Christian world."[2] He adds:

> Much of our preaching in Church at the present day would not have been recognized by the early Christians as *kerygma*. It is teaching, or exhortation (*paraklesis*), or it is what they called *homilia*, that is, the more or less informal discussion of various aspects of Christian life and thought, addressed to a congregation already established in the faith.[3]

Dodd's distinction between *kerygma* and *didache* has had a significant impact on our understanding of the preaching ministry, and it raises important questions for contemporary practice if we are to appeal to Paul as a model. His claim that evangelistic preaching is limited to non-Christian audiences requires scrutiny, especially in our own times. In a culture that is in transition between Christian and post-Christian, we are not likely to make these sharp distinctions. We may expect a continuum among our listeners that extends from those who have been shaped by the Christian heritage to others whose relationship to the Christian faith is marginal at best. Consequently, I suggest that we examine Dodd's sharp distinction between evangelistic and pastoral preaching in light of both the ancient evidence and the modern situation.

Dodd's view that we speak "to a congregation already established in the faith" was more plausible in 1936 than it is in 2000. His argument reflects his situation within the Christian culture of England in that era. Unlike Dodd, we live in a culture that is largely post-Christian, as I argued in the introduction. Nevertheless, despite the changed situation, the popular percep-

---

1. C. H. Dodd, *The Apostolic Preaching and Its Developments* (1936; reprint, New York: Harper & Row, 1964), 7–9.
2. Ibid., 7.
3. Ibid., 7–8.

tion of evangelistic preaching remains largely that of Dodd. Evangelism is regarded as the work of the televangelist or the missionary, not the work of one who preaches to the established congregation. We assume that our own churches were evangelized long before us. Consequently, we think of our own preaching almost exclusively as *didache* rather than *kerygma*, and we assume that we preach "in a Christian land" to those who have already heard.[4] This assumption is reflected in the homiletic literature, where one finds an abundance of titles that offer guidance on preaching to the needs of those who are already converted, but few works on evangelistic preaching.[5]

In the previous chapter, I argued that the letters of Paul provide the models, not only for specific sermons, but for the entire ministry of preaching. However, if the popular perception is correct— if the letters provide only the one-dimensional portrait of Paul as a pastoral preacher who speaks to his churches with dense theological arguments—I must concede that I will have difficulty making my case. On the surface, the letters do not appear to tell us about Paul's evangelistic preaching, nor do they appear to describe the full range of preaching activities before he wrote the letters. The epistles record what the communities heard at one moment in Paul's relationship with them, but neither the story that preceded the letter nor the continuing conversation. We hear the intricate argument of Romans 9–11, for example, but we lose the texture of the entire event. We come into the middle of a conversation between Paul and the Galatians on the topic of circumcision, but we miss some of the argument because we did not hear the earlier discussion. These intricate arguments make difficult models for preaching. As a result of this popular perception, as I noted in the introduction, Paul is rarely the model for preaching. We have difficulty imagining our congregations responding to this dense

---

4. Note the subtitle of Fred Craddock's *Overhearing the Gospel: Preaching and Teaching the Faith to Persons Who Have Already Heard* (Nashville: Abingdon, 1978).

5. See, for example, J. Randall Nichols, *The Restoring Word: Preaching as Pastoral Communication* (San Francisco: Harper & Row, 1987). See also the list of titles in the "Preaching About" series (Westminster/John Knox): David H. C. Read, *Preaching about the Needs of Real People* (1988); William H. Willimon, *Preaching about Conflict in the Local Church* (1987); Elizabeth Achtemeier, *Preaching about Family Relationships* (1987).

theological argumentation. We prefer a story that speaks to the narrative of our own lives.

In this chapter, I wish to place Paul's preaching in a wider context in order to demonstrate that his pastoral and discursive preaching actually participates in a larger narrative. The epistles are, in fact, the continuation of a conversation. This larger story involves *Paul's own story, the story of his listeners, and the story that Paul has communicated to his congregation.*[6] Paul's discursive preaching is not the only dimension to his communication, but it is the necessary sequel to his earlier evangelistic preaching. If we probe beneath the surface of the epistles, we discover a preaching ministry that involves a progression from evangelistic and narrative preaching to discursive reasoning. Each of the epistles, like a still photo, portrays a single moment frozen in time, and for the trained observer, they imply a story. Just as we look at the pictures in our family album and recall the story that lies behind the pictures, we look at Paul's letters and begin to reflect on the larger narratives that involve the intersection of stories. Behind Paul's letters lie the story of his evangelistic preaching, his listeners' initial response to that message, and the continuing story that culminates in Paul's communication with his churches.

The narrative of the epistles is not limited to past events; it projects a story that moves into the future. He anticipates a continuing intersection of his story with that of his congregations. His letters prepare the way for the visit of emissaries (Rom. 16:1–2; 1 Cor. 16:8–10; Phil. 2:19–30) or his own reunion with his congregations (Philemon 22). Occasionally, he writes in order to overcome misunderstandings and prepare the way for his continuing relationship to his churches. In the meantime, his congregations live between their new existence and their ultimate destiny in Christ—"between the resurrection and the return of Christ."[7] Because the story is not yet complete, Paul writes letters to help his listeners reach their final goal.

---

6. See Ben Witherington, *Paul's Narrative Thought World: The Tapestry of Tragedy and Triumph* (Louisville, Ky.: Westminster John Knox, 1994); Norman Petersen, *Rediscovering Paul: Philemon and the Sociology of Paul's Narrative World* (Philadelphia: Fortress, 1985), 43–53. Cf. Richard B. Hays, *The Faith of Jesus Christ*, SBLDS 56 (Chico, Calif.: Scholars Press, 1983), 20–23. Cf. Richard Hays, "ΠΙΣΤΙΣ and Pauline Christology," in E. Elizabeth Johnson and David M. Hay, eds., *Pauline Theology* (Atlanta: Scholars Press, 1997), 4.37.

7. Witherington, *Paul's Narrative Thought World*, 340.

If we read Paul's letters carefully, we can learn very much about this intersection of stories and discover the Pauline model for a preaching ministry that progresses from evangelistic witness to pastoral care. *I am convinced that our avoidance of Paul as a source for preaching is the result of our failure to see the narrative behind his letters.* My task in this chapter is to observe the stories that precede the snapshots. My focus is on Paul's actual preaching ministry prior to his literary activity. I suggest that Christians in a post-Christian era can learn much about preaching from one who preached in the pre-Christian era.

Evangelistic Preaching:
The Story of Paul and His Converts

Paul's pastoral work in the letters occasionally requires that he tell his own story, for only by telling that story can he explain the circumstances that ultimately led to his pastoral work (see 1 Cor. 9:1–23; Gal. 1:10–2:21; Phil. 3:2–16) with his churches. At the center of Paul's story is the encounter with the risen Lord, who called and commissioned him for service. This event was nothing less than a prophetic call. Paul does not hesitate to compare his call with that of the Old Testament prophets (see Gal. 1:15; Jer. 1:5; cf. Isa. 49:1, 6). Just as the prophets were *called* and *sent* to speak for God, Christ called him to "proclaim [Christ] among the Gentiles" (Gal. 1:16). Just as Jeremiah was overwhelmed by the call and compelled to speak God's word (Jer. 20:7–8), Paul says, "Woe to me if I do not proclaim the gospel!" (1 Cor. 9:16). As a result he knows that he is under a divine necessity (ἀνάγκη, 1 Cor. 9:16) to preach.[8] He is not his own master, but the captive who is being led

---

8. Ἀνάγκη refers to the "power of grace," a destiny by which God makes humans his instruments for service. One may compare the divine necessity that compels prophetic activity in the Old Testament. Moses, Amos, and Jeremiah have been compelled by the divine necessity. See Exod. 3:11f.; 4:10ff.; Amos 3:8; Jer. 1:5f.; 20:9; Ezek. 3:17f.; Jonah 1:2ff. W. Schrage, *Der erste Brief an die Korinther*, EKK (Neukirchen: Benziger, 1995), 323–24. Cf. K. O. Sandnes, *Paul—One of the Prophets? A Contribution to the Apostle's Self-Understanding*, WUNT 2/43 (Tübingen: J. C. B. Mohr, 1991), 125–29. See also Seyon Kim, *The Origin of Paul's Gospel* (Grand Rapids: Eerdmans, 1981), 289–90; Carey C. Newman, *Paul's Glory Christology: Tradition and Rhetoric*, SNTSMS 69 (Leiden: E. J. Brill, 1992), 165–67.

through the streets in a triumphant processional (2 Cor. 2:14).[9] His preaching is the consequence of the event when God said, "Let light shine out of darkness," and "shone in our hearts to give the light of the knowledge of the glory of God in the face of Jesus Christ" (2 Cor. 4:6). In the context of explaining a mission that has resulted in rejection by his fellow Jews, Paul recalls the words of Isaiah 28:16, according to which "everyone who calls on the name of the Lord will be saved" (Rom. 10:13, RSV). Then he adds, "But how are they to call on one in whom they have not believed? And how are they to believe in one of whom they have never heard? And how are they to hear without someone to proclaim him?" (Rom. 10:14–15). Paul answers with the claim that "faith comes from what is heard, and what is heard comes through the word of Christ" (Rom. 10:17). He knows that people come to salvation only through preaching and that the preacher must be *sent* by God (10:15). Paul is the preacher whom God has sent for a special purpose. As he indicates later in the epistle to the Romans, his mission is to be God's "priestly servant" (λειτουργός) to the nations and to "proclaim the good news, not where Christ has already been named" (Rom. 15:20). When he adds that he has preached already in the eastern half of the Mediterranean world (Rom. 15:19), he alludes to his story. When he describes his plans (Rom. 15:25–29), he projects his story into the future. Without the event that transformed his life, Paul's story would not have intersected with that of his churches.

---

9. For the view that Paul is the captive of God in the processional, see Gerhard Barth, "Die Eignung des Verkündigers in 2 Kor 2,14–3,6," in *Kirche*, Fs. G. Bornkamm, ed. D. Lührmann and G. Strecker (Tübingen: J. C. B. Mohr, 1980), 261. The opponents have looked to Paul's sufferings as a sign that he is not an apostle. Paul claims to be involved in the victory processional. Cf. Scott Hafemann, *Suffering and Ministry in the Spirit, an Exegetical Study of II Cor. 2:14–3:3 within the Context of the Corinthian Correspondence*, WUNT 2.19 (Tübingen: J. C. B. Mohr, 1986), 25. Hafemann compares Paul's self-portrayal in 2 Cor. 2:14 with ancient texts involving the triumphal processional. Plutarch describes how the king, his family, and their friends and personal attendants were led through the streets as representatives of the vanquished in prelude to their execution. Even the children were led as "slaves," unaware of the fate that awaited them at the end of the parade. Cf. Plutarch, *Rom.* xxv.4–xxxiv. Cf. also Plutarch, *Vit. Ant.* xxvi: Cleopatra cries to the Manes of Mark Anthony, "If the gods of Rome have power or mercy left . . . let them not suffer me to be led in living triumph to your disgrace." See also Frances Young and David F. Ford, *Meaning and Truth in 2 Corinthians* (Grand Rapids: Eerdmans, 1987), 19.

We know more of Paul's story from those occasions when he describes the ongoing activity that has resulted from his call. In 2 Corinthians he responds to the attacks on his preaching ministry with a contrast between his preaching and that of others who claim to be servants of Christ. In contrast to those who, like the sophists, "peddle" their message (cf. 2 Cor. 2:17), Paul graphically describes his continuing activity as a minister as one who speaks, refusing to "tamper with God's word" (2 Cor. 4:2, RSV).[10] In response to the attacks on his ineffectiveness as a preacher, he reaffirms the content of his message: "We do not proclaim ourselves; we proclaim Jesus Christ as Lord" (2 Cor. 4:5). If people reject his gospel, the fault is not that of the preacher; rather, it is the fact that "the god of this world has blinded the minds of the unbelievers, to keep them from seeing the light of the gospel of the glory of Christ, who is the image of God" (2 Cor. 4:4). Any alteration is a "gospel contrary to what we proclaimed" (Gal. 1:8; cf. "different gospel," 2 Cor. 11:4). The "truth of the gospel" must be preserved at all costs (Gal. 2:5, 14), and any violation of it would bring one under condemnation. Hence his preaching will not be affected by market demands; he will not be deterred by apparent failure. Nor will his preaching be determined by its potential results. In his preaching activity he acts as an ambassador for God, speaking on behalf of Christ, when he announces that "in Christ God was reconciling the world to himself" (2 Cor. 5:19). Paul's continuing activity is thus the consequence of the prophetic call that changed his life.

Paul commonly refers to his proclamation with the term *gospel* (εὐαγγέλιον) and the verbs *preach the gospel* (εὐαγγελίζομαι) and *preach* (κηρύσσω).[11] In many instances Paul refers to the content of his preaching with εὐαγγέλιον, which may appear as the object of either verb (1 Cor. 15:1; 2 Cor. 11:7; Gal. 1:11; 2:2; Col. 1:23; 1 Thess. 2:9). In other instances, the verb εὐαγγελίζομαι stands without an object (1 Cor. 1:17; 9:16, 18; 2 Cor. 10:16; Gal. 1:8–9; 4:13) because the object is implied in the verb. The language

---

10. Καπηλεύοντες, used by Paul in 2 Cor. 2:17, is the common term used in the philosophic tradition for the Sophists, who sold their instruction as merchandise. Cf. Plato, *Protag.* 314c, d. See Gerhard Barth, "Eignung," 263.

11. The term κήρυγμα appears in the Pauline literature only in Rom. 16:25; 1 Cor. 1:21; 2:4; 15:14; 2 Tim. 4:17; and Titus 1:3; and elsewhere in the NT only in Matt. 12:41; Luke 11:32.

echoes early Christian reflection on Isaiah 40–55, especially Isaiah 52:7, where the prophet announces, "How beautiful upon the mountains are the feet of the messenger who announces peace, who brings good news, who announces salvation, who says to Zion, 'Your God reigns.'" Paul's gospel is, therefore, the declaration of God's saving events announced by the prophet.

Paul's frequent references to his preaching indicate the central place of evangelistic preaching in his ministry. However, his numerous references to his evangelistic preaching leave the reader at first uncertain about the precise content of his proclamation of the gospel.[12] The variety of expressions indicates that the gospel could not be reduced to a *singular fixed formula*. Nevertheless, one can see a *common narrative* according to which the good news awaited in Isaiah 52 is equated with the story of Jesus. Whether Paul refers to the subject of his preaching as *Jesus Christ* or *the gospel*, he is actually referring to the narrative of God's actions in Jesus Christ, which are a portion of the larger Jewish narrative world.[13] His references to Jesus function within the letters as ministories that reflect his transformation of the basic biblical story.[14]

Paul's frequent summaries of the εὐαγγέλιον indicate the narrative quality of his gospel. In the opening words of Romans (1:3–4, RSV), he elaborates on his message by summarizing "the gospel concerning his Son, who was descended from David according to the flesh and designated Son of God in power according to the Spirit of holiness by his resurrection from the dead, Jesus Christ our Lord." The arguments throughout the epistles refer to the basic narrative. His announcement in Romans, "[b]ut now, apart from law, the righteousness of God has been disclosed" (3:21), recalls the Christ event. The simple phrase "who was handed over to death for our trespasses and raised for our justification" (Rom. 4:25) also indicates the narrative quality of the gospel. In his ringing declaration "[b]ut God proves his love for us

---

12. See R. H. Mounce, "Preaching, Kerygma," in *A Dictionary of Paul and His Letters*, ed. Gerald Hawthorne, R. P. Martin, and Daniel Reid (Downers Grove: InterVarsity, 1993).

13. N. T. Wright, *The New Testament and the People of God* (Minneapolis: Fortress, 1992), 407.

14. Contrary to the claim of Bultmann that Paul is not concerned with the κατὰ σάρκα Christ (2 Cor. 5:16), Paul's story included the narratives about Jesus.

in that while we were still sinners Christ died for us" (Rom. 5:8), he again summarizes the gospel as narrative. In instructing the strong and the weak Christians, he recalls that "Christ did not please himself" (Rom. 15:3). Paul's arguments rest on an appeal to the narrative that changed his life—the story that intersected with his own life story.

Paul assumes that his readers are acquainted with the story. Indeed, a familiar topic in his letters is the recollection of his evangelistic preaching. He reminds the Galatians of the occasion when he "first announced the gospel" (Gal. 4:13) to them. In 1 Corinthians he recalls his original preaching activity when he says, "[W]e preach Christ crucified" (1:23, RSV), and then adds in 2:1–5, RSV,

> When I came to you, brethren, I did not come proclaiming to you the testimony of God in lofty words or wisdom. For I decided to know nothing among you except Christ and him crucified. And I was with you in weakness and in much fear and trembling; and my speech and my message were not in plausible words of wisdom, but in demonstration of the Spirit and of power, that your faith might not rest in the wisdom of men but in the power of God.

Paul refers again to his earlier preaching activity in 3:6 and 3:10 in the words "I planted" and "I laid a foundation" and in the subsequent statement, "in Christ Jesus I became your father through the gospel" (4:15; cf. Philemon 10). He later initiates the discussion of the resurrection with the reminder of his earlier preaching: "I would remind you, brothers and sisters, of the good news that I proclaimed to you, which you in turn received, in which also you stand" (15:1). The subsequent argument is based on the foundation of the *kerygma* that he had originally preached: "that Christ died for our sins in accordance with the scriptures, and that he was buried, and that he was raised on the third day in accordance with the scriptures" (15:3–4).

In Paul's constant reminders of what he had preached, we have a window into his evangelistic preaching, which consisted of telling the story that had intersected with his own story. Althou preached both to Jews and pagans, the letters are addr Gentile churches, and they recall the narrative that preached to pagans. While the details of Paul's evangelistic preaching probably varied slightly in different situations, the epistles indicate that Paul's evangelistic preaching to pagan audiences included the following plot:

> God, the Creator of heaven and earth, has a plan for the world.
>
> God has planned since ancient times to bless the world with good news, and now that moment has come.
>
> God has sent his Jesus, who is the fulfillment of God's plans, to redeem the world.
>
> Jesus died on a cross to rescue all humanity.
>
> God has raised Jesus from the dead, conquering death and all principalities and powers.
>
> This creator God summons you to acknowledge his saving deeds and to turn to him.
>
> On the basis of what God has done in these events, we know that this world is going somewhere. Consequently, you do not need to live your lives in hopelessness or despair, for the God who created the world will also bring it to completion. We have a future as we wait for God to send his son from heaven! (1 Thess. 1:10)

My reading of Paul's evangelistic preaching does not vary greatly from C. H. Dodd's description of Paul's *kerygma*.[15] I suggest that Paul delivered the standard evangelistic sermons in numerous contexts and that he elaborated on the details and implications of the story as the situation demanded. Undoubtedly, when he preached to Jewish audiences, he developed his case with references to the scriptures. Nevertheless, for both Jewish and Gentile audiences Paul's evangelistic preaching involved telling a story. It was the true story of the world, informing listeners that events that had happened in recent history had changed the course of the world and of their lives.[16] Paul was inviting his listeners to come to terms with reality, a reality that was defined in a series of events,

---

15. Cf. also Richard Hays, "Crucified with Christ," in *Pauline Theology*, ed. Jouette Bassler (Minneapolis: Fortress, 1991), 1.234; Dodd, *Apostolic Preaching*, 17. See also John M. G. Barclay, "Conflict in Thessalonica," *CBQ* 55 (1993): 516–17.

16. See N. T. Wright, *What Saint Paul Really Said* (Grand Rapids: Eerdmans, 1997), 89.

and to be incorporated in a history that was not yet completed.[17] His recollection of his own preaching is basically consistent with Luke's portrait of Paul's preaching in Acts. Both Luke and Paul portray a preaching that moves from the narrative of God's deeds to an invitation to the hearers to respond to the message.[18]

Paul assumes that his pagan listeners, prior to their hearing of the gospel, have their own story, although he rarely describes it in detail. Although Acts portrays Paul as carefully adapting his message to the listeners—even employing the Stoic categories of that culture—in the speech at Athens (Acts 17:22–33), the letters provide no indication that Paul's evangelistic preaching involved allowing the listeners to set the agenda. From his perspective, their story consists of hopelessness (1 Thess. 4:13) and enslavement to idols (1 Thess. 1:9; 1 Cor. 12:2; Gal. 4:3, 8) and passions (1 Thess. 4:5). When he says that "Jews demand signs and Greeks desire wisdom" (1 Cor. 1:22), he acknowledges an aspect of their story in the form of their common pursuits. Paul's evangelistic preaching is a challenge to his listeners' story, for his evangelistic preaching always culminates in a call for the listeners to turn from the old existence to a new plot that is determined by the story of

---

17. Ibid., 90.

18. In comments on Paul's sermon at Antioch of Pisidia in Acts 13:16–41, Lawrence Wills demonstrates that the "word of exhortation" (Acts 13:15) is a homily that "exhibits an identifiable three-part pattern which can be found in many early Christian and Hellenistic writings." The sermon's rehearsal of salvation history in part one (13:16–37) provides authoritative exempla that state the basis for the conclusion that is drawn in part two (13:38–39, "Let it be known to you therefore, brethren, that through this man forgiveness of sins is proclaimed to you"). In part three the sermon concludes with the exhortation (13:40–41), which contains an "unmistakable hortatory tone." Paul's challenge to his readers ("Beware, therefore, lest this come upon you") is a call for decision.

The sermon at the Areopagus also contains the triadic arrangement that moves from exempla in the form of a theological argument (17:22–28), including the quotation of ancient authorities, to a conclusion (v. 29, "Being then, God's offspring") that is followed by an exhortation to repent. Here, as in the earlier sermons, Luke presents a Christian preaching that consists of the proclamation of Christ and the summons to respond in faith and repentance (Lawrence Wills, "The Form of the Sermon in Hellenistic Judaism and Early Christianity," *HTR* 77 [1984]: 278–80). C. Clifton Black argues that the pattern of argumentation identified by Wills is consistent with the Greek tradition of deliberative rhetoric that had been adapted in the Jewish synagogue ("The Rhetorical Form of the Hellenistic Jewish and Early Christian Sermon: A Response to Lawrence Wills," *HTR* 81 [1988]: 1–18).

Jesus. Just as Acts commonly records the response of the listeners to Paul's preaching, his letters also describe evangelistic preaching that calls for a decision. Paul summarizes this intersection of stories when he says to the Corinthians, "So we proclaim, and so you have come to believe" (1 Cor. 15:11). He recalls in 1 Thessalonians that the listeners had "turned to God from idols" (1:9–10). Listeners hear and believe (Rom. 10:17). They "receive" the gospel (2 Cor. 11:4), and they are baptized (1 Cor. 12:13; Gal. 3:27). Paul's evangelistic preaching, therefore, is always a call for the response of the listeners.

Our interest in Paul's involvement with those who received his message in Corinth, Thessalonica, and the other cities may obscure from us the fact that most of Paul's listeners did not respond favorably to his preaching. In fact, as I have noted above, Paul often finds it necessary to defend himself against the charge that his preaching has been ineffective. Unlike the book of Acts, the letters tell us little about the numerical response to Paul's preaching. We know more about the apparent failures of his preaching. By refusing to treat the gospel as merchandise (2 Cor. 2:17) or to "tamper with God's word" (2 Cor. 4:2, RSV), Paul demonstrated his concern to be faithful to a trust, even if his faithfulness produced few results. Although he knew that his audience considered his story "foolishness," he nevertheless preached "Christ crucified" (1 Cor. 1:22–23) in a direct challenge to an alternative way of viewing reality. His proclamation was neither a response to the questions that the people were asking nor an attempt to present Christianity as the answer to their own pursuits. In his claim that God had acted in the events of the cross and resurrection, he knew that he was challenging a culture's myths and that his listeners would consider the message scandalous (1 Cor. 1:18–25; Gal. 5:11). Paul gave his listeners a clear choice, a message that they could reject! We easily forget that most of them did. A challenge to the world's view of reality and a summons for listeners to conform their story to the larger story is not likely to result in easy victories.

Paul does not assume the responsibility for the results of his preaching; God has called him to be faithful, not successful. Where Paul's preaching results in a rejection of his message, he knows that the fault is with neither the message nor the messenger, but with the blindness that lies over the eyes of unbelievers (2 Cor. 4:4).

Where his preaching has positive results, he knows that it is God's power and not his own preaching that has been effective. The gospel is "the power of God for salvation" (Rom. 1:16). Unlike the rhetoricians, he does not preach with "plausible words of wisdom, but with a demonstration of the Spirit and of power" (1 Cor. 2:4). God's power is present in the preaching event, awakening faith in the listeners. Consequently, Paul is not the evangelist who depends on his cleverness, sermonic technique, audience manipulation, or adaptation of the message for the sake of having maximum results. His task is to confront the audience with a message that it does not want to hear, leaving the response to God.

Paul's evangelistic preaching in a pagan culture provides an important model for preaching in a culture that faces a new form of paganism.[19] He reminds us, in the first place, that evangelism is not based on market analysis and the desire to attract new consumers. It does not involve the preacher's reaffirmation of the dominant cultural values. In the second place, he reminds us that evangelism involves a clear affirmation of a message that disturbs the pluralism of our culture. The declaration that God has acted in Jesus Christ and makes a claim on our lives is a challenge to the reigning values of our time. This model of evangelism challenges a culture that has no defining narrative, offering a clear voice that listeners may either reject or accept. In the third place, Paul reminds us of the risks of evangelistic preaching. We cannot program the results in advance. Without Paul's faith in God's role in the preaching event, his evangelistic preaching would have been an exercise in frustration.

Evangelistic Preaching: Paul and the Thessalonians

Although the epistles are written to converts and are, by definition, pastoral communication, they provide considerable insight into the relationship between evangelistic proclamation and pastoral communication. The relationship between Paul's evangelistic and pastoral preaching is most clearly indicated in 1 Thessalonians, which is probably his first epistle. In 1 Thessalonians, as in his other epistles, Paul builds his case for appropriate conduct on the

---

19. N. T. Wright, *What Saint Paul Really Said*, 94.

basis of the community's memory of his missionary preaching. The
opening thanksgiving begins with his gratitude for the present condition of the readers—their "work of faith and labor of love and
steadfastness of hope" (1:2–3). These present circumstances are
rooted in the past events that formed the community, as Paul indicates in 1:4–2:12. He recalls their *election* (1:4) as the occasion when
the gospel "came to you not in word only, but also in power and in
the Holy Spirit and full conviction" (1:5). Here, as in his other
epistles (see 1 Cor. 1:18–2:4; Gal. 4:13; cf. Philemon 10), he recalls
his original proclamation as he lays the basis for his message. In
recalling how the gospel "came" to them (v. 5), what they
"became" (v. 6), and what Paul "proved to be" (v. 5),[20] Paul
describes his proclamation and their response. Indeed, all of
1:5–2:12 describes the circumstances of Paul's original coming
(εἴσοδος, 1:9; 2:1) as the occasion when he first preached to the
Thessalonians.

Paul describes his message as *gospel* (1:5; 2:4, 9), *the word* (1:6),
the *word of the Lord* (1:8), the *word of hearing* (2:13, my translation),
and the *word of God* (2:13), which he contrasts with human words
(see 1:5; 2:5, 13). His reference to his preaching as *the word* is especially striking inasmuch as he uses the same term to describe the
written word of the Old Testament.[21] Unlike the popular orator or
popular philosopher who speaks to "please mortals" (2:4), Paul
speaks God's own word (2:13). He will later make a similar claim
in the defense of his ministry when he says that "God is making his
appeal through us" (2 Cor. 5:20). Although Paul never explicitly
summarizes the content of his gospel as he does in the other letters
(1 Cor. 1:18–25; 15:3; 2 Cor. 4:4), his consistent appeal to confessional statements that are apparently familiar to the Thessalonians
indicates that this community has heard the same missionary
preaching that was preached in the other churches. In 4:14, he
appeals to his readers' own knowledge of the death and resurrection when he says, "For since we believe that Jesus died and rose
again, even so, through Jesus, God will bring with him those who
have died." In 5:10, he recalls the confessional statement about the

---

20. Forms of γίνομαι appear in the aorist tense in each case, focusing attention on this
past occasion.
21. K. Runia, "What Is Preaching According to the New Testament?" *Tyndale
Bulletin* 29 (1978): 23.

"one who died for us" as he encourages the community. Scholars have pointed out that the recollection of the community's conversion in 1:9–10 also contains a confessional statement that would call to mind Paul's original preaching.[22] The readers "wait for his son from heaven, whom he raised from the dead—Jesus, who rescues us from the wrath that is coming" (1:10). Thus the word of God, according to 1 Thessalonians, was the missionary preaching that consisted of the basic christological confession about the saving event in Jesus Christ. To preach is to speak for God. The content of the missionary preaching, as we know it from 1 Thessalonians, is consistent with the summary of Paul's preaching to the Thessalonians in Acts when Luke says that he "argued . . . from the scriptures, explaining and proving that it was necessary for the Messiah to suffer and to rise from the dead" (Acts 17:2–3).

In recalling his preaching as God's word, Paul places his preaching in proper perspective and invites his listeners to recognize the difference between preaching and all other forms of discourse. The community needs to recognize that preaching is a trust and that the preacher's task is to act as trustee of the message on God's behalf (1 Thess. 2:4–5). Paul's reminder of his own preaching as a *trust* actually instructs the congregation in how to listen to a sermon and what to expect of other preachers. The task of preachers is to confront the congregation with God's own words as they are mediated in scripture.

In 1 Thessalonians, as with the other epistles, proclamation was more than the announcement of God's saving deeds; it was also a summons for hearers to respond. The Thessalonians "received the word with joy inspired by the Holy Spirit" (1:6). According to 2:13, they "received the word of hearing" (my translation); hence they received "the word of God."[23] They "turned to God from idols, to serve a living and true God" (1:9), and they believed that Jesus died and arose from the dead (see 4:14). Thus the gospel that is

---

22. For the view that 1 Thess. 1:9–10 restates Paul's original missionary preaching, see the discussion in J. Munck, "1 Thess. 1.9–10 and the Missionary Preaching of Paul," *NTS* 9 (1963): 95–110. On the form of the Pauline confessional statement, Vernon H. Neufeld, *The Earliest Christian Confessions* (Grand Rapids: Eerdmans, 42–51.

23. On δέχομαι as technical term for reception of the gospel, cf. Luke 8:13; 11:1; 17:11; James 1:21. Cf. G. Petzke, δέχομαι, *EDNT*, 1.293.

preached is not merely informational about the saving significance of Jesus Christ, nor is it merely the offer of salvation.[24] Preaching contains the summons to the hearers to receive it, believe, repent, and be incorporated into the people of God.

Paul's recollection of his original preaching and the community's response is the basis for his pastoral preaching. The church is composed of people who have committed themselves to live faithfully in response to God's initiative. Paul's preaching recalls those commitments. This understanding of the preaching ministry appears, at first glance, to be an unworkable model in a Christian culture, in which church membership is unrelated to the community's memory of a radical decision. In American and European society, church membership belongs to the fabric of civic life that is inherited from previous generations. In this context, churches are often composed of individuals who have no shared understanding of normative beliefs, shared commitments, or common memories.[25] Without a continued reminder of the church's common faith and commitment, the church will never be an authentic community.

Paul's insistence that the gospel came "not in word only but also in power and in the Holy Spirit" recalls the similar assurances that are given elsewhere in his letters. According to 1 Corinthians 2:4, his word and his preaching were "not with plausible words of wisdom, but with a demonstration of the Spirit and of power." In Romans 1:16, he says that the gospel is "the power of God for salvation." With this claim that the preached message contains power, Paul indicates the wide gap that separates preaching from the human words of the orator or popular philosopher. Preaching is not a human word, and the response is not a human response. The distinguishing fact about Christian preaching is the presence of God's power in the midst of human weakness. Because the content of preaching is the word of God, it is accompanied by the power of God, which is evident in the brief history of the Thessalonian church, as 1:6–10 indicates. The new community overcame the afflictions that were present when they first heard

---

24. O. Hofius, "Wort Gottes und Glaube bei Paulus," *Paulusstudien*, WUNT 51 (Tübingen: J. C. B. Mohr, 1989), 170.

25. See Richard Osmer, *A Teachable Spirit* (Louisville, Ky.: Westminster/John Knox, 1990), 31.

the gospel (1:6), soon becoming examples to the believers in Macedonia and Achaia. The power of the λόγος was present not only in Paul's preaching, but in the way it "sounded forth" in Macedonia and Achaia (1:8): "For the word of the Lord has sounded forth from you not only in Macedonia and Achaia, but in every place." In the parallel phrase in 1:8, he says, "Your faith has gone out" (my translation). With the musical metaphor of "sounding forth," Paul depicts the power of the word of the Lord.[26] This power is finally indicated in the comments of others (1:9–10) who recall the change that has taken place in the lives of those who had turned from idols to serve the living and true God. The word of God was not only informational or challenging. It was the power that transformed the lives of the hearers and created a community.

This power is still at work among the listeners. In 2:13, Paul refers to "God's word, which is also at work in you believers." The word of God, therefore, was not only the initial message. It was the power at work in the community.[27] Thus when Paul expresses thanks in the opening of the letter for this community's "work of faith and labor of love and steadfastness of hope" (1:3), he recalls that their progress is rooted in the enduring power of Christian proclamation.

Pastoral Preaching for New Converts

In describing his "coming" (1:9; 2:1) among the Thessalonians, Paul recalls both their response to the message (1:6–10) and his own preaching activity (2:1–13). He moves in 2:1–13 from recalling their response to the gospel (1:6–10) to describing his own missionary preaching. Although Paul's purpose in this section is to distinguish his own character from that of the popular philosophers, with whom he could easily be confused, and to lay the basis for the instructions that he gives in chapters 4–5, he also offers important insights into his preaching ministry. We may assume that Paul's ministry was of sufficient duration for him to engage in a pastoral ministry with this community. Indeed, Paul's reference to his manual labor in which he "worked night and day" (2:9)

---

26. See John Beaudean, *Paul's Theology of Preaching*, NABPR Dissertation Series 6 (Macon, Ga.: Mercer Univ. Press, 1988), 42.

27. Note ἐνεργέω in 1 Cor. 12:6, 11; 2 Cor. 1:6; 4:12; Gal. 2:8; 3:5; Phil. 2:13.

presupposes an extended period of time. Furthermore, the many references in 1 Thessalonians to what the community already knows (see 2:1, 2, 5, 9; 3:3; 4:1–2) also suggest an extended pastoral ministry among the Thessalonians.

In rehearsing what the Thessalonians already know (2:1), Paul recalls his preaching ministry. His character is attested by the fact that, despite the abuses he had received in Philippi, he had declared "the gospel of God in spite of great opposition" (2:2). That Paul would not distinguish radically between his preaching ministry and his subsequent teaching is indicated in his rehearsal of his interaction with the community. The reference to declaring "the gospel of God in spite of great opposition" in 2:2 serves as the heading to the section in 2:3–12, in which Paul establishes his ethos, reminding the community of his integrity as a spokesperson and preparing the way for the appeals that he will make later in the letter. When he makes the transition from declaring "the gospel of God" in verse 2 to "our appeal does not spring from deceit" (v. 3), he indicates the essential link between his preaching of the gospel (v. 2) and his *appeal* to the community. *Paraklesis*, rendered in most translations as "appeal," is Paul's summary term for his ministry of the word. His declaring the word "of God" (v. 2) cannot be separated from his "appeal" to the community. One cannot distinguish evangelistic preaching from preaching to the community of believers as if Paul had two separate audiences. K. Runia has correctly noted, "The message of redemption is not only 'announced', but it also demands the unfolding, the exposition of its meaning. In this sense 'teaching' and 'preaching' belong together, whereby 'teaching' is the necessary consequence and follow-up of 'preaching.'"[28] The preaching of the gospel involved an *appeal* for response, and the message to the community of believers involved the reiteration of the gospel!

This terminology recalls Paul's reflection on his preaching ministry in 2 Corinthians 5:19–20. After he announces the saving events in 5:19, he says, "So we are ambassadors for Christ, since God is making his appeal through us; we entreat you on behalf of Christ, be reconciled to God." Paul's proclamation, therefore, was both announcement and summons. This summons is not only the

---

28. Runia, "What Is Preaching According to the New Testament?" 15.

invitation to receive the gospel at the moment of conversion. As his comments in 2 Corinthians indicate, Paul's proclamation involved the continuing summons to obey its demand. The entire preaching of the gospel can thus be called simply *paraklesis*, a term that is the most comprehensive in its implications of all of the words in the Pauline epistles for public proclamation.[29] The term is related to the verb παρακαλέω, which is Paul's most common verb in making a polite request. The root word has the connotations of *comfort* (2 Cor. 1:3–7; 7:6b, 7, 12f.), *entreat, challenge,* and *encourage.*[30] Although the emphasis may vary in different contexts, one cannot distinguish sharply among the separate connotations. Paul's preaching, therefore, involved both the announcement of the good news and the challenge to incorporate the good news into the lives of the recipients. Consequently, it is an appropriate term for Paul's own preaching ministry. It indicates that preaching consists of not only proclaiming the good news, but appealing to the community in light of the good news of the gospel.

The nature of this *paraklesis* and its relation to missionary proclamation is indicated throughout this section. Paul speaks as one "entrusted with the message" (1 Thess. 2:4), avoiding the flattery and greed characteristic of the popular philosophers (2:3–8). He imparts not only the gospel, but his own soul (2:8). Instead of being a burden to the community, he works with his hands while he "proclaim[s] . . . the gospel of God" (2:9). This ongoing proclaiming of the gospel was his address to the community of believers. Undoubtedly, Paul continues his evangelistic preaching in the context of the assembly of believers. He recognized no distinction between preaching to believers and nonbelievers. He did not cease evangelizing his congregation; he continued to announce the good news of Christ to communities that were undoubtedly composed of both believers and nonbelievers, and he continued to urge his listeners to receive his evangelistic message.

---

29. Stanley Marrow, *Speaking the Word Fearlessly: Boldness in the New Testament* (New York: Paulist, 1982), 6. Cf. J. Thomas, Παρακαλέω, *EDNT,* 3.23: "On the basis of statistics alone, παρακαλέω/παράκλησις are among the most important terms for speaking and influencing in the NT." See Christian Möller, *Seelsorglich Predigen,* 2d ed. (Göttingen: Vandenhoeck & Ruprecht, 1990), 72–73.
30. Anton Grabner-Haider, *Paraklese und Eschatologie bei Paulus* (Münster: Aschendorff, 1985), 7.

The nature of this *paraklesis* is also apparent in the images of nurse and father that Paul employs for his work (2:7, 11–12). In the latter reference, he describes his role as a father, "urging and encouraging you and pleading that you lead a life worthy of God, who calls you into his own kingdom and glory." We note first Paul's paternal role, a role he often claims as the founder of churches. The three participles indicate the paternal role that Paul claimed for himself. In the participles of *urging* (παρακαλοῦντες), *encouraging* (παραμυθύμενοι), and *pleading* (μαρτυρόμενοι), Paul elaborates on the nature of the preaching ministry, which he describes as *paraklesis* in 2:3. Παρακαλοῦντες, the verb form of παράκλησις in 2:3, is synonymous with παραμυθύμενοι (cf. Phil. 2:1). Both words have the connotations of *urge* and *encourage*. In 1 Corinthians 14:3, both terms are used (in the noun form) for the prophet whose task is to build up the entire community. Both terms imply the paternal role of one who gives loving encouragement to his children. In *pleading* (μαρτυρόμενοι, literally "witnessing"), Paul has reassured the community of believers and indicated the special urgency of their continuing response.[31] *Paraklesis*, therefore, involves the proclamation of the gospel associated with a father's challenging, encouraging, and testifying to his children.[32]

These three participles suggest the nature of Paul's preaching ministry. Paul is a father speaking to his children (cf. 1 Cor. 4:14–15). Thus the parent-child imagery suggests that his preaching was to a community. As a father who had brought the community into existence, he extends his concern beyond their initial response. His preaching ministry involves the continual concern for the formation of the community. This parental concern involves not only individuals, but the community that has come into being through the preaching of the gospel.

The content of Paul's preaching ministry is indicated in the object of the three participles. Paul encouraged his new community to "lead a life worthy of God, who calls [them] into his kingdom and glory" (2:12). In Philippians 1:27 Paul employs the expression "live your life in a manner worthy of the gospel of Christ." This expression suggests that the gospel Paul preaches also implies and

---

id., 11.
d., 12. See also Peter Stuhlmacher, ed., "The Pauline Gospel," in Stuhlmacher, *Gospel and the Gospels* (Grand Rapids: Eerdmans, 1991), 159.

embraces standards of the Christian life.[33] Thus ethical exhortation is an essential component of Paul's gospel. For Paul faith in
this Lord embraces both trustful confession and obedient discipleship.[34] Thus the gospel itself summons those who respond to do so
in a conduct that is worthy of the message.

The continuing ministry of the word is to be seen in the fact that
Paul commissions Timothy, his coworker in the gospel of Christ to
return to Thessalonica in order to "strengthen and encourage"
(εἰς τὸ στηρίξαι καὶ παρακαλέσαι) the church. Timothy's role
indicates that Paul shared his preaching ministry with others and
that the task of encouragement continues in the ministry of others.
We cannot distinguish a "preaching" ministry from the continued
ministry of encouragement, for preaching continued throughout
Paul's interaction with this church. Here the use of "strengthen"
(στηρίξαι) as a synonym for "encourage" (παρακαλέσαι) gives
the latter word a special nuance. This parallelism recalls Paul's
expression of his desire to come to see the Roman church in order
to impart a spiritual gift and "to strengthen you" (εἰς τὸ
στηριχθῆναι) and to "be encouraged by you" (συμπαρακληθῆναι
ἐν ὑμῖν) as well as the comment in Acts that Paul and Silas went
through Galatia "strengthening the churches." *Paraklesis*, therefore, involves strengthening the faith of believers in the context
of threats to the community. Indeed, the nature of this exhortation
is indicated in the statement that Timothy's task was to confirm
their faith, see to it that no one was shaken in the midst of afflictions (3:3), and remind the community of Paul's previous teachings on the problems posed in this hostile society. Exhortation
involves preparing the community for the continued struggle.
Stanley Marrow is correct in his assessment of the nature of
preaching:

> To live out this response in our day to day lives, to resist all the
> allures and enticements of other means of salvation . . . is some-
> thing that requires the constant entreaty, exhortation, supplica-
> tion, and consolation of the ministry of the word, which Paul
> describes as *paraklesis*. This is ultimately why there must be
> preachers, teachers, catechists and instructors in the church

---

33. Grabner-Haider, *Paraklese und Eschatologie bei Paulus*, 12.
34. Ibid.

everywhere. Their task is never ended no matter how thriving and vibrant the community they address is. They have to call the community to a life, a life "in Christ Jesus." . . . They have to call the believers to a conduct "worthy of the gospel of Jesus Christ" (Phil. 1:27), nor are they ever finished bringing that same gospel to non-believers.[35]

Moreover, according to 3:13 God is the one who strengthens the hearts of the community. Here the teaching/preaching ministry involves supporting the community in the context of the hostility from outside and reminding them of past teaching.

The nature of the *paraklesis* is also indicated in the continued references to the task of "encouraging." Not only does Paul send his emissary to participate in the task of encouraging the community; 1 Thessalonians is, in fact, the continuation of the pastoral conversation, as I shall argue in chapter 4. Indeed, Paul's rehearsal of recent events in the first three chapters is actually the prelude to chapters 4 and 5, where he continues the task of "encouraging" the community and reminding them of the very things he had taught them while he was in Thessalonica. As I have observed previously in this chapter, the purpose of the epistle is stated in 4:1–2, where Paul says, "[W]e ask and urge you in the Lord Jesus that, as you learned from us how you ought to live and to please God (as, in fact, you are doing), you should do so more and more. For you know what instructions we gave you through the Lord Jesus." The use of παρακαλοῦμεν with the synonym ἐρωτῶμεν brings further clarification of the nature of the παράκλησις that Paul had given in the past (2:12). These words introduce the instructions that follow and remind the church of the specific instructions that were involved when he taught them to "live a life worthy of God" (2:12). The life that is "worthy of God" consists in concrete obligations for community life. The letter is, therefore, the continuation of the task that had occupied Paul's ministry during his original visit. He continues the task mentioned in 2:12: encouraging and urging. When the letter is read in the assembly, it will function as the reminder of what the community has heard from Paul already.

From Paul's description of his ministry with the Thessalonians, one can see that this letter offers a useful insight into the continu-

---

35. Marrow, *Speaking the Word Fearlessly*, 8.

ity between preaching and teaching. The original proclamation results in the formation of the community and the continued ministry of encouragement. Paul portrays Christian evangelistic preaching as leading inevitably to pastoral work. Paul is, in the words of Reinhold Reck, "caught in an ambiguous situation." He is "caught between his call for worldwide evangelization, which drives him to seek out new areas and lands, and the care for the churches that are the fruit of his proclamation. For the problem is not completed with the first proclamation. It has only begun."[36] The mission work of Paul involves both evangelism and *paraklesis,* and Paul does not distinguish between these two aspects of his preaching ministry.[37] This pastoral work prepares the community for what it might expect and grows inevitably from the original message.

The missing dimension in the contemporary understanding of preaching is this dialectical relationship between evangelistic and pastoral preaching. The Christian preacher continues to live in the same ambiguous situation that faced Paul. To preach is not to speak our own words, but to speak for God, trusting in God's power to awaken a response. C. H. Dodd's distinction between the non-Christian world and the believing community might have been credible when he wrote *The Apostolic Preaching and Its Developments* in 1936, but it is hardly credible in our contemporary post-Christian society. Lesslie Newbigin describes the post-Enlightenment culture as a "missionary problem" in which we confront a pagan society that "is far more resistant to the gospel than the pre-Christian paganism with which cross-cultural missions have been familiar."[38] Because Christian congregations are "formed not only by baptism, but by a host of other masters,"[39] the preacher must continue to recall the foundation of the church's existence by retelling the Christian story. Indeed, the pastoral sermon should be rooted in the saving event of the death and resurrection of Christ. Just as Paul continued to evangelize those who

---

36. Reinhold Reck, *Kommunikation und Gemeindeaufbau,* SbB (Stuttgart: Katholisches Bibelwerk, 1991), 199.

37. Grabner-Haider, *Paraklese und Eschatologie bei Paulus,* 4.

38. Lesslie Newbigin, *Foolishness to the Greeks: The Gospel and Western Culture* (Grand Rapids: Eerdmans, 1986), 20.

39. William Willimon, *Peculiar Speech* (Grand Rapids: Eerdmans, 1992), 75.

were already converted, the preacher continues to restate the Christian story for a community that is composed of a diversity of listeners: people who constantly hear other voices and priorities, seekers, children, believers, doubters, and cultured despisers. As a result of the pluralism of our society, the preacher may never assume that the congregation has already been converted. As Paul's preaching ministry indicates, the announcement of the good news is not intended only for the non-Christian world; the congregation must be reminded regularly of the saving events that are the foundations of its existence. The listening audience is always composed of people who are at different stages of Christian existence. For some, the announcement of God's saving deeds is news that has not yet been considered; for others the proclamation is a reminder of the church's common faith. Therefore, in the ministry of preaching one cannot distinguish proclamation from the words of encouragement to the community. Consequently, evangelistic preaching is the task of every preacher.

Paul's ministry is the reminder that pastoral preaching always builds on the foundation of the gospel. This response is not limited to the initial change in the lives of the listeners that we call conversion. It continues as the preacher presents the congregation with the good news of God's deeds in Jesus Christ and the summons to live "a life worthy of God."

This preaching model has too often been ignored in the preaching tradition of Europe and North America. The close interrelationship between *kerygma* and *paraklesis* in Paul is forgotten both in the tradition of evangelistic preaching that focuses on the initial response of the listener and in the preaching tradition that offers instruction and comfort. The Pauline model that combines evangelistic and pastoral preaching remains a helpful model in our own culture.

Chapter Three

The Shape of Paul's Preaching

In *Amusing Ourselves to Death*, Neil Postman laments that the power of television is so pervasive in the modern society that it has influenced all forms of communication.[1] Schoolteachers must speak to the short attention spans that have been shaped by *Sesame Street*. The nightly news must communicate its message in brief segments that correspond to the film footage. Political discourse, reduced to sound bites because of the short attention spans created in the television age, avoids the kind of dialogue that was formerly a part of the democratic process. Christian communication is also shaped by television entertainment, according to Postman. Many of the changes in liturgy reflect the church's need to shape its discourse to accommodate the culture.

To what extent should Christian preachers adapt to the prevailing forms of communication within their own culture? When Amos Wilder described Christian communication as a "new utterance,"[2] he explained that the Bible avoids some well-known forms of communication and creates others. "The whole compendium of Israel's literature is built upon peculiar rhetorics that find no place in the textbooks of Aristotle and Quintilian."[3] One might infer from the Bible's "new utterance" that Christian communication never adapts completely to the popular forms of communication in any culture.

Several comments in Paul's dialogue with his listeners suggest that he did not accommodate to the prevailing modes of communication in his own day. He preached to the Corinthians, "not with

---

1. Neil Postman, *Amusing Ourselves to Death* (New York: Penguin Books, 1986).
2. Amos Wilder, *The Language of the Gospel: Early Christian Rhetoric* (New York: Harper & Row, 1964), 13.
3. Ibid., 15.

eloquent wisdom, so that the cross of Christ might not be emptied of its power" (1 Cor. 1:17). His speech was "not with plausible words of wisdom" (1 Cor. 2:4). According to 2 Corinthians (10:10–11), Paul's opponents would have agreed that his speech failed to meet the standards of his time. However, Paul's comments are not the only source of our knowledge of his preaching. We learn about the shape of Paul's preaching not only from his comments about his preaching, but also from the letters themselves, which have many of the qualities of the spoken word.

Aristotle claimed that all rhetoric could be delineated into the categories of *invention, arrangement, style, memory,* and *delivery.*[4] In our analysis of Paul's communication, as with any speaker known to us only through written texts, our knowledge of the shape of his preaching is limited to the categories of invention, arrangement, and style. *Invention* involves the nature of the argumentation and the proofs that make the argument convincing.[5] *Arrangement* is the rhetorically effective composition of the speech into a unified structure,[6] and *style* involves the clarity and ornamentation of the author's expression.[7] Although these categories are used primarily to analyze speeches, they also provide the categories for our examination of what I characterize here as the shape of Paul's preaching.

I have shown in chapter 2 that the Pauline evangelistic preaching has a consistent shape that involves the announcement of the good news and the summons for the listeners to respond. The letters, with their movement from theology to paraenesis, also have a consistent shape and provide especially important insights into the distinctive form of his preaching. Although his letters range in complexity from the essay-like quality of Romans to the personal

---

4. Cicero, *Inv.* 1.7.9; *De or.* 1.31.142; *Her.* 1.2.3; Quintilian, *Inst.* 3.3.1.

5. Heinrich Lausberg, *Handbook of Literary Rhetoric*, Eng. trans., ed. David E. Orton and R. Dean Anderson (Leiden: E. J. Brill, 1998), §260–442. See also Malcolm Heath, "Invention," in Stanley Porter, ed., *Handbook of Classical Rhetoric in the Hellenistic Period* (Leiden: E. J. Brill, 1997), 89–120. See also George Kennedy, *New Testament Interpretation through Rhetorical Criticism* (Chapel Hill, N.C.: Univ. of North Carolina Press, 1984), 14.

6. See Wilhelm Wuellner, "Greek Rhetoric and Pauline Argumentation," in *Early Christian Literature and the Classical Intellectual Tradition*, Fs. Robert Grant, ed. W. R. Schoedel and R. L. Wilken, TH 54 (Paris: Beauchesne, 1979), 51–87.

7. Galen O. Rowe, "Style," in Stanley Porter, ed., *Handbook of Classical Rhetoric*, 121–58.

and private concerns expressed in Philemon, they nevertheless contain so many common features that we may speak of a distinctively Pauline mode of persuasion—what Aristotle calls *invention, arrangement,* and *style.* Like practically all communicators, Paul works from a basic template that he adapts to changing circumstances.[8] These common features are most evident at the beginning and end of the letters, as the students of epistolography have noted. Paul identifies himself and his readers and follows quickly with the phrase "Grace to you and peace from God our Father." With the exception of Galatians, his letters follow with a thanksgiving. At the conclusion of the letters, Paul sends greetings and ends with a benediction.

Although the body of the letter varies in length and subject matter, all of Paul's letters have the three characteristics that letter theorists have identified for ancient letters. Paul's letters served the purpose of *philophronesis,* in which writers expressed the friendly relationship between themselves and the recipient; they served the purpose of *parousia,* the extension of the writer's presence; and they functioned as the *homilia,* the writer's part in an extended dialogue.[9] Within the dialogue, the reader may expect to find many of the same features in all of the letters of Paul. These features include thanksgivings, autobiographical reflections, travel plans, biblical commentaries, and ethical instructions that are frequently introduced by the verb παρακαλῶ and its synonyms. The prominence that Paul gives to Christian conduct, which this verb signifies, reflects the persuasive character of his correspondence. All of the letters in the Pauline correspondence are distinguished by the aim of instructing the readers about future conduct. This fact is instructive when we consider the nature of Paul's communication with his churches. The letters are, therefore, the continuation of his prior ministry, in which he had "urged," "encouraged," and "pleaded with" (see 1 Thess. 2:12) his readers to live worthily of the gospel.

The common components in Paul's letters tell us much about Paul's preaching to a community of believers. Nevertheless, we are

---

8. For the template of Paul's letters, see William G. Doty, *Letters in Primitive Christianity* (Philadelphia: Fortress, 1973), 43.

9. See Heikki Koskenniemi, *Studien zur Idee und Phraseologie des griechischen Briefes bis 400 n. Chr.* (Helsinki: Akateeminen Kirjakaupa, 1956).

left with the question: Did Paul create a new form of communication that was determined by the Christian story? Or did he adapt to the prevailing modes of communication of his day? The answer to the question will be instructive for our understanding of preaching today. If, as I suggest, Paul is a model for preaching, we gain insights about the shape and style of the Christian sermon and the nature of Christian persuasion today.

Paul as Letter Writer

For most of this century, scholars have focused on the continuity between Paul's communication and the forms of communication in his time. Adolf Deissmann examined the papyrus letters from Egypt and concluded that the parallels to the Pauline letters were so striking that they provide the appropriate background for reading the Pauline literature. According to Deissmann, "A letter is something non-literary, a means of communication between two persons who are separated from each other." Confidential and personal in nature, it is intended only for the persons to whom it is addressed. He distinguished the private letter from the epistle, which was similar to the letter only in form. The letters of the papyri, he demonstrated, began with the identification of the author and recipient and the greeting (χαίρειν) and concluded with greetings similar to those at the end of Paul's letters. In some cases, they opened with a thanksgiving, and their purpose for writing was expressed in the Greek word παρακαλῶ. He suggested that Paul's letters present a mode of communication much like that of the papyrus letters of the common people and that Paul made only slight adaptations to the papyrus letters when he communicated with his readers.[10]

Although Deissmann's successors continued to compare the letters of Paul with ancient papyrus letters,[11] the papyri proved to be of only limited value in explaining the Pauline mode of persuasion, for the differences between Paul's letters and the papyri are extraordinary. Despite the parallels between the papyrus letters and the

Deissmann, *Light from the Ancient East* (1922; reprint, Grand Rapids: 965), 227.

n White, *The Body of the Greek Letter*, SBLDS 2 (Missoula, Mont.: 2); John White, *Light from Ancient Letters* (Philadelphia: Fortress, 1986).

Pauline letters, the papyrus letters ultimately explained only the frame of the Pauline letter and some transitional formulae. The papyri did little to explain the content of the Pauline letters, for the papyrus letters were brief and lacking in the substantive dialogue that one finds in the epistles of Paul. Even Paul's shortest surviving letter, the epistle to Philemon, is long by the standards of the papyri.[12] Moreover, some parallels were more apparent than real. Klaus Berger has shown that the opening formula, "Grace to you and peace," is more than a slight Christianization of the Hellenistic letter opening, for the words belong to Jewish liturgy.[13] Furthermore, the thanksgiving at the beginning of the letter is more the exception than the rule in Greek epistolography and hardly to be compared to the Pauline thanksgivings.[14] Παρακαλῶ, which commonly appears in the letters, does not introduce ethical advice as it does in Paul's letters. The papyrus letters do not argue a case or offer extensive moral advice. Thus they offer little assistance in helping us understand the nature of the Pauline persuasion.

The meager results from the papyrus letters in offering a genuine parallel to Paul's mode of communication have led scholars to look for parallels in that literature that Deissmann excluded from consideration: the epistles that were meant to function as part of an extended dialogue or "sermo absentium." The letter became a primary means for communication and the exchange of ideas. Epistolary theorists described a variety of letter types, each with its own social function. They also discussed types of letters and their social setting. The social setting included the family, the circle of friends, and official government relationships.[15] Among the letter

---

12. E. Randolph Richards, *The Secretary in the Letters of Paul*, WUNT 42 (Tübingen: J. C. B. Mohr, 1991), 213: "In the approximately 14,000 private letters from Greco-Roman antiquity, the average length was about 87 words, ranging in length from about 18 to 209 words. . . . The thirteen letters bearing [Paul's] name average 2,495 words, ranging from 335 (Philemon) to 7,114 (Romans)."

13. Klaus Berger, "Apostelbrief und apostolische Rede," *ZNW* 65 (1974): 199. See below, p. 81.

14. Ibid., 219. See also Peter Arzt, "The 'Epistolary Introductory Thanksgiving' in the Papyri and in Paul," *NovT* 36 (1994): 32.

15. Abraham Malherbe, *Moral Exhortation*, LEC (Philadelphia: Westminster, 1989), 80–81. Note Stanley Stowers, *Letter-Writing in Greco-Roman Antiquity*, LEC (Philadelphia: Westminster, 1986), 39–40, on Epicurus and Plato.

types were those of comfort, encouragement, admonition, and advice. In some instances the letter was the vehicle by which a philosopher communicated his teachings to his students. The letters of Epicurus to his people scattered around the Mediterranean offer some parallel to the letters of Paul to his distant communities.[16] H. Cancik has examined the epistles of Seneca and demonstrated the presence of the letter form in which philosophical argument preceded moral advice. The letters of Seneca, for example, can be divided into a "teaching" section and a "hortatory" section in a way that is parallel to the Pauline letters. One can note significant parallels between the actual advice given by Seneca and the advice that Paul himself gives in the Pauline letters.[17]

Despite these helpful parallels, ancient letter writing only partially accounts for the nature of Pauline speech. The social context of the ancient letter was the family or the circle of friends, not the community of faith. Paul's letters, however, function to build communities, not encourage private moral formation. The Pauline letters are intended to develop the corporate identity of his churches and to discuss the major theological themes that will guide the community in its development.

Paul as Orator

In light of Paul's comments about eloquent wisdom (1 Cor. 1:17; 2:5), one might conclude that Paul's preaching bore no resemblance to the accepted norms of oral communication of his time. However, much of the recent literature reflects a dissatisfaction with the assumption that Paul's letters were shaped entirely by the conventions of ancient letter writing. Because of this dissatisfaction, a view widely held in previous centuries has reemerged: Paul's letters are actually influenced by the conventions of ancient oratory.[18] This influence may reflect either Paul's intentional adoption of the art of rhetoric as he might have learned it in the

16. Stowers, *Letter-Writing*, 114–18.
17. H. Cancik, *Untersuchungen zu Senecas Epistulae morales* (Hildesheim: Olms, 1967), 16.
18. See Frank Hughes, *Early Christian Rhetoric and 2 Thessalonians*, JSNTSS 30 (Sheffield: JSOT, 1989), 19. The rhetorical study of Paul's letters was commonplace in antiquity. Among the most prominent commentators was Augustine, in his work

schools, or the less intentional appropriation of the rhetoric that he had naturally absorbed in the Hellenistic cities.

The oratorical handbooks classified speeches into three categories: the judicial, the deliberative, and the epideictic.[19] Judicial rhetoric was intended for the law courts, and its goal was to bring the audience to a judgment over an event of the past. Deliberative rhetoric functioned in the democratic assembly, and it called for a decision on future action. Epideictic rhetoric was intended to effect praise or blame and to reinforce the community's values. Although the settings envisioned for oratory in the handbooks did not include the Christian assembly,[20] Aristotle's three categories have been of some value in the analysis of Paul's letters, for Paul's letters occasionally have functions similar to those of the speeches envisioned by Aristotle. Hans Dieter Betz argued, for example, that in Galatians Paul appeals to his readers to make judgments over past conduct; thus he places the book under the category of judicial rhetoric.[21] Since 2 Corinthians also appeals to the readers to make judgments over past conduct, it too has some of the elements of judicial rhetoric. However, both of these epistles call for a

---

Doctr. chr. bk. 4. Augustine cited Paul's letters as examples of Christian eloquence par excellence. The rhetorical analysis of Paul's letters diminished after Eduard Norden's *Die antike Kunstprosa* (Reprint, Darmstadt: Wissenschaftliche Buchgesellschaft, 1958). Norden argued that Paul's rhetoric was lacking in eloquence: The rhetorical study of Paul's letters reemerged in the 1970s, beginning with Hans Dieter Betz, *A Commentary on Paul's Letter to the Churches of Galatia*, Hermeneia (Philadelphia: Fortress, 1979).

Opinions vary on the extent to which Aristotelian rhetorical analysis is appropriate for Paul. For example, Betz's student Margaret Mitchell has given a thoroughgoing rhetorical analysis of 1 Corinthians (*Paul and the Rhetoric of Reconciliation* [Louisville: Westminster/John Knox, 1992]). Others argue that, while Paul did not know rhetorical theory, a functional equivalence exists between parts of his letters and the categories of rhetoric. See Stanley Porter, "Paul of Tarsus and His Letters," in Stanley Porter, ed., *Handbook of Classical Rhetoric in the Hellenistic Period*, 533–85.

19. Aristotle, *Rhet.* 1.3.1.

20. Thomas H. Olbricht, "An Aristotelian Rhetorical Analysis of 1 Thessalonians," in *Greeks, Romans, and Christians*, ed. David Balch, Everett Ferguson, and Wayne Meeks (Minneapolis: Fortress, 1990), 225: "Aristotle did not include the Christian assembly, since it did not as yet exist. Had Aristotle lived in the fourth century A.D., his modus operandi would have driven him to this fourth genre."

21. Betz, *A Commentary on Paul's Letter to the Churches of Galatia*, 24. Other writers have made the more persuasive case that Galatians, with its call for future conduct (chaps. 5–6), is deliberative rhetoric. See J. Smit, "The Letter of Paul to the Galatians: A Deliberative Speech," *NTS* 35 (1989): 1–26.

change in future conduct; thus they have definite deliberative elements. In the other letters of Paul, the apostle both reinforces community values (epideictic rhetoric) and calls for a change in future conduct (deliberative rhetoric). Because these categories overlap in Paul, as they did in Aristotle, the classification of Paul's mode of persuasion into Aristotelian categories is of limited value in our analysis of his letters. I suggest that Paul's letters all aim at future conduct; hence deliberative rhetoric provides a background for the analysis of Pauline discourse.[22]

Invention

One may analyze the letters of Paul according to the categories of invention, arrangement, and style that are mentioned above. According to the rhetorical handbooks, the orator may argue from his own personal character (*ethos*), from the appeal to reason (*logos*), or from the emotions (*pathos*). In ancient oratory, the argument from the speaker's character had a decisive importance, for the speaker's power of persuasion depended on his trustworthiness before his listeners.[23] Autobiographical arguments were most often given at the beginning of the oration, but they could be scattered throughout the speech.[24] Philosophers and rhetoricians presented themselves as examples to their listeners, and the teacher of rhetoric acted in loco parentis in relationship to his students.[25] The argument from *ethos* was the primary mode of argumentation in numerous orations, including those of Isocrates and Demosthenes.

---

22. See Mitchell, *Paul and the Rhetoric of Reconciliation*, 50–55, on the use of παρακαλῶ in deliberative rhetoric.

23. Aristotle, *Rhet.* 2.1.2–3: "It is not only necessary to consider how to make the speech itself demonstrative and convincing, but also that the speaker should show himself to be of a certain character and should know how to put the judge into a certain frame of mind. For it makes a great difference with regard to producing conviction (especially in demonstrative, and next to this, in forensic oratory) that the speaker should show himself to be possessed of certain qualities and that his hearers should think that he is disposed in a certain way towards them; and further, that they themselves should be disposed in a certain way towards him." See George Lyons, *Pauline ...phy: Toward a New Understanding*, SBLDS 73 (Atlanta: Scholars, 1985), 27.
...s, 27.
... Fiore, *The Function of Personal Example in the Socratic and Pastoral Epistles*, (Rome: Biblical Institute, 1986), 177.

The argument from *ethos* is a pivotal feature of the Pauline letter.[26] In some instances, as in 1 and 2 Corinthians, the argument from *ethos* is given in response to attacks on his ministry. Paul demonstrates in 1 Cor. 2:1–5 that, in coming to the Corinthians "in weakness and in fear and in much trembling" (2:3), he embodied the message of the cross. His appeal to an *ethos* shaped by the cross is further in evidence in 4:6–13, where he contrasts his own "weakness" (4:10) with the hubris of his listeners. He makes the argument once more in chapter 9, where he describes himself as the embodiment of the selfless behavior he encourages the Corinthians to adopt.

The argument from *ethos* is the central issue of 2 Corinthians, where Paul's ministry is under attack. His summary of recent events in 1:12–2:13 and of the resumption of his past history with the Corinthians in 7:5–16 conforms to Aristotle's description of the argument from ethos that can be used at the beginning of a presentation and resumed later. In addition to describing his recent history with the Corinthians, he also describes those aspects of his life that "always" (see 2:14; 4:10) distinguish his ministry. He is the embodiment of the life that is shaped by the cross (4:10–11). When he compares himself to others at numerous points in the argument, he demonstrates that he has been forced into the self-praise that characterized much of ancient oratory. Hence Young and Ford have suggested that 2 Corinthians has points of contact with Demosthenes' *Epistle 2* insofar as the speaker is engaged in the argument from *ethos* occasioned by the charges that have been made by his opposition.[27]

Paul appears to argue from personal *ethos* also when he is not directly under attack. Philippians (1:12–26) and 1 Thessalonians (2:1–12; cf. Gal. 1:10–2:21) have extended personal arguments in which Paul demonstrates how he embodies the message he preaches. Although scholars have conjectured that these arguments are given in response to attacks on his demeanor, the epistles themselves leave no indication of that claim. More likely, Paul's major concern was the establishment of his credibility as a speaker rather than the defense against criticism.

---

26. See André Resner, *Preacher and Cross* (Grand Rapids: Eerdmans, 1999).
27. Frances Young and David F. Ford, *Meaning and Truth in 2 Corinthians* (Grand Rapids: Eerdmans, 1987), 37–39.

Recent rhetorical analyses have shown that Paul's appeal to *logos* also has points of contact with the tradition of Greek oratory, in which one might argue from expediency, the exempla from the past, or logical demonstration in the form of enthymemes or syllogisms. Margaret Mitchell has shown that the common appeal to the "expedient" (τὸ συμφέρον, 1 Cor. 6:12; 10:23; 2 Cor. 8:10; 12:1; cf. 1 Cor. 7:25; 10:33) reflects the fact that the argument from advantage was the chief argument in Aristotelian rhetoric.[28] Paul's appeal to scripture has been compared to the appeal to exempla from the past in Aristotelian rhetoric, and his appeal to creedal statements (see 1 Cor. 8:6; 11:23–26; 1 Cor. 15:1–3) can be compared to the common appeal to knowledge shared by the group.[29] The appeal to reason could include the argument from common knowledge, ancient opinion, logical demonstration, or the advantage of the listeners.

The argument from *pathos* is common in the Pauline letters.[30] Paul argues from *pathos* in Galatians 4:19, for example, where he says, "My little children, for whom I am again in the pain of childbirth until Christ is formed in you." The argument from *pathos* is clearly evident also in Paul's passionate defense of his conduct in 2 Corinthians 10–13, where he employs the metaphors of the bride's father (11:1–4) and father of the community (12:14–21) to indicate the nature of his relationship to his hearers. His frequent appeals for Corinthian acceptance of his ministry are also arguments from *pathos*. In the defense of his ministry, he exclaims, "[O]ur heart is wide open to you. There is no restriction in our affections, but only in yours" (2 Cor. 6:11–12). Such appeals to the emotions are common in Paul's letters.

---

28. Mitchell, *Paul and the Rhetoric of Reconciliation*, 25–39. On the argument from expedience, see also Aristotle, *Rhet.* 1.3, 1358b, 22; Quintilian, *Inst.* 3.8.22; 3.8.33. Cf. Lausberg, *Handbook of Literary Rhetoric*, § 61.2; § 196.1
29. Aristotle, *Rhet.* 1.2.13; Quintilian, *Inst.* 5.11.1.
30. Aristotle argues for the importance of pathos in *Rhet.* 1.2.5: "The orator's purpose is actually to make his hearers feel in some of these ways, and prevent them from feeling in other ways, toward specific persons on given occasions and circumstances (toward his client in a judicial case, for example), and to use the feelings to direct or influence their judgment." Pathos is necessary, according to Aristotle, because things appear different to someone under the influence of emotion. Consequently, persuasion takes place "through the hearers when they are led to feel emotion by the speech, for we do not give the same judgment when grieved and rejoicing or when being friendly and hostile."

In the Pauline *inventio*, one sees also the use of the proofs that were commonly employed within the Aristotelian tradition. The Greek listener would have recognized the arguments from *ethos*, *logos*, and *pathos* in the Pauline persuasion. The extent to which Paul subverts or transforms the normal argument will be seen below.

Arrangement

The rhetorical handbooks gave instructions for the orderly arrangement. Aristotle and his successors noted that the persuasive power of the oration depended on its orderly arrangement. The effective oration included the *exordium, narratio, propositio, probatio,* and *peroratio.*[31] The functions of the *exordium* were to introduce the topic and to make the audience favorably disposed to the speaker. The *narratio* covered the history of the case at hand and was commonly followed by the *propositio*, which provided a thesis statement for the argument. The *probatio* consisted of the proofs of the case. In the *peroratio*, the speaker summarized the case and made an emotional appeal to the audience.[32]

The most productive use of rhetoric in the study of Paul in recent years has been in the area of arrangement, where recent studies have demonstrated the rhetorical power of the entire letter as a discourse that has been carefully crafted. Although there is considerable variation in the development of the argument in Paul's letters, the argument of the letters is arranged in a way that corresponds, at least in part, to Aristotelian rhetoric. The Pauline thanksgiving functions as the *exordium* insofar as it introduces the topic and makes the audience favorably disposed to the message. After the opening thanksgiving, Paul commonly makes the transition to a brief summary of recent events (see 1 Thess. 2:1–3:10; Gal. 1:10–2:14; 1 Cor. 1:10–17; 2 Cor. 1:18–2:13; Rom. 1:11–15) that are composed of autobiographical reflections, which function as the *narratio* for the argument. In most of Paul's letters the *narratio* is followed by a thesis statement consisting of the case that is to be argued, which functions as *the propositio* (see 1 Thess. 4:1–2; 1 Cor. 1:10; Gal. 2:15–21; 2 Cor. 1:12–14). This thesis statement

---

31. See Cicero, *De or.* 2.80. Aristotle lists only two parts of the speech (*Rhet.* 3.13).
32. On the functions of each part of the oration, see Lausberg, *Handbook of Literary Rhetoric,* § 263–442.

is then followed by the main argument of the letter, which functions as the *probatio*. Paul's concluding summary in his letters has an emotional appeal in which he provides a restatement of the case (see Rom. 15:14–29; 2 Cor. 10–13; Gal. 6:11–17). Although the application of Aristotelian terms for arrangement should not be employed as a Procrustean bed for analyzing Paul's letters, Aristotelian categories have been a valuable tool in demonstrating the essential coherence of Paul's letters. Paul's sermons are carefully arranged deductive arguments that are intended to reinforce the values that he has already instilled in his communities and to change their behavior in the future.

Attention to rhetorical arrangement in recent research has been of great value in demonstrating the coherence of Pauline argumentation. At least some of the arguments against the integrity of the letters lose their force when one observes that Paul employed principles of arrangement that were suitable in an oral culture.[33] For example, interpreters have argued that 1 Corinthians presents multiple problems for us in determining its literary coherence. Because Paul moves rapidly from one topic to another, many have read 1 Corinthians as Paul's ad hoc response to numerous issues confronting the Corinthian church. Margaret Mitchell has employed rhetorical categories to demonstrate the essential coherence of 1 Corinthians. After noting the problem of factionalism in Corinth, Paul moves from the *exordium* (1:4–9) to the *propositio* of 1 Corinthians in 1:10, in which he demands that the listeners all "speak the same thing" (literal translation). After a brief history of the case (1:11–17), Paul presents his argument. He lays the basis for the specific issues in 1:18–4:21 by subverting the arrogance that has caused the factionalism. Instead of regarding the remainder of the book as ad hoc responses to problems about which the Corinthians had inquired, Mitchell shows that the separate issues in 5:1–11:1 (incest, prostitution, marriage, food offered to idols) fit together as a unified section on the topic of relationships with outsiders, while 11:2–14:40 treats the topic of relationships with insiders. Chapter 15 treats a topic on which the Corinthians were divided (the resurrection), and Paul provides the basic view that should allow them to "speak the same thing."

---

33. See Casey Wayne Davis, *Oral Biblical Criticism: The Influence of the Principles of Orality on the Literary Structure of Paul's Epistle to the Philippians*, JSNTSS 172 (Sheffield: JSOT, 1999), 19.

In numerous cases, interpreters have been perplexed by the interruptions within Paul's arguments, concluding either that Paul was not a careful letter writer or that letter fragments have been inserted within his letters. For example, the subject of meat offered to idols (1 Cor. 8:1–13) is interrupted by the autobiographical section of 1 Corinthians 9 and the treatment of the failure of the wilderness generation in 10:1–22 before it is concluded in 10:23–11:1. Similarly, the discussion of spiritual gifts in 12:1–31 is interrupted by the section on love in 1 Corinthians 13 before it is concluded in chapter 14. Wilhelm Wuellner has demonstrated that each of these two units has an *aba* pattern in which Paul has digressed from the stated topic in order to illustrate his argument. In each case, he shows that such a digression was a common oratorical device.[34]

Style

The handbooks also gave instructions for the orator's style, distinguishing between the *grand style*, *middle style*, and *plain style*. The complicated, or grand, style involved the use of periods composed of two or more dependent clauses.[35] The middle style was typified by parataxis and associated with narrative, while the plain style was associated with spontaneous conversations and bore no indication of refinement.[36] Paul, like most authors, displays examples of all three levels of style, although the grand style is rare in his work.[37] Paul's sentences are commonly paratactic, lacking the elaborate subordinate clauses that were characteristic of Greek literature.

---

34. Wuellner, "Greek Rhetoric and Pauline Argumentation," 185–87.
35. R. Dean Anderson Jr. (*Ancient Rhetorical Theory and Paul* [Leuven: Peeters, 1999], 184) gives the restricted definition of period as a "sentence containing at least two subordinate clauses wherein the main clause, interrupted by the subordinate clauses, is left in suspense and only completed by the last few words of the whole sentence." He cites Luke 1:1–4 as a good example of the period.
36. Porter, "Paul of Tarsus and His Letters," 577.
37. Ibid. Augustine (*Doctr. chr.* 4) examined Paul's speech and saw evidence of considerable rhetorical power by the standards of the rhetorical profession. Augustine focused primarily on the Pauline style, supplying the technical rhetori̇ for stylistic features of Paul's letters. He shows, for instance, that Paul'ṣ 5:3 ("suffering produces endurance, and endurance produces characte produces hope") are arranged in an ascending order that the Greeks examines the "fool's speech" of 2 Cor. 11:16–12:10 and concludes, " eloquently he speaks!"

Hence Paul's letters conform primarily to the middle style. In his extensive use of rhetorical questions, a commonplace in all of his letters, one finds a characteristic of conversational speech and the *plain style*. Paul's use of rhetorical questions may also reflect his use of the diatribe, as Rudolf Bultmann argued in his classic study of the style of Paul's preaching.[38] Stanley Stowers has shown that the diatribe form was a favorite pedagogical device in the teacher's dialogue with his students.[39] Other studies have examined the ornamentation in Pauline style, demonstrating the rich variety of figures that Paul employs.[40]

Rhetorical analysis is a useful tool in understanding the nature of Pauline persuasion and in analyzing the power of the rhetorical unit. Paul's letters consist primarily of appeals for a new form of behavior that grows out of the Christian message. He commonly makes his appeal on the basis of deductive argumentation. Paul's use of deduction should serve as a reminder to homileticians that the story is not the only mode of Christian persuasion and that inductive preaching was never the only form of Christian communication. Christian preaching may also involve deductive argumentation that builds a persuasive case in order to effect community transformation. If Paul is the model, arguments from the preacher's *ethos* have a place in Christian preaching, for the convincing embodiment of the speaker's message in his own character is an appropriate argument in every generation. Arguments from the church's own foundational convictions that are intended to shape consciousness and draw out the implications of the Christian confession are also an essential part of Christian preaching. In addition, the argument from *pathos* always functions as a demonstration of the life-and-death issues relating to the Christian life.

Analysis of the Pauline style has served to demonstrate that Christian preaching is neither *Hochliteratur* of the poet or playwright nor a haphazard and careless flow of words. The epistles are intimate and conversational. Nevertheless, Paul demonstrates, as

---

38. Rudolf Bultmann, *Der Stil der paulinischen Predigt und die kynisch-stoische Diatribe*, FRLANT (Göttingen: Vandenhoeck & Ruprecht, 1910).
39. Stanley K. Stowers, *The Diatribe and Paul's Letter to the Romans*, SBLDS 57 (Chico, Calif.: Scholars Press, 1981).
40. Porter, "Paul of Tarsus and His Letters," has a thorough catalog of the tropes and figures employed by Paul.

Augustine noted, the rhetorical turns of phrase in numerous places. Paul's preaching moved between the plain style and the carefully crafted expression that was suitable for the occasion and the subject matter.

The Pauline persuasion allows us to reflect once more on the issues of Christ and culture as they relate to preaching. To what extent is Christian preaching shaped by the modes of popular speech? Although we do not know whether Paul had a formal education in rhetoric, his speech was undoubtedly influenced by the orators whom he had heard and by the art of persuasion that influenced every aspect of Hellenistic life. Paul's interaction with Hellenistic rhetoric, however, does not mean that, as a preacher, he set out to affect Hellenistic rhetorical features to "reach" his audience. Such rhetorical features were a part of the essential education that he shared with his audience. Similarly, the preacher and the audience are inevitably shaped by the modes of persuasion in their culture. Nevertheless, as we shall observe in the next section, Paul brought to his culture a dimension of persuasion that transformed and subverted the oratorical tradition that he had inherited.

The Distinctiveness of Paul's Preaching

To what extent is the Pauline letter a distinctive form of Christian persuasion? It is in the area of *inventio* that we discover most clearly the distinctiveness of Paul's preaching. Although we have noted that Paul appeals to some of the common proofs of rhetoric, many of these similarities of argument are more apparent than real, for Paul's relationship to his churches is central to his argumentation. Despite the apparent parallels to Paul's mode of discourse in ancient letter writing and oratory, there is something very different about his letters.[41] This distinctiveness may be seen, in the first place, in the relationship of the speaker to his listeners. In most of his letters, Paul identifies himself as an apostle, signifying his authority and indicating the nature of his persuasion. Even in those letters where he does not make apostolic claims (Philippians, 1 and 2 Thessalonians, Philemon), he speaks in the

---

41. See Anders Eriksson, *Traditions as Rhetorical Proof: Pauline Argumentation in I Corinthians*, CB 29 (Stockholm: Almqvist & Wiksell, 1998).

authoritative tones of a father admonishing his children (1 Thess. 2:11–12). His "appeals" (παρακαλῶ, 1 Thess. 4:1; 5:14; Philemon 9) and "requests" (ἐρωτῶμεν, 1 Thess. 4:1; 5:12) to the community are only polite substitutes for the commands that would be appropriate (cf. Philemon 8). His use of the imperative in all of the letters also reflects his authoritative role among the churches. This tone of authority distinguishes Paul's persuasion, for he writes as a father who chooses to request compliance with his wishes rather than demand obedience from his children (Philemon 8–9).

In 1 and 2 Corinthians we gain special insight into the distinctiveness of Paul's communication. In both epistles he specifically identifies himself as "an apostle of Christ Jesus by the will of God" (1 Cor. 1:1; 2 Cor. 1:1), and he regards himself as a father to his churches (1 Cor. 4:14–21; 2 Cor. 12:14–15). This relationship is central to his persuasion, for the dominant aspect of his persuasion is the note of authority that accompanies his role as apostle and father to his churches. Paul's apostolic role is clearly indicated in the beginning section of 1 Corinthians. His thesis statement is "I appeal to you . . . by the name of our Lord Jesus Christ" (1:10). That is, he speaks on behalf of Christ. His persuasion rests not on "plausible words of wisdom," that is, oratorical proofs, but on the "demonstration of the Spirit and of power" (1 Cor. 2:4). In 1 Corinthians 2:6–16 Paul claims a privileged position that is rooted in "God's wisdom, secret and hidden" (2:7), but that is now known among the "mature" (2:6). Paul's gospel is not subject to normal rules of persuasion, for "God has revealed [it] to us through the Spirit" (2:10). Here, as George Kennedy has said, Paul appears to challenge the entire tradition of Greco-Roman rhetoric.[42] Matthew and Paul "make extensive use of the forms of logical argument, but the validity of their arguments is entirely dependent on their assumptions, which cannot be logically and objectively proved."[43] His arguments can be evaluated only by those who have the Spirit of God. Where his hearers evaluate preachers according to their own criteria, Paul declares that he is nothing more than a διάκονος (3:5) through whom they believed. He and Apollos are nothing other than ὑπηρέται καὶ οἰκονόμοι ("servants and stewards") of the

---

42. Kennedy, *New Testament Interpretation*, 17.
43. Ibid.

mysteries of Christ (1 Cor. 4:1). Such mysteries are not subject to rational proofs because they are the revelation from God.

One notes the nature of Paul's radical Christian rhetoric throughout 1 and 2 Corinthians. Although Paul often appeals to standard forms of argumentation, his privileged position as authoritative apostle is always evident. He is a father who admonishes his children (4:14), and he persuades with the paternal rights of discipline (4:21). Paul is a preacher who threatens to come "with a stick" (1 Cor. 4:21). In his instructions involving the man who is living with his father's wife, he writes as one who has made a prophetic judgment (1 Cor. 5:3). Although he appeals to community values in 5:6b ("[d]o you not know that a little yeast leavens the whole batch of dough?") and to the kerygma in 5:7 ("our paschal lamb, Christ, has been sacrificed"), his arguments are reinforced by his personal authority when he writes with words of command (5:9, 11) that dictate the community's behavioral norms.

One may note Paul's use both of standard forms of argumentation and of "radical Christian rhetoric" throughout the Corinthian letters. When he argues from his personal *ethos*, he transforms the concept of *ethos* by demonstrating that he embodies the "foolishness of the cross." When he appeals, in Aristotelian fashion, to that which is "expedient," he transforms this concept by indicating that expediency is defined by the interests of the community of faith.[44] His frequent appeals to what the community knows[45] may be understood in rhetorical terms as an argument based on the values he shares with the community.[46] However, Paul is the interpreter of the community's traditions. When he appeals to scripture (1 Cor. 14:21, 34) as the basis of his argument, he speaks from the privileged position of one who knows that scripture was written "for our instruction" (1 Cor. 10:11; cf. 9:10). As one who has been commissioned by God, he reveals a mystery (15:51) that provides the ultimate answer on questions involving the resurrection.

However, here also Paul speaks as the privileged interpreter of the authorities that are known to the community. In developing his

---

44. Mitchell, *Paul and the Rhetoric of Reconciliation*, 38.
45. Cf. οὐκ οἴδατε in 1 Cor. 5:6; 6:2, 3, 9, 15, 16.
46. In addition to arguments based on what the community knows already, Paul also argues on the basis of traditions available to the community. Cf. 8:6; 11:2, 23–25; 12:2; 15:1–3. See also Eriksson, *Tradition as Rhetorical Proof*, 73–137.

argument from scripture and the traditions that are known within the community, Paul proceeds in a way that is in accord with Aristotle's dictum that the basis of one's argument is the ground one holds in common with the audience.[47] However, in his apostolic role Paul is the privileged interpreter of the community's traditions.

This tone of authority is even more graphically demonstrated in 2 Corinthians, where Paul's work is challenged by the "super-apostles" (2 Cor. 11:5), who have made common cause with the opposition from 1 Corinthians. Here, as in 1 Corinthians (1:18–25), Paul claims that his proclamation is a public spectacle that has life or death consequences (2 Cor. 2:14–17). As the minister of the new covenant (2 Cor. 3:6), he is the counterpart to Moses, who has been made "competent" (2:16; 3:5) to deliver God's covenant despite his own insufficiency. If the glory of his work is not widely acknowledged, it is not because of his own incapacity, but because his listeners are as blinded from hearing the word of God as Israel was blinded at the giving of the Mosaic covenant.[48] In his capacity as God's apostolic servant, he failed to keep a previous promise to visit the Corinthians because he wished to "spare" them (2 Cor. 1:23). He promises in the future, however, that he "will not be lenient" toward his disobedient children (2 Cor. 13:2), for he has taken on the prophetic role of Jeremiah insofar as he has been called for "building you up and not for tearing you down" (2 Cor. 10:8; 13:10).

---

47. See Eriksson, *Traditions as Rhetorical Proof*, 31. The truth argued in rhetoric can be persuasive only if it is acknowledged by the interlocutors and the truth is limited to what is accepted by both partners. "The speaker trying to persuade his audience is therefore dependent on the opinions shared by himself and his audience. Aristotle calls these opinions ἐνδόξαι and understands them as those opinions that commend themselves to all or to the majority or to the wise—this is, to all of the wise or the majority or to the most famous and distinguished of them" (*Top.* 1.1.100b). The same insight is developed in the "new rhetoric" of Perlman and Olbrechts-Tyteca, who stress that the premises held by the audience are the necessary starting point for argumentation. See C. Perelman and L. Olbrechts-Tyteca, *The New Rhetoric: A Treatise on Argumentation* (Notre Dame: Univ. of Notre Dame Press, 1969), 65–74; cited in Eriksson, *Traditions as Rhetorical Proof*, 32.

48. Cf. Kennedy, *New Testament Interpretation through Rhetorical Criticism*, 8: "The Christian orator, like his Jewish predecessor, is a vehicle of God's will to whom God will supply the necessary words, and his audience will be persuaded, or not persuaded, not because of the capacity of their minds to understand the message, but because of God's love for them which allows their hearts to be moved or withholds that grace."

As 1 and 2 Corinthians indicate, Pauline preaching is the authoritative preaching of the prophetic tradition. Paul does not fight with the ordinary human weapons of rational persuasion. His weapons are mighty to God for the tearing down of strongholds (2 Cor. 10:4) in his quest to take every thought captive to Christ. If Paul is a model for preaching, he is the reminder that Christian speech rests ultimately on the apostolic authority that is mediated by the apostolic witness. The preacher, therefore, is not "one without authority," but one who mediates authoritative instruction to the church. The preacher is the heir of the prophetic tradition, recalling the words of those who spoke only the words of God. Preachers do not speak for themselves, but they act as "stewards" whose task is to be faithful in upholding what has been given to them. The preacher functions as the emissary of the apostle, "explaining his ways" to the believing community.

Preaching, the Community, and the Grammar of Faith

The setting of the Pauline letter is also a distinctive feature of his letters. Whereas Aristotle envisioned the setting of the law court, the democratic assembly, or the festive occasion, Paul writes "to the church of the Thessalonians in God the Father and the Lord Jesus Christ" (1 Thess. 1:1) and to other communities of faith. All of the letters, including Philemon, are written to churches and intended to shape congregational consciousness. The ἐκκλησία is composed of those who have responded to Christian preaching and have come together as a community. One must recall that Paul's address to these assemblies has no parallel in Greco-Roman rhetoric, for Aristotle did not envision the Christian assembly.[49]

Paul speaks to his communities in the most intimate familial terms, thus creating a consciousness among the listeners that they are bound to their founder and to each other by family ties. He addresses the Galatians in maternal terms: "My little children, for whom I am again in the pain of childbirth until Christ is formed in you" (4:19). The familial and intimate terms with which he addresses

---

49. Olbricht, "An Aristotelian Rhetorical Analysis of 1 Thessalonians," 225.

the Thessalonians also indicate the nature of preaching to the corporate body. His absence from them was an occasion when "we were made orphans by being separated from you—in person, not in heart" (1 Thess. 2:17), and he describes his churches as his "joy" (1 Thess. 2:20) and his "boast" (2 Cor. 1:14).[50] He recalls that he was, in his relation to them, gentle "like a nurse" (1 Thess. 2:7 [NIV: Like a mother taking care of her children]). In his relationship to them, he was "like a father with his children" (1 Thess. 2:11). The paternal image is pervasive in Paul's writings. He employs the image in 1 Thessalonians to describe his role as the community's teacher (2:11). In 1 and 2 Corinthians he employs the image to describe his authority to discipline (1 Cor. 4:21) and his reasons for not accepting financial support. As a father, he demonstrates his love by giving aid to his children (2 Cor. 12:14). Throughout Paul's letters he addresses his readers in the language of family, addressing the readers as "beloved" and "brothers." In the ancient world this language belonged to the world of family. His common forms of address are "beloved" (1 Cor. 10:14; 2 Cor. 7:1; 12:19; Phil. 2:12; 4:1), "brothers," and "beloved brothers."

He appeals not only to the intimacy of his relationship with Christians, but also to their intimate relationship to each other. One may note Paul's appeal to Philemon's intimate relationship with Christians. In the thanksgiving he says, "The hearts (σπλάγχνα) of the saints have been refreshed through you" (Philemon 7). At the conclusion of the epistle, he says, "Refresh my heart (σπλάγχνα) in Christ" (v. 20). The familial language reflects Paul's engagement with his churches. It explains also the passion with which he speaks of his churches.

The corporate nature of preaching is also evident in the liturgical elements that are present in Paul's letters. This distinctive setting of Pauline speech in Christian liturgy is to be seen throughout Paul's letters, for he speaks with a liturgical grammar that has no parallel in ancient speeches and letters. This distinctive grammar of faith may be seen in the fact that the Pauline letter begins and ends with a word of grace. Paul opens his letters with "Grace to you and peace from God the Father and the Lord Jesus Christ,"[51]

---

50. Reinhold Reck, *Kommunikation und Gemeindeaufbau*, SbB (Stuttgart: Katholisches
erk, 1991), 212.
om. 1:7; 1 Cor. 1:3; 2 Cor. 1:2; Gal. 1:3; Eph. 1:2; Phil. 1:2; Philemon 3; cf. Col.
Thess. 1:1.

and he closes them with a benediction that also offers a word of grace. The benediction at the end of 1 Corinthians (16:23) is typical: "The grace of the Lord Jesus be with you." More elaborate is the benediction at the end of 2 Corinthians (13:14): "The grace of the Lord Jesus Christ, the love of God, and the communion of the Holy Spirit be with all of you." Paul's opening and closing words are taken from the liturgy and reflect his preaching style.[52]

Klaus Berger has demonstrated that the words "Grace to you and peace from God the Father and the Lord Jesus Christ" are not merely a slight Christianization of the familiar Greek letter opening. The wish form that is expressed in the phrase "grace to you and peace" is deeply rooted in Jewish literature and liturgy. The best known of the Old Testament benedictions is Numbers 6:24, which expresses the wish for the divine blessing.[53] Similarly, the phrase "from God the Father and the Lord Jesus Christ" is distinctive in the Pauline correspondence. Berger has said, "For Hellenistic contemporaries this could only be a strange, archaic, unusual introduction to the letter. Here it is given because it is the apostle who writes."[54] The words constitute a word of blessing from one who has been authorized to transmit God's grace and peace to his people. Undoubtedly, this form of benediction reflects the continuation of the Jewish blessing form in the early church. Thus Paul's opening and closing benedictions are drawn from the liturgy of the church. Their presence in his letters suggests that his own preaching contained the homiletic benediction in which he expressed the wish for the divine grace and peace upon the community of faith.

Paul's distinctive liturgical grammar may also be seen in the opening thanksgiving of his letters. Although one may point to parallels

---

52. See Raymond Collins, "1 Thes and the Liturgy of the Early Church," *BTB* 10 (1980): 53, on the liturgical patterns in 1 Thess.: "If it is reasonable to suggest that 'Grace to you and peace' is a pre-Pauline liturgical formula which the apostle has taken over into his letter, it may well be that elements of a liturgical pattern have also been taken over in the closing of the letter (1 Thess. 5:23–28). It has been suggested that the grace-kiss-peace formulary is the conclusion to the liturgy of the word. This suggestion may be supported by an analysis of the prayer found in vv. 23–24: 'May the God of peace himself sanctify you wholly.'" Cf. G. Wiles, *Paul's Intercessory Prayers*, SNTSMS 24 (Cambridge: Cambridge Univ. Press, 1974), 28–40.

53. See Terence Y. Mullins, "Benediction as a NT Form," *AUSS* (1977): 61–62.

54. Berger, "Apostelbrief und apostolische Rede," 99.

in ancient letter writing and rhetoric to the opening thanksgiving (or blessing), the significance of the parallels has been exaggerated. The thanksgiving was rare in the Hellenistic letter, and the resemblance to the opening of Greek orations is minimal.[55] The thanksgiving, like the benediction, is rooted in Jewish liturgy. The Dead Sea Scrolls offer a significant parallel to the thanksgivings of the Pauline letters.[56] The blessing form in 2 Corinthians is also based on Old Testament and Jewish models.[57] The thanksgiving of Paul's letters reflects the Christian liturgy of his churches, which is indebted to the Jewish liturgy. One may assume that the opening thanksgiving in Paul's letters offers a glimpse of the early Christian liturgy and that Paul is the preacher who leads the community in the liturgy. Thus the "social construction" in which Paul is involved includes the shaping of communal identity through the medium of benedictions and prayers.

Other liturgical elements are also commonplace in the Pauline letters. Doxologies, thanksgivings, and petitions punctuate Paul's speech. He frequently interrupts his discourse with the phrase "thanks be to God!" (Rom. 6:17; 7:25; 1 Cor. 15:57; 2 Cor. 2:14; 9:15). Robert Jewett has identified six such homiletic benedictions in the Thessalonian correspondence (1 Thess. 3:11, 12–13 and 5:23; 2 Thess. 2:16–17; 3:5, 16), each beginning with a stylized αὐτὸς δὲ ὁ θεός or δέ ὁ κύριος and expressing a wish in the optative mood.[58] Paul prays for reunion with his community (1 Thess. 3:11), for its sanctification (1 Thess. 3:11; 5:23) and growth in faith and love. Paul's "grammar of faith" undoubtedly reflects his preaching, which in turn is influenced by the Jewish liturgy.

---

55. Ibid.
56. James M. Robinson, "Die Hodajot-Formel in Gebet und Hymnus des Frühchristentums," *Apophoreta*, Fs. E. Haenchen, ed. W. Eltester and F. H. Kettler (Berlin: Töpelmann, 1964).
57. The form commonly begins with εὐλόγητος and the praise of God, followed by the relative clause that describes the works of God. Cf. Gen. 9:26; 14:20; 24:27; Exod. 18:10; Ruth 2:20; 1 Sam. 25:32, 39; 2 Sam. 18:28; 1 Kings 1:48; 5:7; 1 Esd. 4:40, 60; 8:25; 2 Esd. 7:27; Tobit 3:11; 8:5, 15, 16; 9:6; 11:14, 17; 13:18; LXX Pss. 17:46; 28:6; 40:13; 65:20; 67:19; 71:18; 88:52; 105:48; 118:12; 123:6; 134:21; 143:1.
58. R. Jewett, "Form and Function of the Homiletic Benediction," *ATR* 51 (1969): 18–34.

Preaching as Theology and Exhortation

As the continuation of his personal ministry among his churches, Paul's letters all aim at the formation of communities who live "worthily of the gospel." Indeed, although the letters vary in length and subject matter, all of them move toward a call for a change of conduct among the listeners supported with careful theological argumentation. The ethical exhortations, which are most often (but not always) found near the end of the Pauline letter, are not to be regarded as the appendix to a theological treatise, but rather as the climax of the argument in which theological argument provides the basis for change. Paul frequently introduces moral demands with words of request (παρακαλοῦμεν, ἐρωτῶμεν) or speaks in the imperative mode, giving specific instructions on the moral implications of Christian faith. His use of lists of vices and virtues and his concrete demands reflect a preaching that calls for concrete change in the life of the community.

The fact that all of his letters employ theological argument in support of exhortation provides an important model for preaching that is often overlooked in contemporary discussions of preaching. Christian preaching not only forms the communal identity of the people but also gives specific instructions that indicate concretely how one lives the life that is "worthy of the gospel."

Paul and Contemporary Preaching

The preaching ministry of Paul offers important insights for contemporary preaching. The Christian preacher is engaged in authoritative speech. This fact should raise questions about the exclusive reliance on inductive preaching, which is rooted in a nonauthoritative understanding of preaching. The preacher takes on the role of Paul's emissary, communicating and explaining the apostle's words, re-presenting their persuasive power. Like the public reader of Paul's letters, the Christian preacher acts in Paul's absence, interpreting his words for the believing community. The authority does not belong to the preacher, but to Paul.

The analogies between Paul's persuasion and Greco-Roman rhetoric remind us that Greco-Roman rhetoric was not an alien intrusion into Christian rhetoric, for it played a role in shaping Paul's communication from the beginning. Moreover, deductive argumentation, which Paul shares with the rhetorical tradition, has a place in Christian preaching. Christian communication involves a variety of modes of speech, including both induction and deduction. The shaping of congregational consciousness requires that issues be argued and listeners be persuaded in order to determine the church's identity and future course of action.

Although Christian preaching is never totally divorced from the modes of persuasion known within the culture, Pauline preaching is a reminder that our persuasion is never precisely the same as other modes of speech. Christian preaching involves an authoritative word from God that is mediated by the preacher. It shapes the consciousness of the listeners and leads them in doxology, prayer, and praise. Preaching initiates the listeners in a new "grammar of faith" in which the congregation learns the words of prayer, praise, and doxology. Preaching also creates and sustains a community consciousness in which individuals come to recognize that their identity cannot be separated from the corporate identity of the church.

Chapter Four

What Is Pastoral Preaching?

Although the pastoral task has never been limited to the regular sermon, the sermon has always been central to it. Throughout the history of the church, one of the major functions of the sermon has been to provide pastoral instruction to guide the congregation in living the Christian life.[1] Preaching has provided direction for the community, guiding individuals and the corporate community toward faithful living. Two changes in recent years have diminished the pastoral dimension of the sermon. In the first place, with the development of multistaff churches, pastoral care has become a specialized ministry. Consequently, the tasks of preaching and pastoral care have been clearly demarcated into two areas of specialization. If this separation works as planned, the preacher focuses on preaching while the pastoral counselor cares for the needs of the people.[2] In the second place, with the recent emphasis on narrative preaching, the traditional pastoral aspect of preaching has diminished. Where narrative is the predominant mode of communication, the sermon speaks by indirection rather than confronting the listeners with the call for changed lives. This trend toward separating preaching from the pastoral task represents an extraordinary change in our understanding of the preaching ministry, for throughout the history of the church preaching has been pastoral.

For reasons that will become clear in this chapter, I am

---

1. Harry M. Byrne, O. P., "Preaching and Pastoral Care," in *In the Company of Preachers*, ed. Regina Siegfried and Edward Ruane (Collegeville, Minn.: Liturgical Press, 1993), 165. See also Hughes Oliphant Old, *The Reading and Preaching of the Scriptures in the Worship of the Christian Church* (Grand Rapids: Eerdmans, 1998), 2.5–18, for the patristic period.

2. See Christian Möller, *Seelsorglich Predigen*, 2d ed. (Göttingen: Vandenhoeck & Ruprecht, 1990), 9.

convinced that this experiment in specialization is both impractical and theologically inappropriate. The impracticality of this move will be apparent as the people perceive that preaching cannot be separated from the pastoral task. The community will not accept the preacher who prepares sermons that are remote from the concerns of the congregation. The biblical witness, especially the ministries of Jesus and Paul, consistently points to the relationship between preaching and pastoral concern. In chapter 2, I observed the relationship between Paul's evangelistic preaching and his pastoral activity prior to his literary activity, arguing that the letters provide evidence that evangelistic preaching inevitably resulted in pastoral preaching. In this chapter, I shall argue that the letters reflect the next stage in the pastoral conversation. Paul's work is a reminder that one cannot separate preaching from the pastoral task, for preaching is inherently pastoral.

What is pastoral preaching? Although the ideal of pastoral preaching is held in high regard, precisely what we mean by pastoral preaching is a matter of debate, especially in a therapeutic culture. The term "pastoral" has taken on a new meaning in contemporary speech. In ordinary usage, the word "pastoral" has come to be associated with support, acceptance, care, affirmation, healing, even unconditional positive regard, given to individuals. Pastoral care is regarded as individualized care given by the shepherd of the sheep.[3]

This understanding of the pastoral task has had an extraordinary influence on our understanding of pastoral preaching. Thomas Long has said that the image of the preacher as pastor "almost inevitably views the hearers of sermons as a collection of discrete individuals who have personal problems and needs rather than as a group, a community, a church with a mission. The public, corporate, and systemic dimensions of the gospel are often downplayed in favor of more personalistic themes."[4] Consequently, books of pastoral sermons and books about pastoral preaching tend to identify these needs with problems of the individual and the family, for example, loneliness, family conflict, the midlife crisis, unfulfilled

---

Donald Allen, "The Relationship between the Pastoral and the Prophetic in *ounter* 49 (1988): 174.

ong, The Witness of Preaching (Louisville: Westminster/John Knox,

potential, the search for happiness, or self-esteem. In the sermon, the preacher identifies the problem and offers a solution.[5] Therefore, pastoral preaching comes to be identified with "counseling on a group scale."

Harry Emerson Fosdick, who became a model for many preachers earlier in this century, described his method of preaching as the "project method." Fosdick began with the questions of people in his congregation and attempted to provide answers from scripture. In his famous article "What's the Matter with Preaching?" Fosdick wrote: "Start with a life issue, a real problem, personal or social, perplexing the mind or disturbing the conscience; face the problem fairly, deal with it honestly, and throw such light on it from the spirit of Christ, that people will be able to think more clearly and live more nobly because of that sermon."[6] Preaching was largely addressed to individuals and their questions and problems. It closely approximated personal counseling. The test of a good sermon, according to Fosdick, was the extent to which people wished to see the preacher for personal counseling.

The influence of Fosdick's view of preaching has been considerable in our culture. Thus we have seen a long tradition of preaching that is addressed to "felt needs." Such preaching has the advantage of being relevant, for it is based on a sensitive reading of the audience. In our therapeutic age, such preaching is likely to be well received. Through Fosdick's influence, pastoral preaching has since been identified with problem solving. A sermon of this type moves from a vexing personal problem to a psychologically sound "Christian" answer.[7] It has been "problem oriented," tending toward comforting truths instead of the comfort that includes demand as well as succor. The literature of the past thirty years has been influenced by an understanding of "preaching as counseling on a group scale" and pastoring or shepherding as "tender and solicitous concern."[8]

This understanding of pastoral preaching is problematic for several reasons. In the first place, it owes more to modern therapeutic

---

5. Ibid.
6. Harry Emerson Fosdick, "What Is the Matter with Preaching?" *Harper's* 107 (July 1928): 134.
7. Gary D. Stratman, *Pastoral Preaching* (Nashville: Abingdon, 1983), 9.
8. Ibid., 16.

understanding than to the roots of its image in the life of a shepherd, whose responsibilities involved far more than comfort and support for those in his charge. The shepherd's task was not only to comfort and support but also to guide, protect, and ensure the general welfare of those in his charge. In the second place, this view of pastoral preaching, with its emphasis on acceptance, never confronts the listeners with a word of judgment; nor does it offer guidance on the concrete demands of the Christian life.[9] In the third place, the image is understood in almost exclusively individualistic terms; that is, "How can I be happy?" or "How can I have a happy marriage?" In the fourth place, this form of pastoral preaching has difficulty distinguishing between the legitimate needs of the listeners and the wants that have been created in our own society. In the fifth place, the *pastoral* image is only one of many images that the Bible employs to express the concern of leaders for the welfare of their people.

The New Testament offers a variety of images for the task of the preacher's active concern for the welfare of the people. But we employ the pastoral image as the umbrella term. Paul uses imagery from family life (see 1 Cor. 4:14–21) and construction (see 1 Cor. 3:16–17) to describe preaching as the active involvement in ensuring the well-being of the community. In all of these terms, the underlying assumption about the purpose of preaching is the same. This preaching seeks to effect some beneficial change in the hearers and strives to be a catalyst for more responsible living on the part of those who hear.[10]

Paul as Pastoral Preacher in 1 Thessalonians

In describing his relationship to his churches, Paul never describes himself as pastor. Nevertheless, if we mean that pastoral preaching is a term for all preaching that focuses on the needs of the hearers, Paul's preaching is deeply pastoral, and he is an appro-

---

9. Möller (*Seelsorglich Predigen*, 103) speaks of the "antinomian trend" of contemporary pastoral care in which cheap grace is extended: "Whoever has difficulties with God's commandments is absolved, as if Jesus had said to the adulteress, 'Go and keep doing what you have been doing. Others are not doing anything different.'"
10. Long, *The Witness of Preaching*, 31.

priate model for pastoral preaching. As I noted in chapters 2 and 3, he prefers the images of parenting to describe his work as preacher. In Galatians (4:19), he describes himself as the mother who suffers labor pains until "Christ is formed" in the community. In most instances, he prefers the image of father to describe his continuing work with his churches. This paternal role is most clearly described in 1 Thessalonians 2:11–12, where Paul describes his ministry with this infant church: "As you know, we dealt with each one of you like a father with his children, urging and encouraging you and pleading that you lead a life worthy of God, who calls you into his own kingdom and glory." We may assume that Paul's ministry in all of the cities contained the same pastoral (or paternal) dimension and that his letters continued this pastoral conversation.

All of Paul's letters are written for a pastoral purpose. As the continuation of earlier conversations or as the attempt to shape a church's future (as in Romans), they are written to ensure the stability and vitality of his churches. In this chapter, I wish to focus on the pastoral task as it is especially apparent in 1 Thessalonians, Paul's earliest letter, and to demonstrate that the pastoral task in 1 Thessalonians is parallel to Paul's pastoral role in the other letters. This epistle is especially useful for illustrating Paul's role as pastoral preacher because it lacks the complexity of the other letters. Unlike Galatians, the Corinthian letters, or Romans, the book does not appear to engage in elaborate theological debate. Although scholars who are accustomed to extensive mirror-reading of Paul's epistles have argued that the epistle is a response to a crisis occasioned by either the community's distrust of Paul (see 1 Thess. 2:1–12) or confusion over the return of Christ (see 1 Thess. 4:13–5:11), nothing in the epistle explicitly indicates that this is the case. Indeed, if we may take Paul at his word, he writes 1 Thessalonians in response to Timothy's favorable report about conditions in the Thessalonian church (1 Thess. 3:6). As a minority community in a hostile environment, it was vulnerable to harassment and persecution (1 Thess. 3:2). After encouraging the Thessalonians to withstand the trials facing them, Timothy brought back the report of their "faith and love" (3:6). Thus Paul's task in 1 Thessalonians is to speak to a community that was doing well and to encourage the continued health of the church. Indeed, he writes to encourage the people to do "more and more" they are already doing (4:1–2). Paul's challenge, therefore

TH of *god — under shepher —
in an under shepher an day?
in day?
p 86

90   *Preaching Like Paul*

speak to a church on an occasion when there are no heresies to
combat, no controversies to resolve, and no new pressing issues
that call for a decision. Paul's major concern is the ongoing health
of the church in the midst of the various trials they will inevitably
face (see 1 Thess. 3:2). Thus 1 Thessalonians is a model of pastoral
preaching.

The Larger Agenda for Preaching:
The Eschatological Horizon

All pastoral preaching is intended to address the needs of the listeners. Much of our pastoral preaching has been focused on
addressing either the immediate needs that individuals express or
the questions that they ask. Preachers may have little difficulty
finding topics for preaching if they consistently preach in response
to crises in the community or the personal crises of the people.
The problem with such preaching is that it lacks any larger agenda
for the preaching task.

This larger agenda is what we find in 1 Thessalonians. Here, as
in all of the letters of Paul, pastoral preaching is shaped by the
larger agenda of his preaching ministry: *the continued formation of a
community that awaits the parousia.* Paul speaks, therefore, not to
individuals but to churches. His pastoral concern for their lives
must be seen in the context of his eschatological vision of the triumph of God. The church, which lives in anticipation of this ultimate triumph, is God's unfinished business. Because the churches
are Paul's "glory and joy" at the parousia (1 Thess. 2:20; cf. 2 Cor.
1:14; Phil. 2:16) and the ultimate test of whether he has run in vain
(Phil. 2:16; 1 Thess. 3:5), he is deeply anxious about their welfare
(cf. 2 Cor. 11:28) and "orphaned" (ἀπορφανισθέντες, 1 Thess.
2:17) from them when he cannot see them face to face. This anxiety for his church motivates him to send Timothy to encourage
them in the face of the tribulations (3:2–3). He sees the obstacles
that could prevent his work from coming to an appropriate conclusion at the day of Christ. Thus his pastoral preaching is the
expression of a loving father (cf. 2:11–12) who has a clear understanding of the actual needs of his community. His preaching,
therefore, is driven by his engagement with his churches and his
concern for their ultimate welfare.

The larger agenda of Paul's preaching is determined by his conviction about what God is doing in the world.[11] Paul frequently refers to this agenda in both personal and eschatological terms. Consequently, he consistently refers to this larger agenda of his preaching. In the creedal statement of 1 Thessalonians 1:10, he recalls the church's eschatological self-understanding as the community that awaits the return of the Son. This eschatological dimension continues to be a theme in the constant references to a community that lives in anticipation of the return of Christ (4:13–5:11). The prayers in 3:13 and 5:23 also indicate the larger agenda for his preaching. Paul prays that God will "sanctify you entirely" (5:23; cf. 3:13) before the parousia. His instructions indicate both the activity of God in sanctification and the community's responsibility for conduct that is the embodiment of sanctification (4:3, 8).

Paul employs a variety of images throughout his epistles to develop this understanding of the larger agenda for his pastoral work and preaching. The images of farming and construction in 1 Corinthians, mentioned above, describe the community that grows and is continually under construction until the end (1 Cor. 3:10–17).[12] The imagery suggests the priority of the community over the individual, for the corporate community is God's vineyard (1 Cor. 3:6–9) and building (1 Cor. 3:16). Consequently, the ministers' task is the "watering" and "upbuilding" of the church as it awaits God's triumph. The test of the preachers' work is the endurance of their construction work through the ultimate trial, when the eschatological day reveals the quality of their work (1 Cor. 3:13–15).

Paul extends the imagery of the building (οἰκοδομή) with his frequent references to the task of individuals to *edify* (οἰκοδομεῖν). He charges all participants to "encourage one another" (1 Thess. 4:18), and he makes *edification* the criterion for individual conduct in the context of decision making (cf. 1 Cor. 8:1; 10:23) and worship (1 Cor. 14:3–5, 17). Contrary to much contemporary usage, which focuses on the *edification* of the individual, Paul's concern is

---

11. See Richard Hays, *The Moral Vision of the New Testament* (San Francisco: HarperSan Francisco, 1996), 32.
12. The imagery of building and planting echoes Jeremiah's prophetic task (cf. Jer. 1:10).

the construction of the corporate community as the edifice that will survive the ultimate test at the parousia.[13]

In Galatians, as I noted above, Paul is the mother in travail; the church is the infant that is being formed ("until Christ is formed in you"). The mother's task is to participate in the *formation* of the infant. In 2 Corinthians he is the father of the bride who will present his daughter a pure virgin to Christ (2 Cor. 11:2) at the end. In Romans (12:2) and 2 Corinthians (3:18), he employs the language of transformation to describe the progress of the community as a process of being re-formed. Paul envisions his churches as eschatological communities that are being transformed as they await the parousia (cf. 1 Cor. 1:8). His task in preaching, therefore, is to provide the guidance for his communities as they are transformed into the image of Christ. For Paul, preaching involves participation with God in the task of community formation. Communities are changed as God's word is "at work" among the believers (1 Thess. 2:13).

The eschatological dimension provides the larger agenda for Paul's pastoral preaching. If Paul is a model for pastoral preaching, the needs of the community define the content of preaching. These needs are, however, ultimate needs, not the community's desires for the tranquility of the moment or individual satisfaction. Eschatological preaching focuses the attention of the congregation not only on matters of the individual's future but on God's future as it impinges on the present moment.[14] Preaching that is genuinely eschatological demonstrates the provisional nature of our own commitments and values, reminding us that God's future places our own priorities in a new perspective. The focus on God's ultimate purpose also confronts a culture of narcissism that aims at individual fulfillment and pleasure with the challenge to live faithfully and morally in expectation of the future.

---

13. See Charles Campbell, *Preaching Jesus* (Grand Rapids: Eerdmans, 1997), 222. Campbell's distinction between the edification of the individual and of the community is critical for the discussion of the postmodern emphasis on the experience of the individual: "Preaching focused on individual experiential events, in which the primary function is the eventful transformation of individuals, still operates within a basically modern, not to mention liberal, American framework."

14. Thomas Long, "Preaching God's Future: The Eschatological Context of Christian Proclamation," in *Sharing Heaven's Music: The Heart of Christian Preaching, Essays in Honor of James Earl Massey*, ed. Barry L. Callen (Nashville: Abingdon, 1995), 195.

Eschatological preaching is the missing dimension in much of contemporary homiletic thought.[15] Paul's preaching is a reminder that pastoral preaching transcends the questions of the moment in order to ensure that the focus for preaching is directed toward the triumph of God. This ultimate horizon is a corporate perspective that initiates the church into a common vision of its journey together, its common purpose, and its shared renunciation of a narcissistic culture.

Establishing Corporate Identity

The task of community formation provides the agenda for Paul's preaching ministry on all occasions. Thus in the absence of a crisis in 1 Thessalonians, Paul continues the task of Christian formation that began with his original preaching in that community. This task involves answering the fundamental questions that had always been at the center of Israel's consciousness: Who are we and what are we to do? Paul writes to establish corporate consciousness and answer corporate questions about the identity of the community. He writes not to individuals but "to the ἐκκλησία of the Thessalonians in God the Father and the Lord Jesus Christ" (1:1). He addresses them, with language drawn from Israel's past, as "beloved of God" and "elect" (1:4, my translation), language that echoes the election terminology of Deuteronomy 7:6–7, according to which Israel's identity as God's "elect" is rooted in the fact that God loves his people. The distinctive language of election also occurs later in the epistle when he calls on his listeners to live "worthy of God, who calls" the community "into his own kingdom and glory" (2:12).[16]

---

15. Ibid. Long points to three basic distortions in contemporary approaches to eschatology. One is the fundamentalist preaching with its charts and calculations and its chronicling of contemporary events in order to watch for the signs of the end. The second is the exclusive focus on the eschatology of the individual. The third is the mainline and liberal embarrassment with eschatological language.

16. Paul consistently establishes the identity of his communities with the terminology drawn from Israel's status: holy (Rom. 1:7; 16:2, 15; 1 Cor. 1:2; 6:12; 14:33; 16:15; 2 Cor. 1:1; 13:12; Phil. 1:1; 4:21–22); "children of God" (Phil. 2:15/Deut. 32:5); elected (Rom. 8:33; 1 Thess. 1:4); loved (1 Thess. 1:4); called (1 Thess. 2:12; 5:24); known (1 Cor. 8:3; Gal. 4:9). This language demarcates communal identity sharply from the culture in which they live.

Because the Pauline communities live as minorities within the social world, Paul's preaching reinforces their identity by demarcating the community from its surrounding culture. He associates the readers with him in the bonds of affection (1 Thess. 2:17; 2:19; 2:20). He describes the non-Christian majority society as "the others" (οἱ λοιποί, 4:13; 5:6) and as "the Gentiles who do not know God" (4:5).[17] Thus his preaching reinforces their Christian identity as a community separated from its culture.

The shape of the entire letter demonstrates that, for Paul, community ethos is based on the identity of the people. Paul does not turn to the specific instructions that comprise the cohesive ethos of the community (chaps. 4–5) until he has reaffirmed the community's essential identity. As a minority community facing the inevitable tension with the larger society (see 2:1–2; 3:1–5), this community, like all minority communities, needs the reaffirmation of its identity. In the first three chapters Paul reaffirms this identity by recalling the common memory that he shares with the readers and that they share with each other. The opening thanksgiving moves from his word of gratitude for their present condition (1:2–3) to a recollection of their corporate history. In 1:5–10, Paul describes not an individual response to the gospel but a corporate response in which the whole community "turned to God from idols" (1:9) in such an extraordinary way that they became models for believers in the larger region (1:7). The countercultural existence that he encourages on the readers was already apparent from the beginning of their existence. Paul is appealing to their corporate memory, recalling their past in order to focus on their future. Thus Paul recalls the circumstances under which individuals became a community of faith in response to his preaching.

Paul's recollection of his ministry among them (2:1–12) recalls his ties with the community, reminding them that the content of the letter is nothing new. At the very beginning of their Christian life, Paul had devoted himself to the gospel and to the community. He recalls that the gospel that was the foundation for their corpo-

---

17. This is a consistent feature in all of Paul's letters. Note the reference to "outsiders" (οἱ ἔξω, 1 Cor. 5:12, 13) the ἄπιστοι, ἄδικοι. The minority culture, by contrast, has a πολίτευμα in heaven (Phil. 3:20). They are "God's temple" (1 Cor. 3:16) and "those who are being saved" (σωζόμενοι, 1 Cor. 1:18; 2 Cor. 2:15). Cf. Michael Wolter, "Ethos und Identität in paulinischen Gemeinden," *NTS* 43 (1997): 434.

rate life was a trust that Paul had communicated to them (2:5). Paul describes his personal relationship as that of a "nurse" (2:7) and father who had encouraged them to walk "worthy of God" (2:12). In his recollection of his own personal conduct in 2:1–12, he demonstrates that he has been a model of the conduct that he expects from his listeners.[18] Thus their collective past as his children and their memory of the word that brought them into existence serve as the foundation for their identity.

The continued rehearsal of the community's progress in the faith (2:13–3:10) also reminds the listeners of their corporate history as a people of faith and provides the background for the specific instructions that define the community's boundaries in chapters 4–5. Paul reminds the church of their shared response to the gospel, their endurance in faith and love (3:6), and their intimate ties to Paul.

The occasional creedal statements in 1 Thessalonians reflect Paul's attempt to reinforce the community's identity with the memory of what the people have believed from the very beginning. In recalling their conversion, in which they had "turned to God from idols . . . to wait for his Son from heaven, whom he raised from the dead" (1:9–10), Paul is recalling the community's faith. In 4:14 Paul reinforces communal identity by recalling that they, not their neighbors, have a hope, arguing, "Since we believe that Jesus died and arose again, even so, through Christ Jesus, God will bring with him those who have died" (4:14). What the community has always believed is the foundation of its solidarity and the mark of its identity.

Paul's proclamation is a reminder that preaching involves corporate consciousness. Preaching is not counseling on a group scale. Fred Craddock has said correctly that one preaches not to an audience but to a congregation. The forming of corporate identity is no easy task in our individualistic society.

---

18. Paul's claim that he did not act with uncleanness (ἀκαθαρσία, 2:3) anticipates his call for the Thessalonians not to behave with uncleanness (ἀκαθαρσία) in 4:7. His claim that he did not take advantage of anyone with greed (πλεονέξια) anticipates his instruction for believers not to take advantage of others (πλεονέκτειν) in the congregation in 4:6. His memory that he worked with his hands (2:9–12) anticipates his instructions to the congregation in 4:9–12. See Abraham J. Malherbe, *Paul and the Thessalonians* (Philadelphia: Fortress, 1987), 75.

Covenantal preaching, by implication, moves against individualistic hearing toward a more corporate listening. The preacher
addresses the faith community as such. This may seem obvious;
but in a society that so highly prizes individual rights against the
constraints of any community, it may be more counterculture
than we realize.[19]

Through the corporate language, the sermon is engaged in
"social construction," drawing together the individuals and smaller
groups into a corporate identity. As is the case with the epistles of
Paul, the sermon addresses the issues that face the community. As
I have noted in chapter 2, the sermon appeals to the community's
traditions (see 1 Cor. 11:2) and corporate memory to interpret the
situation that now confronts the community's identity. Walter
Brueggemann has described this corporate identity of the church:
"The congregation, as a community in crisis, gathers to decide one
more time about its identity and its vocation. The people gathered
have been bombarded since the last gathering by other voices of
interpretation that also want to offer an identity and a vocation."[20]
Paul's pastoral preaching took the individuals who had
responded to the gospel and formed a corporate consciousness.
Paul wrote to instruct and sustain congregations. He did not envision an individual reader (or viewer) reading the letters silently in
the comfort of home.[21] Paul speaks to community identity here, as
in all of his letters. For a variety of reasons, this dimension is
largely lacking in the modern understanding of pastoral preaching.
In the first place, Paul's clear demarcation between the church and
the world demonstrated the need for the support system of the corporate community. A community composed of individuals who had
left families to become a part of this new family could recognize
the corporate nature of its faith. In the second place, the intimacy
of the house church provided the intimacy our congregations do
not provide. In the third place, the ancient communities shared a

19. Arthur Van Seters, "The Problematic of Preaching in the Third Millennium,"
Interpretation 45 (1991): 271.
20. Walter Brueggemann, "The Social Nature of the Biblical Text for Preaching," in
Preaching as a Social Act, ed. Arthur Van Seters (Nashville: Abingdon, 1988), 139.
21. Richard Lischer, "The Interrupted Sermon," *Interpretation* 50 (1996): 177.

common story that involved pain and suffering, which resulted in a corporate consciousness that we no longer share.

Paul's preaching is a reminder that pastoral preaching is addressed to the church. To preach is to act ecclesially, to build on the supposition that this body of listeners intends to believe and act as a community. They belong to one another and to Christ, but they desperately need to know and feel what this means. They need to discover the meaning of commitment to the body of Christ.[22] Pastoral preaching moves against individualistic hearing toward a more corporate listening. To say that pastoral preaching is addressed to the church may seem obvious inasmuch as most preaching takes place in the assembly. In our own therapeutic culture, however, it is no longer obvious that preaching is addressed to corporate concerns, for the contemporary urban church is not likely to possess a corporate identity. Where consumers search for churches that answer their needs and for preachers who speak to their own individual search for self-esteem and significance, preaching that establishes a corporate identity will be countercultural.[23]

William Willimon describes this task of establishing corporate consciousness as "turning an audience into a church."[24] He describes the specific challenge of preaching to consumers who add Sunday church to their other occasions for consuming and meeting their own needs. Consumers ask how the sermon fits into their expectations, which have been formed within our culture. Some judge the sermon by its creativity or its new ideas. Others come in search of a word that is relevant to the issues that they face in their own world. They are not accustomed, however, to listening as a corporate community. To establish corporate listening was a challenge in Paul's time, and it remains a challenge for pastoral preaching today.

Paul's preaching ministry in 1 Thessalonians provides an important model for the contemporary preacher. Paul's insistence on the corporate nature of Christian experience challenges entrenched views of the Christian faith, according to which discipleship

---

22. Van Seters, "The Problematic of Preaching in the Third Millennium," 270.
23. Ibid.
24. William Willimon, "Turning an Audience into a Church," *Leadership* 15 (1994): 28.

involves an individualistic, rather than a corporate understanding of the Christian life. This individualistic understanding of Christian faith is often combined with the American ideals of the "rugged individual" to create a mentality that resists making fundamental commitments to the community.[25] Hence the primary identity of contemporary listeners is shaped by the ideals of self-actualization and individual freedom. We face a major challenge, therefore, if our preaching is to establish corporate consciousness. Perhaps, as Marva Dawn has suggested, we miss the corporate aspect of preaching because the English language does not distinguish between the singular and plural "you."[26] Furthermore, our therapeutic culture, with its focus on individual needs, causes us to miss the corporate aspects of faith. In this context the minister is authorized to lead the community of faith in its construction of reality. This task is an ongoing process by which the preacher educates the community to recognize that God has called individuals into a body in which they are members of Christ and members of each other.

Corporate Community and Insider Language

One is unlikely to establish corporate listening without establishing the community's own distinctive vocabulary. In writing to a congregation composed of new Gentile converts as well as any visitors who might have been present for the reading of 1 Thessalonians, Paul is not content to speak to them only in the language and terminology that they know. Indeed, 1 Thessalonians has numerous examples of "insider language" that would not have been immediately intelligible to those who had received no prior education in the faith. Such terms as "election" (1:4, my translation), "the wrath that is coming" (1:10), "coming" (παρουσία, 2:19), and the frequent reference to sanctification (3:13; 4:3, 7; 5:23) reinforce the community's corporate identity by continuing to initiate them into the "peculiar speech" that distinguishes them from the

---

25. Robert N. Bellah et al., in *Habits of the Heart* (Berkeley: Univ. of California Press, 1985), have described the pervasiveness of this individualism throughout American life. American individualism results in the loss of both civic and religious commitment to the group.
26. Marva Dawn, *Reaching Out without Dumbing Down* (Grand Rapids: Eerdmans, 1995), 212.

larger society.[27] In subsequent letters, Paul develops this vocabulary with extensive explanation of these categories. In 1 Corinthians, for example, he elaborates in considerable detail on the theme of sanctification (cf. especially the radical distinction between insiders and outsiders in 1 Corinthians 5:1–11:1). In Romans, he develops the topics of the wrath of God (1:18–32) and election (chaps. 9–11). Therefore, a vital aspect of Christian formation for Paul was his instruction in a new vocabulary that was taken from Israel's experience. Paul's communication with the larger world and his need to build a bridge to Greco-Roman listeners did not prohibit him from speaking to his converts with a distinctive discourse.

Much of the contemporary literature on worship has focused on the biblical illiteracy of our society and the need for translating our terminology for the benefit of those who do not know Christian discourse. Undoubtedly, Paul was capable of translation into the language of the larger society, and in numerous instances he spoke in the language forms of his culture. Nevertheless, the need for translation did not prohibit Paul from initiating his listeners into this "peculiar speech" of his communities, for a characteristic of cohesive communities is that they have a terminology of their own. George Lindbeck has written that "human experience is shaped, molded, and in a sense constituted by cultural and linguistic forms." He adds, "There are numberless thoughts we cannot think, sentiments we cannot have, and realities we cannot perceive unless we learn to use the appropriate symbol systems."[28] Language, according to Lindbeck, "is a communal phenomenon that shapes the subjectivities of individuals rather than being primarily a manifestation of those subjectivities."[29] Communities define themselves and create corporate expectations by their own use of insider language. They tell stories that contribute to communal identity. To tell a small part of a story, sometimes even to use a single word or image, is to evoke the corporate memory of

---

27. See William Willimon, *Peculiar Speech* (Grand Rapids: Eerdmans, 1992), 6: "No matter our style of preaching, there is no way for us preachers to weasel out of the baptismal truth that we preach within a distinctive universe of discourse. We talk funny."
28. George Lindbeck, *The Nature of Doctrine* (Philadelphia: Westminster, 1984), 34.
29. Ibid., 33.

the community.[30] Because not all Christian experience can be translated, Paul initiated his listeners into their own distinctive insider language.

A major challenge of pastoral preaching is to guide the congregation to become competent speakers of its own language. According to Lischer, this dimension of preaching has been lost, inasmuch as the community of faith has lost its own distinctive language. "In the past fifty years, a great wave of social, political, and cultural developments has eliminated the church as a linguistic base camp not only for a nominally 'Christian' nation but also for believers, who find it increasingly difficult to talk to one another." The church has, according to Lischer, adapted its own story and doctrine to secular ideology. It has championed so-called neutrality in religious matters as the norm for public discourse. "In all this linguistic action, the church thought of itself as a kind of base camp. After all, it was the sponsor of its own experiments with language."[31]

Pastoral Preaching:
Establishing Communal Ethical Norms

As a community that is being sanctified in anticipation of the parousia (3:13; 5:23) and empowered by the word of God and the Holy Spirit (4:8), the church is challenged to live "worthy of God" (2:12). As I have shown in chapter 2, Paul's initial instruction to his converts included specific moral instructions. The moral norms provided the badges of identification and the boundaries for the communities. Paul's preaching moves beyond individual instruction toward an ethical mandate that describes morality in communal terms. His listeners learn to ask "What should we do?" rather than "What should I do?"[32]

Paul's pastoral preaching to new converts was catechetical instruction, giving in detail the concrete demands of the Christian life to listeners who had not previously been enculturated into the communal norms of this movement. He assumed that Gentile con-

---

30. Ronald Allen, "The Social Function of Language in Preaching," in *Preaching as a Social Act*, 169.
31. Lischer, "The Interrupted Sermon," 171.
32. Hays, *Moral Vision*, 197.

verts did not know the norms of the new community.[33] He indicated that their identity, their shared story, and their conduct are inextricably combined, giving them the cohesiveness to live as a minority community in a hostile environment. The lists of vices and virtues (see 1 Cor. 6:9–11; Gal. 5:19–26; cf. 2 Cor. 12:20–21), which were probably derived from Paul's earlier catechetical instruction, provided new converts with a framework for knowing the expectations of the community and the sanctions associated with the violation of these norms. This initiation into the communal norms provided the model for centuries of pastoral preaching.[34]

The opening lines of 1 Thessalonians demonstrate the close relationship between the community's identity and its ethos. In the opening thanksgiving, Paul anticipates the letter's emphasis on the ethos of the community (chaps. 4–5) by giving thanks for their "work of faith and labor of love and steadfastness of hope" (1:3). The triad of faith, hope, and love becomes the unifying thread throughout the letter. Catechetical instruction involves introducing the church to these central Christian values. Paul expresses his gratitude here for the progress of the community. Later he recalls Timothy's favorable report of their "faith and love" (1 Thess. 3:6). This expression of gratitude is the prelude for his prayer that God will make them increase in love for each other before the parousia (3:12) and his paraenetic instructions to them to "put on the breastplate of faith and love, and for a helmet the hope of salvation" (5:8). The triad of faith, hope, and love was a central part of Paul's exhortation in all of his letters. The fact that he mentions it

---

33. The fact that Paul's specific moral demands have numerous points of contact with Hellenistic and Jewish moral expectations has raised questions about the distinctiveness of the ethic that Paul required of his churches. However, the countercultural nature of Paul's ethic consists in the way in which he connects the specific demands with his theological arguments drawn from the Christian story. The church is the eschatological community that has been called into being as a witness to God's reconciling work. The cross of Christ defines its shared vision of morality. See Hays, *Moral Vision*, 41.

34. On the tradition of catechetical preaching in the form of moral instruction, see Hughes Oliphant Old, *The Reading and Preaching of the Scriptures in the Worship of the Christian Church*, vol. 1, *The Biblical Period*, and vol. 2, *The Patristic Age*. According to Old, the earliest Christian catechetical material was moral instruction. One observes the tendency toward more specific instructions in the disputed letters of Paul, in which concrete moral instruction is given for family members. This tendency continues in 1 Peter and in the patristic literature (Old, *Reading and Preaching of the Scriptures*, 1.257).

at the beginning and end of 1 Thessalonians indicates that the larger agenda of Paul's preaching is to create a community that is held together by these values.

Just as Israel was sustained by its *haggadah* and *halakah*—its story and its code of conduct—this minority culture is also sustained by its story and its code of conduct, both of which Paul established in his original visit and now reinforces in the letter. The community's identity is the basis of its ethos. Here the striking fact about Paul's communication with the Thessalonians is the marked lack of originality. As he establishes communal identity, he constantly appeals to the church's memory of what he taught them previously. He introduces the code of conduct by recalling this instruction (4:1–2). He employs the language of tradition to urge his community to maintain its moral traditions. Then he indicates in specific detail the nature of the ethos of this community. In their sexual conduct, they do not live "like the Gentiles" (4:5). Their countercultural identity results in countercultural conduct. Paul describes the nature of sanctification in concrete terms: sanctification involves the abstinence from πορνεία. He spells out the kind of conduct that is expected of this community in his insistence that each one "take a wife in holiness and honor" (4:4, my translation).[35] His pastoral preaching, therefore, involves the reaffirmation of the standards of behavior that are acceptable within this community. Just as their communal identity is rooted in Israel's election and sanctification, the standards of behavior are rooted in the moral instruction that was consistently reaffirmed among diaspora Jews of Paul's time.[36] Although some Greco-Roman moralists declared the importance of the control of the passions and the practice of monogamy,[37] Paul's portrayal of Gentile morality assumes the common depiction of Gentile behavior that one finds in contemporary Jewish portrayals of Gentile morality (see Rom. 1:18–32). Consequently, he gives specific instructions to his Gentile converts on sexual morality as the expression of sanctification.

---

35. On the interpretation of 1 Thess. 4:4, see O. Larry Yarbrough, *Not Like the Gentiles: Marriage Rules in the Letters of Paul*, SBLDS 80 (Atlanta: Scholars Press, 1985), 68–87.

36. Ibid., 76–77.

37. Ibid., 31–63, for texts. Cf. also Abraham J. Malherbe, *Moral Exhortation: A Greco-Roman Sourcebook*, LEC (Philadelphia: Westminster, 1986), 152–61.

In subsequent letters Paul will elaborate on the communal expectations concerning sexual behavior and demand that his churches maintain boundaries of appropriate conduct. When the Corinthians raised questions about his original instructions (1 Cor. 7:1), he elaborated on his original commands by giving instructions for specific situations (1 Cor. 6:12–7:40). In Romans, he also elaborates on this topic with his contrast between the sexual conduct that results in the wrath of God (Rom. 1:18–32) and the new Christian existence that is marked by the control of the passions (Rom. 6:12–7:25).

The relationship between communal identity and conduct may be seen also in Paul's insistence on brotherly love (φιλαδέλφια, 4:9–12). Throughout 1 Thessalonians, Paul consistently addresses his hearers as "brothers" (ἀδελφοί, NRSV, "brothers and sisters").[38] In his opening thanksgiving, he expresses his gratitude for the "labor of love" (1:3) that is manifest in the community. In 3:12 he prays that God will cause them to "increase and abound in love to one another and for all." These reminders form the preface to his challenge to them to conduct themselves as family by practicing "brotherly love." Paul takes individuals who have been strangers to each other and creates in them a sense of family. His listeners knew—or thought they knew—what "brotherly love" was. Ancient writers speak of brotherly love as one of the highest virtues. Paul transforms their understanding of this virtue by giving specific instructions on living as family in the new community. His pastoral task, therefore, is both to shape the corporate identity of the community as family and to encourage an ethic of family life.

The pastoral task for Paul also involves establishing the conditions by which the community can continue to live in Paul's absence. The latter part of 1 Thessalonians is distinguished by the repeated references to the community's pastoral work toward each other. The eschatological instructions of 4:13–5:11, which many have taken to be the primary theme of the book, are actually given in the context of pastoral instructions. Paul is far less concerned about laying down a sequence of events that precedes the parousia than he is with the pastoral concerns about a community's anxiety

---

38. 1:4; 2:1, 9, 14, 17; 3:7; 4:1, 10, 13; 5:1, 4, 12, 14, 25. See Malherbe, *Paul and the Thessalonians*, 47–52, on Paul's use of kinship language.

about its future. He himself writes these instructions in the pastoral role of one who wishes to spare his community from grief (1 Thess. 4:13). He concludes his reassuring words about the certainty of the parousia in 4:17 with the challenge for his hearers to "encourage one another with these words." Similarly, he concludes his reaffirmation of the community's hope in 5:1–11 with the words "Therefore encourage one another and build up each other, as indeed you are doing." Paul's pastoral task is to involve the community in the continued pastoral activity of "encouraging one another."

Paul's continued advice to the community to acknowledge its leaders, to be at peace among themselves (5:12–13), to admonish the disorderly and bear with the weak (5:14) further indicates that pastoral preaching involves initiating the community in the pastoral work of encouraging each other.[39] Pastoral preaching shapes the corporate identity of the community so much that the community is sustained by the continued pastoral activity of the members toward each other.

The constant feature of the letters of Paul is the movement of Paul's message from theology to the morality that grows out of the gospel. Paul's speech is often punctuated with imperatives that spell out the norms for communal living. He recognizes that his listeners live in a pagan culture and have little knowledge of the concrete requirements of the Christian faith. Consequently, the concluding sections of his letters to Rome and Galatia are composed of lengthy treatments of the conduct that he expects of his listeners. His letters to the Corinthians and Philippians are filled with detailed explanations of the life that pleases God.

Paul's instruction to the community indicates that pastoral preaching involves not only acceptance and understanding but the establishment of concrete expectations for those who live within the community. In a culture that is both therapeutic and pluralistic, focusing on individual freedom, the establishment of communal norms is a special challenge for the preacher. To Christians who have been shaped only by the Protestant emphasis on grace and the American emphasis on individual rights, the imperative mood may sound legalistic and oppressive. For listeners who come

---

39. Abraham J. Malherbe, "'Pastoral Care' in the Thessalonian Church," *NTS* 36 (1990): 388–91.

as individual consumers, this form of pastoral preaching is likely to be unwelcome. Listeners do not want to be confronted with communal norms that separate them from the society at large or inhibit their freedom. George Lindbeck has written:

> The modern mood is antipathetic to the very notion of communal norms. This antipathy can be construed, as it is by sociologists of knowledge, as the product of such factors as religious and ideological pluralism and social mobility. . . . The suggestion that communities have the right to insist on standards of belief and practice as conditions of membership is experienced as an intolerable infringement of the liberty of the self. This reaction is intensified by the growing contradiction between the traditional standards and the prevailing values of the wider society as communicated by education, the mass media, and personal contacts.[40]

The pastoral preaching of Paul taught the diverse individuals who "turned to God from idols" (1 Thess. 1:9) how to live as a community. Paul's pastoral preaching involved a parental concern for the ultimate welfare of the community, the establishment of an eschatological vision of God's ultimate purpose for his people, and the instructions for living that consisted of a life that was "worthy of God." Pastoral preaching, therefore, is not limited to the preacher's response to the perceived needs or questions that individuals are asking. Pastoral preaching is determined by the larger agenda of preaching: the eschatological vision of a people who are making a corporate journey toward their destiny in God. The ultimate test of the quality of pastoral preaching is the community's transformation into a holy people. Paul's concluding benediction in 1 Thessalonians 5:23 is, in fact, the agenda for pastoral preaching: "May the God of peace himself sanctify you entirely; and may your spirit and soul and body be kept sound and blameless at the coming of our Lord Jesus Christ."

Paul does not preach only in response to an immediate crisis. Although his preaching may at times come as a response to the questions of his community, his content is determined by a larger agenda that requires that the community be constantly reminded

---

40. Lindbeck, *The Nature of Doctrine*, 77.

of its identity as a separate people summoned to live a countercultural existence. In his preaching task Paul is engaged in "social construction." Because he knows that his church faces another society, which tells a different story, he creates a new identity for his community based on their common memory. He binds strangers together with an identity and an ethos, pointing them to an alternative world and providing specific instructions for a corporate response to God's saving deeds.[41]

To transfer Paul's moral preaching into the contemporary situation is no easy task. Paul does not provide an extensive case law to cover many issues that we face. His advice on head coverings or the eating of food offered to idols, for example, may not appear to provide the model for contemporary preaching. However, we find a deeper level in which his kind of pastoral preaching is both possible and necessary if the church is to maintain its identity. The preacher assists the church in forming a corporate response to our pressing issues. People who live in this community know that the story of Christ's self-giving love is more than their foundational story; it is the norm for community life and a challenge to their own selfishness. Listeners who have heard the biblical story have learned not to think of themselves more highly than they ought to think (Rom. 12:3). They have learned that the lives of others—even those that limit our personal freedom—are more important than our own. From Christian preaching they have also discovered the resources for keeping their marriage vows and emptying themselves of the selfish ambitions that destroy family and communal life. Even where the answers to moral questions are not always clear, pastoral preaching continues to challenge the congregation to ask the moral questions and to discuss them in light of the gospel of Christ.[42]

---

41. Cf. Peter Berger and Thomas Luckmann, *The Social Construction of Reality: A Treatise in the Sociology of Knowledge* (New York : Anchor Books, 1991), 107.
42. On the hermeneutical challenges of using the New Testament ethical norms for the contemporary church, see Hays, *Moral Vision*, 291–312.

Chapter Five

Explaining Ourselves:
Preaching and Theology

R ecently a cartoon appeared in *Leadership* magazine in which
the preacher faced a congregation of people sitting in La-Z-
Boy chairs, with each person holding a remote control for changing
channels.[1] This portrayal of preaching is undoubtedly the perception of those who speak to a generation of people who have been
shaped by the power of television. Under the influence of television, as I noted in chapter 3, the preacher faces the challenge of
adapting to a culture that is unaccustomed to reasoned discourse.[2]
The Christian community is inevitably affected by this culture, and
it has little appetite for the linear reasoning that has characterized
the traditional sermon and little familiarity with the Christian message. Under the pressure of maintaining membership levels and
reaching out to the unchurched, preachers, like politicians and
educators, wonder how to communicate in a climate in which listeners sit impatiently with their channel changers, ready to move
on to another voice at the first onset of boredom. The listeners'
impatience with reflective discourse makes storytelling an especially attractive alternative for the preacher, as I argued in the
introduction.

We face consumers who are accustomed to comparison shop-
ping. They choose their churches in the same way they choose
their appliances and their cars.[3] The loss of denominational loyalty,
which is characteristic of the new generation of church members,

---

1. *Leadership* 15 (1994): 29.
2. See Richard Jensen, *Thinking in Story: Preaching in a Post-literate Age* (Lima, Ohio:
CSS, 1993), 45–58.
3. Robert G. Hughes and Robert Kysar, *Preaching Doctrine in the Twenty-first Century*
(Minneapolis: Fortress, 1997), 3. See also Robert N. Bellah et al., *The Good Society*
(New York: Knopf, 1992), 183.

results in congregations that are not united by a theological tradition or a single doctrinal basis.[4] What unites them may be their
shared social class, leisure-time interests, or a particular liturgical
expression. Consequently, preachers face audiences that view doctrinal beliefs as matters of preference. Under these conditions,
preachers design their sermons to ensure that listeners do not
change channels, trying to create an atmosphere of maximum audience appeal. Preachers who conform to audience expectations hope
to compete in the marketplace of entertainment.

Where preaching is determined by audience ratings, theological
reflection is not likely to have a prominent place, for few people
come to church wanting an elaboration of the great themes of the
faith. If few people come wanting to know, in Harry Emerson
Fosdick's words, "what happened to the Jebusites,"[5] even fewer in
the modern era come wanting an elaboration on the great themes
of the Christian faith. Theology is commonly associated with irrel-
evance and abstraction. "Theology seems often to the outsider just
so much word-spinning, air-borne discourse which never touches
down except disastrously."[6] In the popular mind, theological
reflection belongs to the academy, not to the Sunday sermon.

If the minister and the church associate theological reflection
with the academy alone, generations of theological educators and
publishers bear some responsibility. In the seminary, the studies of
preaching, theology, and biblical studies are compartmentalized
into the domain of specialists in each area. When these subjects are
treated as separate disciplines, the specialists are answerable primarily to other specialists, leaving the task of integration to the
preacher, who has seen no model of integrating preaching with
theological reflection. Consequently, preachers who perceive that
the preaching and theology belong to two different worlds will
hesitate to attempt to preach theology.

---

4. Hughes and Kysar, *Preaching Doctrine*, 3. See Bellah et al., *The Good Society*, 202–4,
on the "deconfessionalizing" in mainline churches. The authors describe a theological
pluralism that results in a "caucus church" that diminishes theological conversation
and education.

5. Harry Emerson Fosdick, "What Is the Matter with Preaching?" *Harper's* 107
(July 1928): 135.

6. Ian Ramsey, *Models for Divine Activity* (London: SCM, 1973), 1; cited in David
Wells, *No Place for Truth* (Grand Rapids: Eerdmans, 1993), 97.

The Pauline Model

Theological reflection is a vital dimension of preaching, as I argued in the introduction. While Paul's letters are all pastoral communication, as I argued in the previous chapter, they are also examples of faith seeking understanding. The modern reader is likely to be amazed at the lengthy theological arguments that punctuate the letters that were meant to be read in the assembly. These arguments reflect Paul's high expectations for his listeners. He undoubtedly assumes his listeners will follow his intricate argumentation. His theological reflection is not, however, abstract and irrelevant. As much as his letters may offer detailed theological argument, Paul never offers treatises on the great doctrines of the Christian faith in a comprehensive and systematic way. He never offers a comprehensive sermon on the incarnation or atonement. His theological discourse appears in the context of questions that have been raised in his congregations or the issues that threaten the identity of the church. Paul's theological discourse is interwoven with his pastoral communication. The issues that he faces are ultimately theological in nature.

Although Paul's letters consistently repeat the instruction already known to the congregations, as we have seen in 1 Thessalonians, they move beyond the mere repetition of previous teaching. We may observe the progression of Paul's theological discourse as we note the sequence of his letters. In 1 Thessalonians, a letter that is fundamentally pastoral in its purpose, Paul introduces theological categories for his listeners. His catechetical instruction includes a lesson on ecclesiology, as he addresses the "ἐκκλησία of the Thessalonians in God the Father and the Lord Jesus Christ" (1:1) and recalls their "election" (1:4, my translation). With his focus on election and sanctification (3:13; 4:3, 7; 5:23), he equates the congregation at Thessalonica with the people of God in the Old Testament, whom God elected for service. His affirmation of the Christian hope also offers the listeners an eschatological understanding (1:9–10; 4:13–5:11) that is rooted in the biblical understanding of God's saving purposes. Although he does not systematically explain these doctrines, he provides his listeners with an intellectual framework for understanding their faith. He introduces a theological vocabulary and provides a coherent intellectual framework for his listeners. Inasmuch as he is not responding to a crisis, but laying a foundation, he is providing a glimpse at the coherent center of his theological instruction.[7]

In subsequent letters Paul engages in an extensive conversation with churches in which his instructions lead to new questions that require clarification. Where crises and new issues arise, Paul elaborates on his original theological instruction. Here his theological discourse is related to the contingent situation, which has required him to articulate theology under new circumstances. Because churches never live in isolation from their culture or from changing problems, their ongoing existence requires that they continue to ask how the Christian message addresses new situations. This extended conversation comes in the form of the theological reflection that fills Paul's letters. New questions and challenges call for theological reflection on the gospel. Paul's sustained and sometimes lengthy arguments presuppose that the communities can follow his argument. In Galatians and Romans, for example, he presents a sustained argument on the implications of the gospel for the inclusion of both Jews and Gentiles within the people of God. His elaboration on the theme of the righteousness of God is a response to the concrete problems of churches that were confronted with the issue of the inclusion of Gentiles in the people of God. If we follow the sequence of Paul's letters, we observe that the theme of the righteousness of God is developed in Galatians (2:21; 3:6, 21; 5:5) and then greatly expanded in Romans. Paul never elaborates on the doctrine of justification by faith in abstract terms. His theological argument is occasioned by a concrete situation in the life of the church. Issues that appeared to be relatively simple— table fellowship between Jews and Gentiles, for example—could not be resolved by majority vote or a compromise between two sides. These issues were profoundly theological in nature.

Paul does not give a systematic treatment of the incarnation. However, the "Christ hymn" in Philippians 2:6–11 is an articulation of the story of the one who "emptied himself" for the sake of others. In this instance also, Paul's recitation of this hymn appears in the context of the pastoral problems that faced the Philippian church. When he encourages his listeners to conduct themselves

---

7. See J. Christiaan Beker, *Paul the Apostle: The Triumph of God in Life and Thought* (Philadelphia: Fortress, 1980), 23–93, for the categories of coherence and contingency in Paul's thought.

"in a manner worthy of the gospel" (Phil. 1:27), he appeals to this great christological formulation. He confronts a community that faces potential division initiated by the quarreling of two women (Phil. 4:2–3) with a profound christological statement that is intended to provide them with the mind of Christ (Phil. 2:5). Thus, for Paul, all of the issues facing the church are theological in nature.

Theology in 1 Corinthians

Although all of Paul's letters guide the congregations in theological reflection, his lengthy conversation with the Corinthians— the most thorough conversation available to us—makes the Corinthian correspondence an especially useful example of preaching as faith that seeks understanding. We may assume that during Paul's ministry in Corinth (see Acts 18:1–18) his preaching ministry involved catechetical instruction that is similar to that which Paul gave to the Thessalonians on his original visit. We may assume, furthermore, that Paul's first letter to the Corinthians reinforced the same instruction (cf. 1 Cor. 5:9). The preaching task, however, is never complete with mere repetition, for preaching involves explanation and follow-up in a sustained conversation with the listeners. Paul's prohibition of relationships with immoral people in the earlier letter apparently elicits new questions that require further explanation. Consequently, he must explain that his instruction involves only church members who are immoral (1 Cor. 5:9–13). In a similar way, the standard instruction about avoiding sexual immorality (see 1 Thess. 4:1–8) has led to new questions that Paul answers in 1 Corinthians 6:12–7:40.[8] His preaching, therefore, involves continued reflection and elaboration over his basic instruction as he engages in a conversation with his listeners. In these instances, preaching involves elaboration over what has been said before.

Paul's conversation with the Corinthians involves more than the extension of the original conversation, for 1 Corinthians indicates that the letter was also occasioned by new questions that required answers. Consequently, Paul's preaching to the Corinthians

---

8. See O. Larry Yarbrough, *Not like the Gentiles*, SBLDS 80 (Atlanta: Scholars, 1985).

involves reflection about new situations and crises in light of the community's faith. Chloe's people have reported a partisan rivalry between the followers of Paul and Apollos that was in some way associated with the high value the Corinthians placed on wisdom and rhetoric (1:10–17). These norms were especially valued by the socially prominent Christians in Corinth, who apparently claimed wisdom for themselves (3:18) and manifested a consistent pattern of arrogant behavior.[9] According to 1 Corinthians, the Corinthian church was divided apparently between the devotees of Paul and of Apollos.[10] Since the subject of public speaking and wisdom is also a part of the discussion, we may assume that many of the Corinthians saw more in Apollos than in Paul—although there is no evidence that Apollos encouraged the comparison.[11] They saw in Apollos the ideals of rhetorical power and wisdom. Paul suffered by comparison. If he could not explain himself, his ability to direct the affairs of the church would be greatly diminished. Paul's challenge, therefore, is to address new questions that have been provoked by the common evaluation of orators in Hellenistic Corinth.[12] The Corinthians evaluated Christian leaders through the filter of their own views of wisdom and oratory, demanding that the speaker conform to their own views.

The numerous issues Paul addresses in 1 Corinthians 5–16 appear at first to be unrelated to the topic of partisan rivalry Paul addresses in chapters 1–4. The issues Paul confronts in Corinth do not appear to be the problems of doctrine. Here Paul's preaching involves responding both to new crises about which he has heard and to new questions that members of this congregation have raised. As in chapters 1–4, one sees the anticommunal factors that

---

9. See Peter Marshall, *Enmity in Corinth: Social Conventions in Paul's Relations with the Corinthians*, WUNT 2.23 (Tübingen: J. C. B. Mohr, 1987), 194–96, on *hubris* as the underlying issue.

10. The reference in 1:12 ("'I belong to Paul,' or 'I belong to Apollos,' or 'I belong to Cephas,' or 'I belong to Christ'") should not be taken as an indication of four factions. In 3:1–5 Paul refers only to himself and Apollos.

11. See Ben Witherington, *Conflict and Community in Corinth* (Grand Rapids: Eerdmans, 1995), 100. See also Stephen M. Pogoloff, *Logos and Sophia: The Rhetorical Situation of 1 Corinthians*, SBLDS 134 (Atlanta: Scholars Press, 1992), 100–103.

12. See Duane Litfin, *Paul's Theology of Proclamation*, SNTSMS 79 (Cambridge: Cambridge Univ. Press, 1994); cf. Witherington, *Conflict and Community in Corinth*, 100.

are present in the lawsuits (6:1–11), the insistence on freedom to eat meat offered to idols (8:1–13; 10:23–11:1), and the chaos at the Lord's Supper (11:17–34) and in the corporate assembly (chaps. 12–14). The Corinthians' perspectives on the nature of Christian preaching, freedom, community, baptism, the Lord's Supper, and the resurrection were thus filtered through the community's own prior experience. Most of these issues reflect the pretensions and values of a socially mobile minority who interpreted Christian experience with the norms of Hellenistic society. These issues are, in fact, rooted in the problems that are first identified in chapters 1–4. They reflect the influence of the socially prominent people who came to the Christian faith with their own understandings of community and their own understanding of Christian freedom, which they have superimposed on their experience of Christian community. Similarly, the insistence of some that "there is no resurrection" (1 Cor. 15:12) is rooted in the Hellenistic understanding of life after death.[13] Paul's opposition did not deny the Christian confession that Christ "died for our sins" and "was raised on the third day in accordance with the scriptures" (1 Cor. 15:3–4). The underlying problem was the Corinthians' desire to see Christian experience through the filter of their own past cultural experience. This Corinthian development took place under the conditions of a newly arisen Gentile-Christian church, which did not simply lay aside its former culture, understanding of religion, and interpretation of the world, or adapt itself fully to the apostle's understanding during his stay in Corinth.[14] Thus the formation of a new Christian culture was no easy task.

The fact that Paul appeals to what the church has "received" (1 Cor. 11:23; 15:3) and believed (1 Cor. 15:12) indicates that the Corinthians had not challenged these basic traditions. Nevertheless, Paul and his listeners apparently have major disagreements over the meaning of these traditions. These disagreements are, in fact, rooted in theological judgments that must be debated as part of Paul's ongoing dialogue with his congregation.

---

13. Despite frequent claims to the contrary in the commentaries, 1 Corinthians offers no evidence that the denial of the resurrection by the Corinthians is rooted in a form of realized eschatology.

14. Jürgen Becker, *Paul: Apostle to the Gentiles* (Louisville, Ky.: Westminster/John Knox, 1993), 199.

For Paul, theological preaching is not a retreat into abstractions that are far removed from the whole congregation, as 1 Corinthians 1–4 demonstrates. Here Paul moves from the concrete issue lying before the Corinthians—the partisan rivalry mentioned in 1:10–17—to a lengthy theological statement in 1:18–2:16 before he comes back to the point at issue in 3:1–5. That is, partisan rivalry cannot be addressed with brief lectures on the church as a family or a simple condemnation of partisan behavior and arrogance. Paul knows that a deeper issue is at stake. Consequently, 1:18–2:16 is a lengthy theological argument that lays the basis for Christian unity. It also provides the introduction to the remainder of Paul's message in 1 Corinthians.

Paul explains himself in the first part of 1 Corinthians by going back to the preaching that called the church into existence. In recalling his original preaching, he returns to the common ground on which no one could disagree. Even Paul's opponents will agree on the basic Christian confession—that Paul had preached "Christ crucified" (1:23). What the opponents apparently had not understood was the implication of the message of the cross for the crisis at Corinth. Hellenistic listeners could easily have interpreted the cross and resurrection of Jesus in terms that were analogous to their own background, according to which the story of Jesus' death and resurrection were interpreted in terms of Greek hero worship. They evidently regarded Christ as the victorious hero who is celebrated after surviving trials. Such an analogous story was available in the Heracles saga, in which Heracles was celebrated as one who endured many burdens and sufferings before he ultimately became victorious.[15]

Under these circumstances, Paul's challenge is not only to repeat the basic preaching that the church had heard, but also to interpret the tradition in the context of the issue that divides the church. Consequently, before Paul returns to the issue of partisan rivalry and arrogance, he interprets the kerygma in 1:18–2:16. In 1:18–25, he moves beyond the traditional recitation of the preaching (see 1 Cor. 15:3) to describe his preaching in such a way as to focus on the humility and shame of the cross. He preaches the "message about the cross" (1:18) and "Christ crucified" (1:23), a

---

15. Becker, *Paul*, 201.

message that is "foolishness to those who are perishing" (1:18), a "stumbling block to Jews and foolishness to Gentiles" (1:23). He then argues that the cross is the reminder that God turns our human expectations upside down: God's wisdom is foolishness to the world, the power that the world has mistaken for weakness. In describing the cross as God's means of "outsmarting" the wise, Paul undermines the pretensions of the "wise" people of Corinth. Therefore, the cross is the living demonstration of the incomprehensible ways of God, who "chooses" to save the world in a way that confounds human arrogance.[16] In other instances Paul explains the story of the cross by using a variety of images for the significance of the cross.[17] In this situation, however, where he confronts the pretensions of the "wise" opposition in Corinth, he declares that the *crucified* Christ reveals God's power and wisdom.

According to 1:26–28, not only did God choose a means of salvation that challenges the world's ideas, but in the people he chose he also has challenged normal expectations. There are "not many . . . wise by human standards, not many . . . powerful, not many . . . of noble birth" (1:26). The Corinthians have not received the gospel because of their superior wisdom, power, or status (1:26), but only by God's call.[18] In the same way, according to 2:1–5, Paul is not the kind of speaker one might reasonably have expected. He did not come to them in fancy words of wisdom (1 Cor. 2:1–5). He further defines his message in 2:6–16 as the mystery that is hidden from this world, but is recognized only by those to whom God has given the Spirit. By claiming that only those who possess the Spirit grasp the mystery of the cross, Paul challenges the epistemology of his opposition. Their understanding had been shaped by their culture. Although they claim to possess the Spirit, the very ways in which they measure spirituality demonstrate that they do not grasp the meaning of the cross.

---

16. See Victor Furnish, "Theology in 1 Corinthians," in *Pauline Theology*, ed. David M. Hay (Minneapolis: Fortress, 1993), 2.66.

17. Note the rich imagery in Rom. 3:21–26, where Paul employs such words as *expiation* (ἱλαστήριον), *redemption* (ἀπολύτρωσις) and *righteousness* (δικαιοσύνη). Here Paul employs both cultic and judicial imagery to explain the meaning of the cross. See Furnish, "Theology in 1 Corinthians," 68.

18. Furnish, "Theology in 1 Corinthians," 65.

The result of this lengthy argument is to undermine the partisan rivalry and arrogance of the socially prominent people at Corinth. This section confronts the readers with a way of knowing God that is different from the understanding that has resulted in factionalism. Paul could have addressed the problem of arrogance and factionalism in more direct terms than in 1 Corinthians. He could have proceeded directly from the statement of the problem in 1:10–17 to the response in 3:1–5, or he could have called for some means of conflict management. He knew, however, that what the church needed was a new theological vision. The concrete problems at Corinth called for a theological response. The emphasis on orators and human wisdom reflected a way of thinking that belongs to this world. Paul and Apollos are nothing more than servants (3:1–5), and anyone who argues over preachers from human standards is still immature. *It was Paul's way of saying that our preaching is not determined solely by our listeners.*

The striking fact is that it took Paul a considerable amount of space to make his point, which becomes the foundation for his responses to the specific problems that plague the Corinthian church. Paul does not answer questions in an ad hoc way, but instead returns to the foundation of Christian experience to correct the abuses at Corinth. The cross has created a new vision of community that will address the anticommunal forces in the church.[19] When he faces the problem of sexual immorality, occasioned once more by Corinthians who claimed their superior wisdom as the basis for their freedom,[20] he argues on the basis of theological commitments involving soteriology (5:7) and anthropology (6:15–17). When he addresses the problems of lawsuits, he argues for a selfless conduct that is based on the appropriation of the cross

---

19. Charles Cousar says, "In the long run behavior can only be superficially changed unless imaginations are changed, unless angles of vision are renewed. Thus the text confronts the readers with an alternative perspective, albeit a radical one, to their way of understanding God and their life in community" ("The Theological Task of 1 Corinthians: A Conversation with Gordon D. Fee and Victor Paul Furnish," in David M. Hay, ed., *Pauline Theology*, 2.97).

20. See Marshall, *Enmity in Corinth*, 285–87. Marshall demonstrates that the phrase "all things are lawful" (1 Cor. 6:12; 10:23) echoes the language of personal freedom in Hellenistic sources, according to which freedom involved the license to do as one likes. For the Stoics, freedom was synonymous with educated moral autonomy. "Only the wise man was truly free" (Marshall, 287). Cf. Dio Chrysostom, *Disc.* 14.13–14.

(6:7–9). In response to the anticommunal conduct of Corinthians who claimed the right to eat meat offered to idols, he reminds his readers of the significance of the cross (8:11). In response to the chaos at the Lord's Supper, he reflects on the meaning of the tradition and then offers instructions that grow out of this reflection (11:17–34). Before he gives specific advice on corporate worship in chapter 14, he first discusses the nature of Christian community in chapter 12. Paul's profound treatment of the church as the body of Christ is a response to the antisocial forces in Corinth. The Corinthian situation could be addressed adequately only if Paul could bring them to see the theological implications of the issues at hand. In response to the Corinthian claim that "there is no resurrection" (1 Cor. 15:12), Paul develops a lengthy argument about the nature of the resurrection (1 Cor. 15:1–58). Without theological reflection, the church would address its problems through the filter of its own cultural values.

Preaching and Theology in 2 Corinthians

Preaching is an ongoing conversation, as the Corinthian correspondence indicates. Preachers may hope that the sermon will resolve the crisis at hand, but 1 Corinthians demonstrates that the sermon does not resolve the crisis. New crises emerge out of the old ones, and the preacher's explanations result in new sets of questions. In the case of 1 Corinthians, Paul's explanations were not particularly successful, for 2 Corinthians is both the continuation of an old discussion and the response to a new crisis that came to Paul's attention as soon as Timothy returned to Paul after delivering 1 Corinthians. This crisis was so severe that Paul had already made a "painful visit" (2 Cor. 2:1) and written a "tearful letter" (2 Cor. 2:4) to salvage the situation at Corinth. Indeed, 2 Corinthians is our final record of a debate that has been taking place since Timothy delivered 1 Corinthians. Outsiders have come to Corinth and joined forces with the minority that has challenged Paul's leadership in 1 Corinthians. Once more, the community compares Paul with other preachers (see 2 Cor. 3:1–3; 10:12–18) and questions his legitimacy as a minister and apostle. In this instance, the newcomers to Corinth have invited comparison to Paul by making claims for their own status as ministers and apostles. They question Paul's integrity, portraying him as the flatterer who tells his audiences what they want to hear (cf. 1:15ff.).[21] They question his refusal to receive remuneration for his work (11:7–11), and they criticize his public persona and speaking ability. They say, "His bodily presence is weak, and his speech contemptible" (10:10). To make matters worse, they argue that Paul does not have the Spirit (10:2).[22] Thus they apparently equate the possession of the Spirit with a strong physical demeanor, speaking ability, and powerful deeds. Once more, as in 1 Corinthians, the Corinthian theology is filtered through the values of the Hellenistic world, which placed great value on power, performance, and effectiveness.[23]

Paul's readiness for theological combat is most evident in chapter 10, where the argument reaches special intensity. In response to the charges against his ministry, Paul portrays his task in military terms. He is a soldier who wages war, not with weapons that are "according to human standards" (κατὰ σάρκα) (10:3), but with spiritual weapons in order to "destroy strongholds" (10:4). He adds, "We destroy arguments and every proud obstacle raised up against the knowledge of God, and we take every thought captive to obey Christ" (10:4–5). Using the language of philosophic debate,[24] Paul describes his preaching ministry. Theological argument is necessary because Paul is engaged in warfare against the presumption of ideas that undermine the Christian faith. This claim, which comes near the end of 2 Corinthians, functions as a description of the argument that pervades the epistle. Paul is a the-

---

21. For the "flatterer" as a stock figure in Greco-Roman literature and the numerous analogies in 2 Corinthians, see Marshall, *Enmity in Corinth*, 70–90.

22. The opponents' charge that Paul conducted himself κατὰ σάρκα suggests that they questioned Paul's possession of the Spirit.

23. One of the major issues in scholarship on 2 Corinthians concerns the literary integrity of the epistle, which few scholars uphold. However, I assume, with most scholars, that the issues addressed throughout 2 Corinthians are fundamentally the same. Although the intensity of the argument in 2 Corinthians 10–13 is greater than in chaps. 1–9, the subject matter throughout the epistle is the same: the defense of Paul's ministry.

24. For the military metaphors to describe the philosopher's task, see Epictetus, *Diss.* 4.16.14: "The philosopher's thoughts are his protection." Philo refers to a "stronghold" as a structure built "through the persuasiveness of argument" (*Prob.* 15). Cf. *Conf.* 128–31. See A. J. Malherbe, "Antisthenes and Odysseus, and Paul at War," *HTR* 76 (1983): 143–73, for extended discussion of philosophic debate as military engagement.

ological preacher who enters the arena where bad ideas tempt the church from its commitments. His church is caught between, on the one hand, the attractions of a Christianity that conforms to the common cultural expectations of the Hellenistic world and, on the other hand, the preaching ministry of Paul.

Paul's defense of his ministry is decidedly theological. The opening section of the epistle (1:1–2:13), which appears on the surface to be more autobiographical than theological, actually offers a theological defense of Paul's conduct. Paul writes to reaffirm his integrity (1:12–14) in response to the charges against him by insisting that he does not tell his listeners what they want to hear; he does not say "Yes, yes," and "No, no" (1:17), like the flatterers. His word is always "yes" because God is faithful (1:20). God keeps his promises, and he has sealed them with the promised Holy Spirit, which has been given to the community of faith. What drives Paul's ministry and dictates his plans, therefore, is not opportunism, but his dedication to others because of Christ. It was to "spare" (1:23) his people that he had failed to keep his earlier promise. In describing himself as one whose ministry is governed by his concern for others, he anticipates the theological argument that forms the centerpiece of the book (see below on 2 Cor. 5:11–6:2).

In 2:14–4:6 we see an eloquent and powerful theological statement about ministry as Paul responds to the challenges to his preaching ministry. Paul describes himself as the captured prisoner on his way to death (2:14) while at the same time affirming that his ministry is a matter of life and death for his hearers. Again, this is not the ministry the consumers want, but it is the ministry of Paul, who has been "captured." He is not like those who "peddle" the gospel (2:17). In order to demonstrate his point, he takes his listeners through a complicated argument in which he declares that his ministry is nothing less than the ministry of the new covenant Jeremiah had announced (2 Cor. 3:1–6). Indeed, as the ministry of the new covenant, it surpasses the ministry of Moses in glory, for his ministry of the Spirit results in the transformation of the people of God (3:18).

To his critics, Paul's ministry does not look glorious. The numerous references to Paul's weakness in 2 Corinthians (11:21, 29, 30; 12:5, 9, 10; 13:4) suggest that the opposition has criticized Paul for his humility and weakness. One evidence of this weakness was to be seen in the ineffectiveness of his ministry, which was evident both in the apparent failure of his preaching ministry and in his ineffectiveness with the Corinthians. Despite the appearances to the contrary, Paul claims that his ministry has profound results. Although he faces unbelief (4:4; cf. 3:14, 15), he will not "tamper with God's word" in order to win converts (4:2, RSV), for the problem with unbelief does not lie with his message, but with the "god of this world" who has "blinded the minds of the unbelievers" (4:4). That is, it is not the effectiveness of the preacher that produces results; the results of Paul's preaching depend on the power of God that creates response (cf. 1 Thess. 1:5; 2:13) and the Satanic power that blinds the hearts of unbelievers. Despite the absence of results, Paul will continue to preach "Jesus Christ as Lord" (4:5) because God has shone in the hearts of believers "to give the light of the knowledge of the glory of God in the face of Jesus Christ" (4:6). Despite his opponents' claim to the contrary, his own human frailty as an "earthen vessel" (4:7, RSV), and his own temporary affliction (4:17), he does not lose heart (4:1, 16) because he "walks by faith, not by sight" (5:7). By the standards of his culture—and of his opposition—he is not a minister of Christ.

Such a countercultural existence requires explanation. In 5:12–21 he gives the most densely theological treatment of his own ministry in the entire book.[25] Here Paul not only engages in theological preaching but also reflects on the task of theological preaching. In 5:11–12, he justifies his theological task by explaining himself to the listeners. Although he refuses some forms of persuasion (cf. 1 Cor. 2:4), he nevertheless "persuades men" (5:11, RSV). Although he is already known to God, he is not content unless he is also known to the consciousness of his listeners (5:11), who need to understand the issues that are before them. He wishes to give the listeners "an opportunity to boast about us, so that you may be able to answer those who boast in outward appearance and not in the heart" (5:12). Just as Paul introduces the entire letter with his desire that this church take pride in him (1:14), he now returns to the same theme in 5:12. In this instance, however, the critical issues that lie before the congregation require not only that the listeners understand his ministry, but that they also be able to

---

25. Steven J. Kraftchik, "Death in Us, Life in You," in *Pauline Theology*, 2.167.

answer Paul's opposition. *The purpose of Paul's theological state-*
ment—and the purpose of theological preaching—is to create in the
church the capability of speaking in theological terms to the issues that
arise. The church will survive the crisis that lies before it only if it
can reflect theologically on its identity. Paul is not content, therefore, with his own functioning as a theologian; he expects the
church to be capable of engaging in theological discussion also.[26]

Marva Dawn speaks of the church as "a community of theologians." She asks, "Do our sermons nourish believers in foundational
doctrines of the faith to equip them to resist heresies and idolatries
and 'folk religion,' with its too simplistic formulations of how faith
applies to life?"[27] William Hendricks, after interviewing people to
find out why they left churches, encourages pastors to teach people
to think theologically, so that they can resist what is "essentially
'McDoctrine'—spiritual fast food of proof-texts and cliches that are
filling and fattening, but not particularly nourishing."[28]

There is an irreducible cognitive content to the Christian faith.
Paul elaborates on this reflective dimension in 5:14b–15.[29] The
church remains incapable of reflecting theologically on its identity
unless it has observed mature theological reflection from its teachers. Consequently Paul proceeds with the theological reflection
that will guide the listeners in their moment of crisis. In 5:13, he
begins to provide theological answers to the Corinthians by
explaining his ministry: "[I]f we are beside ourselves, it is for God;
if we are in our right mind, it is for you." This distinction between
the ecstatic ministry "for God" and the rational ministry "for you"
probably echoes the debating points between Paul and his opposition. While we cannot penetrate to the precise issues that lie
behind this phrase, Paul's major point is transparent: he is describing the "for you" quality of his ministry. As in 2:14, he describes
himself as a prisoner of the love of Christ ("the love of Christ
urges us on") and then recalls the ancient creedal statement "one

---

26. On the church's loss of theological vocabulary, see Bellah et al., *The Good Society*, 193.

27. Marva Dawn, *Reaching Out without Dumbing Down* (Grand Rapids: Eerdmans, 1995), 238.

28. William Hendricks, *Exit Interviews: Revealing Stories of Why People Are Leaving the Church* (Chicago: Moody, 1993), 284; cited in Dawn, *Reaching Out without Dumbing Down*, 238.

29. Witherington, *Conflict and Community in Corinth*, 394.

has died for all" (5:14), which is the basis for all theological reflection on ministry. Those who know the ancient creed recognize that Christ's servants reenact the cross in their lives: "[A]ll have died." To be controlled by the cross is to come to the end of the egocentric existence and the kind of ministry that Paul's opposition values.

Paul's theological preaching here is "faith seeking understanding." He provides understanding to the creedal statement by developing implications that his listeners had not considered.[30] He develops this new understanding even further when he compares his new understanding with his former way of knowing in 2 Corinthians 5:17: "From now on, therefore, we regard no one from a human point of view [κατὰ σάρκα]; even though we once knew Christ from a human point of view [κατὰ σάρκα]." That is, as in 1 Corinthians 1:18–2:16, Paul responds to the concrete issue by arguing from his new epistemology: Christ has transformed his entire way of knowing. Paul invites the church to evaluate the crisis before it with this new understanding, which has been lacking in their evaluations thus far. Without this new understanding the church cannot meet the challenges that face it.

In 2 Corinthians 5:17 Paul develops this argument for a new epistemology further when he explains that the entire community shares the new way of knowing: "[I]f anyone is in Christ, there is a new world" (my translation). The new creation, which had been the object of Jewish hopes (see Isa. 66:22), has now become a reality in the church. The issues that are open for discussion between Paul and the Corinthians cannot be resolved at the level of the old creation, for Christians have experienced an entirely new world.

According to 5:18–6:2, Paul concludes this carefully argued theological statement by emphasizing that this new creation—and the ministry the opponents criticize—is from God. In the twofold repetition statement that God was reconciling the world to himself (5:18, 19), Paul offers an alternative version of the creedal statement that "one has died for all" (5:14) and emphasizes that God was the one who initiated this ministry. The God who reconciled the world to himself in Jesus Christ has also committed to Paul the

---

30. The succession of "so that" (ὥστε) in 5:16, 17 indicates that Paul is developing the implications of the creedal statement in 5:14.

ministry by which he makes the appeal "be reconciled to God" (5:20; cf. 6:1–2).

The theological argument of this section is so dense that the modern reader may easily forget the central thrust of the argument. Paul, unlike his heirs in centuries of theological reflection, is not speaking in abstract terms to offer a comprehensive theology of the atonement. His theological reflection is not an exercise he conducts for the sake of academic peers. It is the unavoidable response to a situation in which his community is tempted by false understandings of the gospel. He expects his communities to follow his argument and to repeat it in the context of theological controversy. Instead of responding to his audience according to the criteria of their culture, Paul offers a way of seeing the world that is both old and new. It is old in the sense that he repeats the creedal statements that had been the foundation of the church, but new in the sense that these creedal statements remind the church of God's new creation, which is interpreted for the sake of changing situations.

Reflections on Theological Preaching

Because of the challenges that face the preacher in our own culture—short attention spans, biblical illiteracy, a pluralism that is hostile to all truth claims—we are likely to be wary of the Pauline model, which does not conform to the community's expectations. However, the Corinthian correspondence is a reminder of the price of not engaging in sustained theological discourse. Clyde Fant has written that "Corinthians sometimes seem to be everywhere"[31] with their insistence on a message that conforms to our cultural expectations. Without theological discourse, "the pulpit can yield to public pressures, follow false messiahs, be hushed in a fearful silence, or strut and preen itself in the warm sun of general approval."[32] Without critical theological reflection, the church mistakes the gospel for the reigning ideologies and popular special interest causes, thus failing to bring listeners to consider what really matters. Sermons that "baptize" nationalism, the pursuit of

---

31. Clyde Fant, *Preaching for Today* (New York: Harper & Row, 1987), 6.
32. Fred Craddock, *Preaching* (Nashville: Abingdon, 1985), 49.

personal happiness, or the cult of self-esteem have lost the capacity for theological critique. Thus in the absence of theological preaching, the church's message is reduced to trivia. Its mission and goals rest on the will of the majority rather than the church's memory.

Theology urges upon the preacher and congregation a much larger agenda: creation, evil, grace, covenant, forgiveness, judgment, and the reconciliation of the world to God. "It is not out of order for theology to ask of preaching, What ultimate vision is held before us?"[33] Theological preaching, therefore, is necessary to bring the church to consider the great themes of the Christian faith as it charts its future course.

To employ the Pauline model is neither to ignore the questions that the community is asking nor to allow the church to set the agenda for preaching. Rudolf Bohren finds an analogy between the preacher and the poet when he cites Paul Valery's reflections on poetry. According to Valery, there is a distinction between works that are created by their audience (i.e., they fulfill its expectations) and works that create their own audience.[34] According to Bohren, the church is a creation of the word of God, and preaching involves initiating the community of faith into a way of thinking that is far removed from audience expectations.[35] We have seen in 1 and 2 Corinthians that, in describing the gospel as a mystery (1 Cor. 2:7) or in describing the "new world" (2 Cor. 5:17) initiated by God, Paul's preaching has created an audience and offered a new vision of reality. Walter Brueggemann suggests this new vision of reality: Just as Paul offered a "new world" to the Corinthians, the preacher guides the church as it envisions an alternative world of values. Such preaching does not aim at immediate outcomes, but, over time, "it makes available a different world in which different acts, attitudes, and policies are seen to be appropriate."[36]

---

33. Craddock, *Preaching*, 49. Cf. Richard Lischer, *A Theology of Preaching* (Nashville: Abingdon, 1981), 19: "Theology requires the preacher to relate all the articles of the broader gospel—creation, fall, providence, sanctification, church, eschatology—all the texts of Scripture to the constitutive core of the Christian faith."
34. Rudolf Bohren, *Predigtlehre* (Munich: Kaiser, 1986), 453.
35. Ibid.
36. Walter Brueggemann, "Preaching as Reimagination," *Theology Today* 52 (1995): 324.

The Pauline model of theological preaching focuses on the essentials of the Christian faith. He returns to the major creedal statements that are known to the church, keeping the church's attention focused on the essential gospel that called the church into existence. Although preachers speak from authoritative texts, they cannot bypass theological reflection on the gospel. This theological preaching maintains coherence in the church's proclamation. Edward Farley has made the important distinction between preaching the Bible and preaching the gospel. He reminds us that the preaching of the Bible is no guarantee of the preaching of the gospel. We may preach the Bible, offering small morsels of scriptural text each week without ever addressing the larger theological themes of scripture.[37] Our task is to see the text within the larger context of God's revelation in Christ. Similarly, Richard Lischer describes the perils of preaching from texts without reflection on the gospel.

> As long as the preacher believes that it is possible to move directly from text to sermon, the sermon will be awash with unassimilated and unordered biblical assertions. For the preacher as theologian must discover how, in the words of Melanchthon, "The Gospel opens the door to a correct understanding of the whole Bible." I am not issuing a license for the preacher to ride rough-shod over the particularity of texts or to dogmatize the Bible. I am inviting preachers to understand their task as broader and more demanding than the serial restatement of a pericope's religious ideas.[38]

Theology, as Paul demonstrates, is never an abstraction that can be divorced from the life of the church. The new situations in the life of the church demand that we continue to reflect on the gospel that brought us into existence. Our congregations, like those Paul addressed, will inevitably judge the Christian experience through the filter of their own experience. Preaching, therefore, must be theological, moving beyond the simple reminder of the church's faith toward a faith that seeks understanding. When we are

---

37. Edward Farley, "Preaching the Bible and Preaching the Gospel," *Theology Today* 51 (1994): 93.
38. Lischer, *A Theology of Preaching*, 19.

seduced by the demands of our audience, theology challenges us to reflect on our essential identity and to recognize that God has called us to look beyond the temporary gains that come when we adapt to the needs of the people and to reflect on the story that challenges all cultures.

Chapter Six

Preaching as Remembering

"There is no lack of information in a Christian land." Fred Craddock describes these words from Søren Kierkegaard as the "text" of his *Overhearing the Gospel*. "We do not share the gospel as pioneer missionaries chopping our way through the jungle to bring the new, first-time word to startled villagers."[1] We preach to those who have heard the message already. We assume that, because we live in a Christian culture, our listeners have heard the sermons of countless preachers before us. Moreover, they have heard our own preaching. Consequently, we face the task not only of speaking to those who know the Christian story but also of preaching to those who have heard the Christian message week after week. In my own tradition, the preacher is accustomed to preaching more than one hundred times each year to the same community of faith. The listeners are, in Craddock's words, "palimpsests"—manuscripts in which one layer of writing is super-imposed on another.[2]

We may actually envy the first-time missionaries who proclaim something new to those who have not been informed. For the first-time hearer, our message may actually be *news*. I once heard—although I do not know the source—that D. H. Lawrence said that, if he had lived in the first century, he would have been a Christian because Christianity was new and vital; but in the early part of this century, it was already old and lifeless. These sentiments have been echoed numerous times, leaving us with the impression that "there is no lack of information in a Christian land." In a culture that

---

1. Fred Craddock, *Overhearing the Gospel* (Nashville: Abingdon, 1978), 24, on Søren Kierkegaard's struggle with this task.
2. Ibid.

places great value on originality, no challenge is greater for the preacher than preaching to those who have already heard. Many of us can identify with Reinhold Niebuhr's description of his early days in the preaching ministry:

> Now that I have preached about a dozen sermons I find I am repeating myself. A different text simply means a different pre-text for saying the same thing over again. The few ideas I had worked into sermons at the seminary have all been used, and now what? I suppose that as the years go by life and experience will prompt some new ideas and I will find some in the Bible that I have missed so far. They say a young preacher must catch his second wind before he can really preach. I'd better catch it pretty soon or the weekly sermon will be a terrible chore.
>
> You are supposed to stand before a congregation, brimming over with a great message. Here I am trying to find a new little message each Sunday. If I really had great convictions, I suppose they would struggle for birth each week. As the matter stands, I struggle to find an idea worth presenting and I almost dread the approach of a new Sabbath. I don't know whether I can even accustom myself to the task of bringing light and inspiration in regularly weekly installments.[3]

Niebuhr was concerned, no doubt, that repetition and predictability would result in congregational boredom—the preacher's greatest fear. The need to find something new generates a worship renewal movement in which classical hymns are discarded for new ones and the traditional prayers are exchanged for expressions that seem spontaneous and new. Just as predictability ultimately dooms the best television serial, we also sense that it reduces our capacity to maintain the vitality of the congregation. Consequently, those of us who preach attempt at all costs to avoid repetition. We hesitate to preach on time-honored texts or to repeat ourselves or what others have said before, and we measure the quality of preaching by its creativity and originality.

The challenge of saying something new may lead the preacher in a variety of ways. A time-honored solution is the preaching of

---

3. Reinhold Niebuhr, *Leaves from the Notebook of a Tamed Cynic* (reprint, Hamden, Conn.: Shoe String Press, 1956), 4.

the *lectio continua:* the preacher works continuously through a book of the Bible. Another time-honored tradition is provided by the lectionary, according to which the preacher's texts have been chosen in advance in accordance with the Christian year. In either case, the preacher is liberated from the agonizing choice of a topic and a text. While either of these solutions to the problem of choosing a topic (or text) liberates the preacher from the agonizing choices Niebuhr described, the preacher nevertheless faces the problem of speaking words that will meet the challenges of the pastoral ministry. The preacher wonders about the relevance of the texts that have been chosen or their appropriateness for the occasion.

Those who do not want to be constrained either by the *lectio continua* or the lectionary may follow the tradition of preaching to the "felt needs" of the hearers. This approach has the advantage of allowing the preacher to address the concerns of the listeners in a way that is more direct than the other two choices. Preachers who exercise this freedom may allow the community to set the agenda for the sermon. They also have the freedom to cover issues in society that are on the minds of the people and to reflect on recent events. As liberating as this approach may sound, however, it leads ultimately to the dilemma expressed by Niebuhr inasmuch as the desire to avoid repetition leads the preacher in a constant search for something new to say. Preachers are left waiting for a community crisis or new issues to tackle. Faced with this difficulty, the preacher searches for more obscure preaching texts or for topics no one has addressed before.

Despite our aversion to repetition, it has a valuable place in the forming of a community. I have shown in chapter 2 that Paul's preaching of the saving events of Christ and his *paraklesis* to the congregation cannot be sharply distinguished. Nor can one distinguish between two kinds of audiences. Today's listening audience, like Paul's listening audience, is a mixture of individuals. Some of the listeners have considerable familiarity with the Christian message, while others do not. The congregation does not know the story as well as we might think, and they are likely to know it much less in the future. Preachers and teachers may face the occupational hazard of thinking that what is shopworn for them is shopworn for others also. Because we heard themes and traditions repeated many times in our formative years, we easily assume that those topics live on in the memories of others even when they have not been repeated. We forget the effects on the memory of the passage of time. Therefore, if we think, with Kierkegaard, that "there is no lack of information in a Christian land," we are likely to be mistaken. We face a culture that has little experience of the Christian faith.

Alec McGowen does the marvelous presentation of the Gospel of Mark in theaters everywhere in good King James English. He tells of people who come to him after his presentation and ask, "Did you write it?" or "Where do you get your material?" That world will increasingly be our own. William Willimon has written, "Today's average churchgoer is largely unfamiliar with Christian speech. People arrive on Sunday morning without a working knowledge of Christianity. They hear our words without some fundamental assumptions of Scripture."[4] The church now confronts the problem of amnesia, in which people know neither the narratives nor the commandments. Future audiences will have much in common with the audiences that Paul faces. A post-Christian society may resemble the pre-Christian society.

The need to find something new to say sends us in search of ever-more-obscure preaching texts or novel twists to an old story. Indeed, preachers, more than anyone else, evaluate preaching by the degree of novelty that it displays. Our enthusiasm for revolutionary new approaches in preaching probably reflects our own sense that the air of familiarity and predictability is ultimately destructive for preaching.

Preaching to Romans and Others

Near the conclusion of Romans, Paul describes the vital importance of preaching as remembering when he writes, "I have written to you rather boldly by way of reminder, because of the grace given me by God" (Rom. 15:15). The passage introduces Paul's final summation of the letter in words that, like the peroration of a speech, restate the case that he has already made. Paul describes his entire epistle to the Romans as a "reminder." He has

---

4. William Willimon, "Turning an Audience into a Church," *Leadership* 15 (1994): 30.

complimented the Roman listeners already (15:14) for their "goodness" and "knowledge"; thus now he describes the epistle as a "reminding again" (my translation).[5] His term for "reminding" (ἐπαναμιμνήσκων) was commonly used in antiquity for the repetition of a tradition.[6] Paul indicates, therefore, that he has said nothing new. His words here may be seen as "a tactical didactic ploy to indicate that everything he has so far written to them was not (or should not have been) strange to them, or at least that it follows directly from the basic faith and understanding of faith which was the common bond of all who believed in Christ Jesus."[7] Paul suggests, therefore, that his preaching to the Romans is a repetition of what they already know. What he has written is nothing less than the church's teaching, which the church must have known.[8] Thus he chooses not to say anything new. He will speak only of what the gospel attests.

Paul's description of Romans as a reminder is in keeping with the emphasis throughout the biblical tradition on remembering as a primary mode of communication. The canonical process involved the appropriation of a memory, the "re-remembering" of earlier traditions. Israel's functional canon provided both stability and flexibility as the community continued to reappropriate the old traditions in new situations. Interpretation involved remembering. Walter Brueggemann describes interpretation as the community's act of recalling the old treasured memory in the context of the new situation. "Interpretation seeks to mediate between the tradition and the situation."[9] This process of interpretation occurs throughout scripture. The sources of the Pentateuch, according to Brueggemann, are responses to new situations. Israel incorporates a new telling of its story to address its changing needs. In the same way, the Synoptic Gospels are reflections on the memory of the

---

5. Ulrich Wilckens, *Der Brief an die Römer*, EKK VI/3 (Neukirchen: Neukirchener Verlag, 1982), 3.117. Cf. ἐπαναμιμνήσκω, *EDNT* 2.18.

6. See Ernst Käsemann, *Commentary on Romans* (Grand Rapids: Eerdmans, 1980), 392.

7. James Dunn, *Romans 9–16*, WBC (Dallas: Word, 1988), 859.

8. Otto Michel, *Der Brief an die Römer*, KEKNT (Göttingen: Vandenhoeck & Ruprecht, 1966), 364.

9. Walter Brueggemann, "The Social Nature of the Biblical Text for Preaching," in *Preaching as a Social Act*, ed. Arthur Van Seters (Nashville: Abingdon, 1988), 135.

early church. Similarly, the Gospel writers assume that their listeners know the story already. The one who first committed the oral tradition to writing addressed a community that was already familiar with the story. If, as I assume, Mark ended mysteriously with the empty tomb at 16:8 without appearances of the resurrected Lord, he could end his gospel in this way, knowing that the community knew the traditions. When Luke wrote a gospel after consulting his predecessors (Luke 1:1–4), he was taking up the tradition and retelling it for a new situation. The church's memory was the basis for continuing reflection.

The appeal to the memory in Romans, therefore, belongs to the larger biblical tradition, for "exhortation in the form of anamnesis is a marked feature of the Christian message."[10] The appeal to memory is a common feature in the epistolary literature. According to 2 Timothy 1:6, Paul writes to "remind you to rekindle the gift of God that is within you." Similarly, in 2 Peter 1:12, the author introduces his letter, "Therefore I intend to keep on reminding you of these things, though you know them already and are established in the truth that has come to you" (cf. Titus 3:1). Jude also introduces the epistle with an indication that the listeners have already heard what the author will say: "Now I desire to remind you, though you are fully informed" (Jude 5). For several decades, scholars have noted the presence of traditional material in Ephesians, Colossians, and 1 Peter. The presence of so much common material suggests that these epistles are largely a collection of catechetical material that was used for the instruction of new converts. The ethical lists, including the household codes, were probably committed to memory by those who had recently been baptized. Thus these letters are largely reminders.[11] A common form of biblical speech is the reminder of what the community already knows.

Paul's Earlier Letters

A survey of Paul's letters indicates the variety of ways in which he appeals to the memory of his listeners. James Dunn points out that three types of traditions may be isolated in Paul: kerygmatic

---

10. K. H. Bartels, "Remember," *DNTT* 3.243.
11. Nils Dahl, "Form-Critical Observations on Early Christian Preaching," in *Jesus in the Memory of the Early Church* (Minneapolis: Augsburg, 1976), 17.

traditions, church conduct traditions, and ethical traditions.[12] One may add to this list also the initiation into the knowledge of scripture. Although these traditions cannot be tightly demarcated from each other, we may make distinctions between them and note their role in the Pauline correspondence. In each instance, Paul reminds the community of the traditions that are known within the church.

According to Nils Dahl, "The church's memory grew spontaneously out of its missionary experience."[13] One may notice the consistent appeal to the church's memory throughout 1 Thessalonians, Paul's oldest letter. In his opening prayer, he refers to his memory of the congregation (1:3). His primary concern, however, is that the Thessalonians also remember what he said to them. Throughout the epistle we find the formula "Just as you know" (1:5; 2:1, 5, 11; 3:3, 4; 4:2; 5:1ff.). When he recalls that he had sent Timothy to prepare the congregation for the inevitable afflictions, he adds, "[Y]ou yourselves know that this is what we are destined for" (3:3).

In the first place, Paul appeals to memory when he enunciates ethical traditions.[14] In 1 Thessalonians 4:1–2, he also employs the language of rabbinic tradition to introduce the entire paraenetic section of the book: the listeners have "received" (παρελάβετε) from Paul the instructions for lives that are pleasing to God (4:1), and he expects them to remember the instructions he gave them (4:2).[15] When he exhorts the Thessalonians, he not only says that they should live in conformity with the precepts he has given them and with the traditions he has transmitted to them, but he also adds "just as you are doing" (4:1, RSV).[16] Such a compliment is, of course, a good tactical move in Paul's communication, but it is more than that. The initial acceptance of the gospel puts the whole of life under oblig-

---

12. James Dunn, *Unity and Diversity in the New Testament* (Philadelphia: Westminster, 1977), 66–69. In large measure, scholarship has succeeded in demonstrating that the epistles bear the mark of the ideas and formulas of kerygmatic, catechesis, or liturgical tradition.

13. Dahl, "Form-Critical Observations on Early Christian Preaching," 15.

14. Dunn, *Unity and Diversity in the New Testament*, 68.

15. Cf. Oscar Cullmann, *The Early Church: Studies in Early Christian History and Theology*, ed. A. J. B. Higgins (Philadelphia: Westminster, 1956), 63: "We find the whole Jewish paradosis terminology, and, what is more, we find it used in a definitely positive way."

16. Dahl, "Form-Critical Observations on Early Christian Preaching," 15.

ation. The community of baptized Christians that has come to share in the gospel and that has received basic catechetical instructions already knows what must be done. They have received the Holy Spirit and they are moving in the right direction. Now they need constant reminders of their original commitments. The first obligation of the apostle in his communal instruction is to make the faithful remember what they have received and already know— or should know.[17]

The paraenesis of 4:3–5:11 is punctuated with consistent indications that he is reminding his readers what they already know. The requirements for appropriate sexual morality (4:3–8) and brotherly love (4:9) and the eschatological instructions (5:1–2) are already known to the community. Similarly, he insists in both Galatians and 1 Corinthians that the ethical norms belong to a tradition that he has already communicated (cf. Gal. 5:19; 1 Cor. 6:19). He reminds the Philippians, "Keep on doing the things that you have learned and received and heard and seen in me" (Phil. 4:9). Paul's appeal to the Jesus tradition in 1 Corinthians 7:10 and 9:14 suggests that he employed the sayings of Jesus as guidelines for his churches. The numerous echoes of the words of Jesus in the epistles (Rom. 12:14; 13:9; 16:19; 1 Cor. 9:4; 13:2) suggest that Paul commonly appealed to the teachings of Jesus in shaping the common life of his communities.[18] These ethical traditions may be what Paul has in mind in 2 Thessalonians 2:15 and 3:6, when he calls on the community to remember the traditions.

In the second place, Paul appeals to the community's memory when he recalls kerygmatic and confessional traditions. As I have noted in chapter 5, kerygmatic traditions commonly function as the basis for Paul's discussion with his listeners. He appeals to the kerygmatic traditions when he recalls how the Thessalonians "turned to God from idols, to serve the living and true God, and to wait for his Son from heaven, whom God raised from the dead—Jesus, who rescues us from the wrath that is coming" (1 Thess. 1:9–10). He appeals to kerygmatic traditions again in 1 Thessalonians 4:14, when the phrase "since we believe that Jesus died and rose again" becomes the basis for his argument about the future hope of this commu-

---

17. Ibid.
18. Dunn, *Unity and Diversity in the New Testament*, 68.

nity. Similarly, 1 Corinthians is punctuated consistently by the memory of the church's traditions. In the opening argument, the memory that he had originally preached "Christ crucified" was an appeal to the community's tradition. When he argues for the future resurrection in 1 Corinthians 15, he begins with the community's tradition that "Christ died for our sins in accordance with the scriptures, and that he was buried, and that he was raised on the third day in accordance with the scriptures" (15:3–4). Paul employs the language of tradition inherited from rabbinic practice. Tradition (*paradosis*) is a fundamental form of Christian communication. Here the community's kerygmatic tradition is "of first importance."[19]

In the third place, Paul appeals to the community's memory of liturgical traditions. In 1 Corinthians Paul appeals to traditions drawn from the conduct of the church to establish communal norms for the assemblies. When he congratulates the Corinthians for keeping the traditions (1 Cor. 11:2), he evidently refers to the common church practices that he has established. After he condemns the Corinthians for their practice of the Lord's Supper, he again employs the language of tradition with the words "[f]or I received from the Lord what I also handed on to you, that the Lord Jesus on the night when he was betrayed took a loaf of bread" (1 Cor. 11:23–25). The tradition of Jesus' words is clearly intended to govern the practice of the Lord's Supper at Corinth. Similarly, when he addresses other practices in the corporate assembly, he appeals to the practices of all the churches (1 Cor. 4:17; 11:16; 14:33b). The appeals to the custom among the churches reflect a pattern of instruction that consisted of the church's tradition.

Romans as a Reminder

To speak of the content of Romans as a *reminder* is remarkable for two reasons. In the first place, Paul has never preached in Rome. Unlike the other communities to which Paul writes, the Roman church was not founded and nurtured by Paul. Indeed, at

---

19. James I. H. McDonald, *Kerygma and Didache: The Articulation and Structure of the Earliest Christian Message*, SNTSMS 37 (Cambridge: Cambridge Univ. Press, 1980), 124. See also M. B. Thompson, "Tradition," in *Dictionary of Paul and His Letters* (Downers Grove, Ill.: InterVarsity, 1993), 944.

the beginning of the epistle, he expresses his eagerness "to proclaim the gospel to you also who are in Rome" (1:15). In the second place, the very length and weightiness of Romans suggests that it is more than a *reminder* of what the community has heard already. When one compares Romans to the similar subject matter in Galatians, one notices the thoroughness of the argument of Romans. Arguments that are made in Galatians in the heat of battle are more developed in Romans, with less passion and a more deliberate tone. Indeed, Romans is so filled with repetition from Paul's previous letters that Bornkamm described it as "Paul's last will and testament"[20] summarizing the major themes from earlier letters. Thus, because we cannot imagine that the original listeners had heard all of Paul's message before, Romans scarcely fits our understanding of a reminder.

It is in the fact that Romans is a reminder, however, that we gain an insight into the nature of Paul's appeal to the memory in his preaching. Romans is apparently written to a concrete situation. Most recent studies suggest that in Romans Paul is facing the rival claims among Jewish and Gentile Christians and that Romans is written to bring the two groups together in order that they might together "glorify the God and Father of our Lord Jesus Christ" (Rom. 15:6).[21] *We may assume, therefore, that Paul's reminder is not the mere repetition of words that they have heard before, but also a statement of the implications of the Christian message for the current situation.* Paul returns to what they know as the basis for his presentation, as Romans 15:15 suggests.

The content of Romans suggests that preaching and reminding cannot easily be separated. Neil Elliott has demonstrated this fact in his comparison of the beginning and ending of the letter. Near the beginning of the letter, Paul expresses his eagerness to preach (εὐαγγελίσασθαι) the gospel to the community at Rome (1:15). In the following verses, he explains the nature of this gospel (εὐαγγέλιον): It is the power of God to salvation to everyone who has faith (1:16). The righteousness of God has been revealed (1:17) in the gospel message. That is, after declaring his intent to preach

---

20. Günther Bornkamm, *Paul* (New York: Harper & Row, 1969), 88–96.
21. See the discussions in Karl Donfried, *The Romans Debate* (Minneapolis: Augsburg, 1991).

the gospel (1:15), Paul proceeds to unfold the implications of the gospel. Romans 1:16–17 function as the thesis statement of the letter, in which he elaborates on the implications of the gospel of the righteousness of God in order to address the issues that face the community. As Elliott has said, "These observations lead to the hypothesis that Paul intends this letter to Rome to serve as the medium of his 'evangelization' of the Romans."[22] Paul's desire to "evangelize" those who have already responded to the gospel is to be seen in the fact that, for Paul, the Christian life is "the continuing answer to God's call through the power of God (1:16) now made available to the congregation in the gifts of the Spirit."[23]

In earlier letters, Paul had employed the terminology of the *righteousness of God, or justification by faith,* to elaborate on the nature of the gospel (Phil. 3:9; Gal. 2:16–21). The new dimension in Romans is the scope of Paul's exploration of the theme of *righteousness.* Drawing upon Israel's heritage, according to which God's righteousness is the covenant faithfulness by which he vindicates his people, Paul declares that the death and resurrection of Jesus "for our sins" was nothing less than the vindication for which Israel had pleaded. Thus he moves beyond the immediate crisis to the larger theological reflection on the theme. Leander Keck has written that what "makes Romans tick" is that "Paul did not allow his immediate situation to govern completely what he had to say, but allowed the inner logic of his gospel to assert itself even if that meant subjecting his first readers to a certain amount of theological overkill."[24] In moving beyond the original situation, Paul demonstrates that his "evangelization" of the Romans cannot be separated from theological reflection. Nor can the reminder of what the listeners know already be separated from the fuller implications of that message. In the first five chapters, therefore, Paul describes the content of his gospel (1:16–17) as the revelation of God's righteousness for all who believe. He elaborates on his thesis by offering the antithesis of God's righteousness for all who believe: the wrath of God (1:18–3:20) upon all human disobedience. He restates this thesis in 3:21–26, declaring once more that

---

22. Neil Elliott, *The Rhetoric of Romans* (Sheffield: JSOT, 1990), 84.
23. Ibid.
24. Leander Keck, "What Makes Romans Tick?" *Pauline Theology,* ed. David M. Hay and E. Elizabeth Johnson (Minneapolis: Fortress, 1995), 3.29.

God's covenant faithfulness (= God's righteousness) extends to Jew and Gentile alike. As a result, according to 3:27–5:11, our only boast is in the saving message of Christ, who has redeemed all humanity (5:12–21). This good news undermines all human arrogance and creates the conditions under which Jew and Gentile can "with one voice glorify . . . God" (15:6). Paul's message was, therefore, a reflection on the community's memory.

Throughout the first five chapters, Paul expects his community to recognize the creedal statements and the scriptures that serve as the basis of his proclamation. In 1:3–4, he describes the gospel of "his Son, who was descended from David according to the flesh and was declared to be Son of God with power according to the spirit of holiness by resurrection from the dead, Jesus Christ our Lord." His citation of this creedal statement suggests that it should be familiar to this audience that is unknown to him. In his recitation of the creed, he declares that it was "promised in advance" (1:2, my translation) in the holy scriptures. He buttresses this claim throughout the argument of chapters 1–5 by arguing on the basis of scripture. He appeals to the community's knowledge of scripture in 1:17 when he cites Habakkuk 2:4, "The one who is righteous will live by faith." He recites the words of scripture when he demonstrates the sinful condition of humanity in 3:9–20. He argues that his gospel of the righteousness of God was "attested by the law and the prophets" (3:21), and he illustrates his message with a lengthy treatment of the story of Abraham drawn from Genesis 15:6. In this argument from scripture, Paul assumes that his gospel is recorded in scripture and that he is only reminding his community of what they know—or should know—already.

Where the gospel is preached, listeners respond in baptism. The Roman community has already heard the gospel, and all have been baptized. In Romans 6–8, Paul's message focuses on the impact of the righteousness of God in the lives of believers, who live between the revelation of God's righteousness (1:17) in the present era and the ultimate vindication. Those who have been baptized into Christ demonstrate the power of the gospel in their own lives by overcoming the disobedience that evoked God's wrath (see 1:18–32). Indeed, Christian existence in the present age opens the possibility of "newness of life" in which those who have been baptized are capable of overcoming the passions of the flesh (cf.

1:24ff.) that characterized unredeemed humanity. Because Christians are empowered by the Spirit (8:1–11), they are now free to yield themselves to the power of righteousness (6:18) and to keep the just requirement of the law (8:4).

In his elaboration of the gospel message, Paul appeals to the community's memory of baptism: "Do you not know that all of us who have been baptized into Christ Jesus were baptized into his death?" (6:3). In recalling the community's memory of baptism, Paul appeals at the same time to the church's confession of the death, burial, and resurrection of Christ. Those who have been baptized share the destiny of the risen one. Appeals to the prior instruction are sprinkled throughout this unit (6:4, 9, 16). Here Paul appeals to catechetical instruction. This instruction "is distinguished from the missionary proclamation in that it does not bring the message of Christ to those who have not yet heard it, but recalls to believers the message they have already heard."[25] The missionary preaching culminates in a call to baptism; in contrast, in his preaching to the community, Paul calls for a recollection of the baptism that has already occurred.

Paul reminds the readers of their own experience when he says, "[you] have become obedient from the heart to the form of teaching to which you were entrusted" (Rom. 6:17). This "form of teaching" (τύπος διδαχῆς) was probably the catechetical instruction that the community had previously received. This instruction involved specific ethical teaching that demarcates Christian existence from the behavior described in Romans 1.

The logic of Paul's gospel of the righteousness of God leads him to argue that "[i]f God is for us, who is against us?" (8:31). Consequently, the argument of Romans moves toward an affirmation that God's faithfulness will inevitably result in the reclaiming of the entire creation (8:18–39). Indeed, the logic of God's covenant faithfulness inevitably results in the salvation of both Jew and Gentile (Romans 9–11). Moreover, the force of Paul's arguments in Romans 9–11 depends on the scriptural evidence for the faithfulness of God to his people. Thus the conclusion of the argument, according to which "all Israel will be saved" (11:26), is developed from Paul's interpretation of the scriptures that are known to

---

25. Dahl, "Form-Critical Observations on Early Christian Preaching," 31.

the community. Paul has reminded the church of what it should know already.

The doctrine of the righteousness of God creates the environment for a Christian community in which Paul urges his listeners "not to think of [themselves] more highly than [they] ought to think" (12:3), but to "[l]ive in harmony with one another" (12:16). The ethical appeals of Romans 12–15 are not new instruction, but the repetition of exhortations that were widely known in the Christian community.

The epistle to the Romans, with its grand theological vision, ultimately leads toward a vision of a community that has been reminded of the gospel of the righteousness of God. A community that has heard the full implications of the righteousness of God can live in harmony and "with one voice glorify . . . God" (15:6). In Romans, as in all of his epistles, Paul reminds the community of the gospel, leading the community to grasp the full implications of the gospel story. Paul continually preached the gospel and reappropriated it in the concrete areas of life.

Remembering in a Post-Christian Society

When Fred Craddock, in *Overhearing the Gospel*, echoed Kierkegaard's word that "there is no lack of information in a Christian land," he addressed the problem of preaching to those who have already heard. Craddock's concern in 1978 was the proclamation of the gospel to those who have already heard. I am not convinced that we face the problem of preaching to a Christian land today. We do not face communities that have been shaped by the memory of the Christian message. Our communities, like Paul's communities, live in a non-Christian culture. Those who have heard the Christian message have also been listening to numerous other voices in our culture, leaving them with a blend of Christianity, pop psychology, and clichés of our own culture. In this cultural climate, we may assume that there *is* a lack of information in a land that is no longer Christian. Paul provided a model for preaching in a non-Christian land when he shaped the memories of his listeners.

In describing his own preaching as a "reminder," Paul both established his continuity with Israel's focus on remembering its heritage and established an important model for the contemporary preacher. Paul's preaching reminds us that, in preaching to those who have already heard, we are not forced to say something new each week. In speaking to one congregation, we speak to a variety of listeners. Some—especially in a post-Christian society—have not heard the Christian message before; others have heard, but they did not hear well. Others will forget the Christian message if their memories are not refreshed. The appeal to the memory will connect the community with its foundational story, reaffirm the liturgical expression by which the community responds to God, and recall the community's moral norms. Paul's preaching, therefore, demonstrates that preachers should not have an aversion to stating what has been said before.[26]

If Paul's appeal to the memory serves as a model for preaching, memory functions in a variety of ways. Because communities are always composed of members who have varying degrees of memory in the church's traditions, the repetition of the fundamentals of the faith creates the memory that is necessary for continued progress in the faith. For others, the repetition of the community's traditions is an appeal to the memory and to traditions that are already familiar to the people. In other instances, the appeal to the memory involves a return to common traditions and a reflection on them as the preacher speaks of the implications of the traditions for the community's life. The epistle to the Romans indicates how the church's tradition forms the basis for future conversation about the changes that take place within the congregation. Reflection on the community's traditions has been the anchor providing the stability and identity of the people of God for millennia. In the new millennium, we shall maintain our identity, not by originality, but by remembering our past.

---

26. See Fred Craddock, "Preaching to Corinthians," *Interpretation* 44 (1990): 163: "Use of the familiar evokes the power of recognition which not only draws in the listeners as knowing and informed participants but also makes them responsible for their own thoughts and decisions. New material belongs to the speaker and may later be owned by the listener, but familiar material belongs to the entire congregation. There can be no shock of recognition without first a nod of recognition."

Reflections on Paul
and the Preaching Ministry

The age of computerized communication, multimedia presentations, and distance learning raises sobering questions about the capacity of preaching to survive in the new marketplace of communications. If the distinguishing feature of the cultus for both Judaism and Christianity is the oral address, as Y. Brilioth noted,[1] we must ask if preaching has a future in this changed climate. If preaching has a future at all, we must ask what form it may take. If the biblical faith is one of hearing rather than seeing, the place of preaching in the new era remains a question.

Despite the questions about the future of preaching, I am convinced that "God decided, through the foolishness of our proclamation, to save those who believe" (1 Cor. 1:21) and that preaching is fundamental to the Christian witness. Preaching has faced major challenges before. Paul was a reluctant competitor in the field of professional oratory, and both he and his detractors agreed that he was undistinguished as a speaker. Nevertheless, his preaching was ultimately powerful, resulting in the formation of communities throughout the Mediterranean world. I suggest that Paul's preaching ministry remains a neglected model for the preaching task. In this study I have observed the dimensions of the Pauline preaching ministry that provide the preacher with important insights about the preaching task. Although Paul understood his call as a unique vocation, he also recognized that he was not alone in preaching Christ. Just as Paul shared the task of preaching the gospel with Silvanus (2 Cor. 1:19), he has shared the preaching task with others through the ages. Contemporary preachers, therefore, share in the preaching task.

---

1. Y. Brilioth, *A Brief History of Preaching* (Philadelphia: Fortress, 1965), 2.

A Distinctive Christian Speech. We have noted that, although Paul's preaching has points of contact with the rhetoric of the time, it has its own distinctive shape. The distinctive nature of Paul's preaching becomes apparent in his own explanation of his work in 2 Corinthians 5:11–6:2. Paul's preaching is distinctive, in the first place, because it is "church rhetoric," as Thomas Olbricht has observed.[2] Paul speaks neither to the judicial assembly nor to the assembly of free citizens, but to the Christian community. His preaching is distinctive, in the second place, insofar as it relies not only on rational modes of persuasion, but on the authority of God. Paul speaks as an "ambassador" for God (2 Cor. 5:20). Paul's preaching is distinctive, in the third place, insofar as his preaching consistently comes in the form of an appeal (2 Cor. 6:1–2) to the community for behavioral change.

The Pauline model suggests that preachers will not be totally separated from the rhetoric of their own time. Preachers are inevitably influenced by contemporary modes of discourse. Nevertheless, they should recognize the distinctiveness of Christian discourse. Preachers remain ambassadors for God, and their words appeal to the authority of God. The Pauline model is a reminder that preaching calls for the response of faith and a conduct that is appropriate to the gospel (Phil. 1:27).

Captivity to the Word of God. For Paul, the preaching ministry is motivated by a captivity to the word of God. Like Jeremiah before him, Paul is the captive of God's word who is under "necessity" to preach (1 Cor. 9:16, RSV). In his role as preacher, he is involved in a victory processional in which he marches as the captive (2 Cor. 2:14). He describes his own preaching as "the word of God" (Phil. 1:14; 1 Thess. 2:13). This description is especially striking, evoking the Old Testament language of God's word, which "will stand forever" (Isa. 40:8) and "shall not return to me empty" (Isa. 55:11). Paul (and the other New Testament writers) also uses the term λόγος for the written word of the Old Testament (Rom. 9:6, 9; 13:9; 1 Cor. 15:54; Gal. 5:14).[3] Thus in describing his own preaching as

---

2. Thomas Olbricht, "An Aristotelian Rhetorical Analysis of 1 Thessalonians," in *Greeks, Romans, and Christians,* Fs. Abraham J. Malherbe, ed., David L. Balch, Everett Ferguson, and Wayne A. Meeks (Philadelphia: Fortress, 1990), 225.

3. K. Runia, "What Is Preaching According to the New Testament?" *Tyndale Bulletin* 29 (1978): 23.

the "word of God," Paul identifies his own preaching with God's own words. Consequently, he speaks with the authority of God. As one who has been conscripted into the service of the word, Paul does not "peddle" or "tamper with" the word of God.

This contrast between his own ministry and that of those who "peddle" God's word echoes the debate between Plato and the Sophists. The Sophists, who took payment for their instruction and were known for making the worse argument appear the better, were only "peddlers," according to Socrates.[4] Like Socrates (and Plato), Paul identified his message with the truth that could not be diluted. Paul is the preacher who has been sent with a message that is not his own. He is only a "steward of God's mysteries" (1 Cor. 4:1). The truth Paul proclaims is nothing less than the "good news" announced by the prophet centuries prior to Paul (Isa. 52:7).

The good news in Jesus Christ. Although Paul uses the Old Testament language of the "word of God" and the "good news" to describe his proclamation, he specifically identifies God's own words with the death, burial, and resurrection of Jesus Christ. Acts and the Pauline letters agree that Paul's missionary preaching focused on the death and resurrection of Jesus of Nazareth. This proclamation was not limited, however, to missionary audiences. Paul consistently reminds his communities of the content of his original preaching of the death, burial, and resurrection of Christ (1 Cor. 15:3–5; 2 Cor. 5:14; 8:9; 1 Thess. 4:14; 5:10). These creedal formulae recall the common ground that is the basis for all future discussion. This reminder of the church's confession undoubtedly served more than one purpose. For Paul's original converts, the recitation of the facts of the gospel served as a needed reminder of the conviction that brought a diverse group together as a community. For the outsiders and new converts, the recitation of the creed was the first announcement of the gospel. Because the house churches of Paul's world were never neatly separated into separate categories in which missionary preaching could be separated from pastoral preaching, Paul's preaching was reconfirmational to some and evangelistic to others. Evangelism involved the articulation of the εὐαγγέλιον for the groups who gathered to hear the reading of Paul's letters. This form of evangelism remained a model for

---

4. *EDNT* 2.249.

Christian proclamation for centuries, and it remains a viable model for the contemporary preacher.

The gospel and the character of the preacher. Unlike the "peddlers," whose teachings are only products to be sold, Paul knows that his captivity to the gospel determines his identity and shapes his character. Like the orators of his own time, Paul frequently appeals to his own conduct as the witness to the truth of his cause. His appeal to *ethos* is, as André Resner has shown,[5] a "reverse *ethos*" by which he demonstrates the extent to which the foolishness of the cross has determined his conduct. When he appeals to his conduct in 1 and 2 Corinthians, he lists the tribulations that demonstrate the effect of the cross in his personal life. He "always" carries around the dying of Jesus (2 Cor. 4:10). His frequent catalogues of sufferings (1 Cor. 4:8–12; 2 Cor. 6:3–10; 11:23–29) also demonstrate that the message of the cross determines the character of the preacher. As a captive of God's word, he suffers for the gospel, preaching in the midst of much opposition (1 Thess. 2:2), and he assumes that his listeners will also suffer because of the gospel (Phil. 1:29; 1 Thess. 3:3). Paul's total identification with the story of the cross—his determination not to give offense to the gospel by his personal conduct (cf. 2 Cor. 6:3)—is, despite his detractors, ultimately a compelling argument for his gospel.

Paul's ministry is a reminder that the content of preaching cannot be separated from the character of the preacher. In an era when preaching cannot compete in the communications revolution, the essential quality that is unique to preaching is the authenticity of the preacher. Preachers who are willing to sacrifice themselves for the sake of their message remain a compelling argument for the gospel.

"Receiving the word of God." The preaching of the gospel summons the hearers to respond in faith and repentance and to be incorporated into the community of faith. As both the Pauline correspondence and Acts demonstrate, evangelistic witness calls for a response. The Thessalonians "turned to God from idols" (1 Thess. 1:9) and "received" the word (1 Thess. 1:6). The Christian response was not only associated with the moment of conversion. The task of preaching is to continue to encourage the community to "lead a life worthy of God, who calls [us] into his own kingdom and glory"

---

5. André Resner, *Preacher and Cross* (Grand Rapids: Eerdmans, 1999).

(1 Thess. 2:12) and to appeal to the Christian community to be "reconciled to God" (2 Cor. 5:20). Thus the continuing task of the preacher is to proclaim God's saving deeds and to call for the community to live in a way that is "worthy of the gospel" (Phil. 1:27).

"When I am weak, I am strong." When Paul defends his failure to compete effectively with the professional orators, he says that he did not come "with eloquent wisdom, so that the cross might not be emptied of its power" (1 Cor. 1:17). He declares that he came "in weakness and in fear and in much trembling," and that his word and preaching were not "with plausible words of wisdom, but with a demonstration of . . . power" (1 Cor. 2:3–4). As the reluctant competitor in the field of public communications, Paul knows his effectiveness rests, not on his own capability, but on the power of God (1 Thess. 1:5; cf. Rom. 1:16). Because preaching is accompanied by the power of God, neither the preaching event nor the human response rests in the preacher's hands. The "god of this world" may blind the hearts of the unbelievers (2 Cor. 4:3–4) or create and sustain the response of faith among believers (cf. 1 Thess. 1:5). The word of God that is active in the preaching event continues to work in the lives of believers (1 Thess. 2:13). By this reliance on the power of God in the preaching event, Paul recognizes that the results of his preaching rest with God. Consequently, the preacher is assured that ultimate responsibility for the success of preaching rests with God. The preacher's task, then, is not to be successful, but rather to be faithful in proclamation.

"Until Christ be formed in you." Paul's consistent reflections on the ultimate aim of his preaching remind us that the preacher looks beyond the community's own perception of its needs to the larger vision of the goal of preaching. Paul uses a rich variety of metaphors to indicate that the aim of preaching is the transformation not only of individuals but of communities whom Paul will present to Christ at the parousia (Phil. 2:16; 1 Thess. 2:19). As the mother (Gal. 4:19), father (1 Thess. 2:11–12), father of the bride (2 Cor. 11:1–4), architect and builder (1 Cor. 3:10–17), Paul recognizes that his churches are unfinished business and that his ministerial task is to present the community to Christ. The eschatological horizon gives direction to the entire preaching task, defining the essential needs of the church.

Paul demonstrates that preaching is always ecclesial. Evangelistic preaching results in the formation of Christian communities, and pastoral preaching is aimed at the transformation of the entire church. Although contemporary churches are separated by time and culture from the churches of the Mediterranean world, many of the challenges of community formation remain the same. The tasks of establishing corporate memory, confronting ideologies that threaten Christian identity, and establishing a corporate ethos face the preacher in every era. If Paul is the wise architect who laid the foundation (1 Cor. 3:10), many of us build on the foundation that others have laid. Paul provides the model for us as we build on his work.

Preaching Paul's Sermons after Him

In the sketches that follow, I bring together my exegetical reflections with the pastoral and theological task. The italicized portions represent exegetical and hermeneutical observations that I intend to develop in the sermon. In the numbered movements at the left, I have provided the basic plot of the sermon in an ordered progression. I wrote these first movements after I determined the communicative focus for the sermon. The statements in bold are my initial attempts to map out the progression of thought. After I supplemented this basic plot with a fuller text, I added the introduction, through which I wish to focus the attention of the listeners on the major concern of the text as it intersects with our own communal concerns. The indented sections represent my attempts to clarify the movements within the text either by answering potential objections and misunderstandings or by illustration and elaboration.

Sanctified or Sanctimonious? (1 Thess. 4:3–8)

Pastoral preaching as community formation involves instruction in the concrete demands of the Christian life and communal commitment to the same norms. Center of gravity: The call of God involves our self-control in matters of sexuality. Because corporate consciousness involves learning a new vocabulary, I shall follow the movement of the text as it defines sanctification in terms of sexuality. Hermeneutical orientation: A community in a post-Christian society, like its counterpart in a pre-Christian society, listens to the concrete demands of the Christian life. The repetition of the same theme (inclusio) *in 4:3, 8 ("this is the will of God," "whoever rejects this rejects not human authority but God") frames the discussion and is important for the sequential arrangement of the sermon.*

The introduction provides a focus, anticipates congregational reaction to the topic of sexuality, and establishes the progression toward the final movement.

Ever since Nathaniel Hawthorne characterized a New England community as sanctimonious and judgmental over a young woman's disgrace, the church has received a bad press in matters of sexuality. Because of her sexual seduction by a lover who was unknown to the community, Hester Prynne had to wear the scarlet letter. Since that time, Christianity has been, at least in some circles, accused of equating sex with sin, of repressing our most basic needs, of restricting sexual liberation, of taking a holier-than-thou attitude toward anyone who challenged the rules laid down by the church. I suspect that we have suffered from such a bad press on this matter that now we are uncomfortable speaking about sexuality for fear of confirming the worst suspicions about the church.

What do we make of these disturbing words from Paul's first letter to the Thessalonians? "This is the will of God, your sanctification: that you abstain from fornication."

1. **[God calls us to sanctification.]** Of course, we don't want to be sanctimonious or "holier-than-thou." Those words may be exaggerations of a very good word. We may not hear much on the street about the words "sanctification" or "holiness," but these are very good words—our words. In fact, they are two ways of expressing the very same idea—the idea that Christians are actually "separated" from the world around them. Yes, we have made a common commitment to separate ourselves from the values of our culture. If we are "set apart," we are likely to get some bad press.

> I recognize that some may have done bad things with sanctification; they may have turned it into sanctimoniousness. But it is a good word, nevertheless. It was the word for ancient Israel, the people whom God separated from the world in order that they might be devoted to him. Separation meant being different enough from their surroundings that they did not simply blend in and they did not share the point of view of the people around them.
>
> A recent movie *Blast from the Past* describes a family that went underground in the 1960s, thinking that a nuclear disaster was beginning. Thirty years later they sent their son, Adam, above ground to find a wife. Adam did not know the world of

the 1990s. He knew the love songs of the 1960s, not the music of the 1990s. He knew ideals of love and marriage, not the ideals of the 1990s. This is the way it is with sanctification. God has called us together into a fellowship in which he challenges us to offer an alternative existence.

2. **[The people of God demonstrate sanctification in their shared commitment to sexual morality.]** Now it is not quite true that Christians cannot talk about sin without talking about sex or that, in matters of sexuality, we are forever sanctimonious. But we do express our sanctification in matters of sexuality. We share values that may very well bring us a bad press. I suspect that Paul's words "This is the will of God, your sanctification: that you abstain from fornication" weren't exactly welcome in the pagan climate of his own day. But sanctification involved saying no to some forms of sexual expression. It still does. If our whole being belongs to God, including our sexuality, we say no to sexual expression apart from commitment, no to relationships that treat others as commodities, no to relationships that fulfill only our own selfish needs.

But if sanctification means saying no to destructive and selfish relationships, it means saying yes to a covenant relationship between husband and wife, yes to a sexual relationship between two people who share not only their bodies but their whole existence.

3. **[This is the will of God.]** I recognize that the words are a challenge to the messages we receive in countless ways in the media. But they aren't my words, not Paul's words, not the words of a repressive church. "This is the will of God." God has called us into this kind of community. It is God who empowers us through the Holy Spirit.

Children of the Day (1 Thess. 5:1–11)

Pastoral preaching involves creating a counterculture in which the church comes to recognize the line of demarcation between the Christian community and its culture. The text focuses the congregation's attention on Christian hope. Hermeneutical orientation: My listeners are not likely to take seriously the contemporary apocalyptic discussions. Hence they tend to dismiss this language. My task is to communicate the major burden of the text: Eschatological consciousness is the driving force in our moral commitment. In the progression of thought, I move from an acknowledgment

*of our own lack of eschatological awareness toward a conclusion in which
I want the congregation to hear Paul's challenge to moral intensity based
on eschatology.*

During the gulf war a decade ago, I spoke with a student who
had been mesmerized by the news of the conflict in Iraq. He indicated that the news was of particular importance because he
wanted to see if Armageddon was about to occur. He was sure that
the *time* had come.

Armageddon—that last cosmic battle between the forces of good
and evil that is described in the book of Revelation—is taken with
absolute seriousness by many people. Televangelists become news
analysts as they speak with Bibles in one hand and their maps in the
other, showing us where the cosmic battle is about to happen and
when Christ will return. They specialize in describing the *time* of
the end.

1. **[Talk about the end-time is not a high priority for us.]** I
find myself very comfortable with Paul's words to the Thessalonians. Paul does not want a church to spend its time speculating
about the end of the world. Most of us are willing to comply with
his wishes and leave this topic to the fanatics. We may even take
pleasure in the absurdity of those calculations, which always turn
out to be wrong.

> I recall Peter DeVries's story about the family that was caught
> between the pious mother and the unbelieving father. The
> atheist father suddenly became a believer—for a short period—
> when the explosion took place at the fireworks factory. He was
> sure it was the second coming, so he had a conversion experi-
> ence. Then he realized what had really happened, and he knew
> that he would lose face completely if he went back to his old
> ways. The second coming was a topic for some humor.

2. **[We face negative consequences when we ignore God's
future.]** But perhaps we make a mistake if we too easily dismiss this
concern for the end. Our understanding of the end makes a major
difference on our priorities today. Our culture long ago dismissed
the idea that God is bringing his world to a conclusion.

> We see the consequences of this dismissal of the future in our
> compulsive consumption and instant gratification. Christopher
> Lasch has chronicled this dimension in our culture in *The*

Culture of Narcissism. With the loss of a consciousness of the end, a culture develops a focus on personal pleasure, consumption of material things, and the incapacity to build for the future.

Ernest Hemingway wrote "The Snows of Kilimanjaro," which tells the story of a dying man who looks back over the decisions he has made and the options he has taken. He looks back with great regret because he has lived blindly, as if he were to live forever. Now the imminence of death has placed life's decisions in a new perspective.

Paul speaks of those who cannot see beyond the moment, and he describes them as the people of the night. "[T]hose who sleep, sleep at night, and those who are drunk get drunk at night." Without a future we squander our time in pleasure.

3. [Consciousness of the end motivates us for action today.] But we are a people with a future. We are the "children of the day." In fact, the distinguishing fact about us is that we believe in God's ultimate triumph. In a culture without hope, we believe in the future. *This belief in God's triumph is not a matter for speculation. It transforms how we live today.* Paul even describes our response as a warfare. There are battles to be fought and preparations to be made.

I recognize that some are skittish about using the martial imagery to describe the Christian life. Some would remove the images of warfare from the hymnal. The fact is, however, that the imagery of warfare helps us recognize the absolute serious-ness of our commitment. Our faith is not only a matter of having our needs met, not a picnic in the afternoon, not a leisure-time religion.

Because we see the future, we declare war on hunger and poverty. We declare war on the insidious self-seeking, and we put on the weapons of faith, hope, and love.

The Better Way (1 Cor. 13)

This classic text belongs to a larger conversation in which Paul confronts the anticommunal forces at Corinth. In this instance, Paul addresses the chaos because of the emphasis of some on the more spectacular gifts. As a digression within the discussion of worship and gifts in 1 Corinthians 12–14, this passage calls for a renewed emphasis on the one fact that can restore community in Corinth. Hermeneutical orientation: Although my own congregation does not experience tension on the issue of the gifts, we do face the challenge of competing ministries. Because familiarity creates a barrier, I attempt to overcome this barrier in the introduction by suggesting that familiarity has dulled the edges of the passage. The sketch follows the progression of the argument in 1 Corinthians 13.

"If I speak in the tongues of mortals and of angels, but do not have love, I am a noisy gong or a clanging cymbal . . ." (I quote the entire passage.)

These words have become public property. We are likely to find the words at weddings of all kinds. They appear in my copy of *Bartlett's Familiar Quotations*. They appear in countless anthologies. The words about love have become a classic.

But this is just the problem. When beautiful words like this enter the public domain, they become so familiar that we scarcely hear them. The words become nothing more than platitudes.

If we had heard the words when they were first delivered, we might not have thought of them as beautiful. In fact, the words came as a censure to the way Christians were behaving.

1. **[We search for the better way.]** These words were written to Christians who were caught up in a rivalry over the gifts of the Spirit. Everyone seemed to be passionately caught up over the question of who had found the better way. Rivalry like that is enough to tear a community apart.

We can identify with them, can't we? It was not easy to hold a church together in Corinth, and it is especially difficult to hold together a community with so much diversity. Rivalries emerge between good ministries. In our love for a particular ministry, we simply feel that we have found the better way.

> Traditional or contemporary worship? We have found a better way!
> A commitment to social justice or evangelism? We have found the better way!
> Bible study or action? We have found the better way!

2. **[What matters is love.]** In the middle of our rivalry, Paul says something like "If I have taken the right stance on worship,

and have not love, I am nothing. If I have devoted myself to evangelism or social justice until I am exhausted, but I have not love, I am nothing."

They ask Paul to explain the better way, and he talks past them. He talks about love when they wanted him to settle their arguments about the better way.

3. **[What is love?]** Of course, no one is really against love. But love has to be put into practice. "Love is patient; love is kind; love is not envious or boastful. . . ." Love is not a matter of platitudes. It must be put on the ground.

> Love is an aged servant of Christ who exhausts himself taking care of his wife, who suffers from Alzheimer's disease.
> Love is a church community surrounding one of its members who has been stricken with Lou Gehrig's disease.
> Love is a couple taking enormous risks by adopting an abused child.
> Love is an attorney who devotes his services to defend the rights of the homeless.

4. **[Love endures forever.]** Love is exhausting. But it is the one thing that lasts forever. "Love never ends. But as for prophecies, they will come to an end; as for tongues, they will cease. . . ." We devote ourselves to the one thing that lasts forever!

> It is easy to lose perspective, to treat smaller goals as ultimate goals. Duane Thomas, the star running back for the Dallas Cowboys in the 1970s, was once asked what it felt like to be playing in the ultimate game. He responded, "If this is the ultimate game, why are they playing it next year?"

In our passion for one good program or another, we lose sight of the one thing that will last forever. "The greatest of these is love."

Promises to Keep (2 Cor. 1:15–23)

This passage is the opening section of Paul's defense of his ministry. The Corinthians have interpreted Paul's change of travel plans as an indication that he is a "flatterer"—the stock figure in antiquity who always told his audiences what they wanted to hear. Paul defends his integrity with a theological answer, indicating that God's faithfulness is a model for his ministry. Hermeneutical orientation: In our infatuation with self-realization, we fail to recognize that the keeping of commitments is fundamental to our Christian self-understanding. (I delivered this homily in the chapel service of the Graduate School of Theology at Abilene Christian University.)

I am not exactly sure when I learned my first Hebrew word, but I know that it was early. In fact, I cannot remember a time when I didn't know the word *amen*. I knew it was the way to end a prayer. I wasn't sure that the prayer counted if we did not say "Amen"—sort of like punching the "send" button when we send an e-mail message. Then someone told me that it really meant "so be it." Through the years, I have heard the word in many contexts. I have heard it in foreign countries where it was the only word I recognized in an entire worship service. The word has entered our popular vocabulary. It is the kind of word that becomes so familiar that we scarcely remember it means something. It is our word. In the reading for today, it is a serious word. Paul reminds the Greek-speaking congregation in Corinth of that moment in worship when they say the Hebrew word *amen*. It isn't just the way we end a prayer. It is more.

1. **[We face inevitable questions about our character and commitments.]** I wouldn't have given much thought to this word if Paul had not explained it. He explains the word only because he is under attack. He faces the cynical charges all ministers and church leaders face: He makes his plans as an opportunist, looking out only for himself. He had told the Corinthians that he would visit them and spend the winter, and he had not come.

It sounds as if someone is making a big fuss about something very small. From his failure to keep his commitment, they draw major conclusions about his character. But then our little decisions form a composite of who we are. We all make little decisions each day that serve as indices of who we are.

It isn't easy to keep commitments—all of them. It limits our freedom to make commitments. We begin a new ministry, and we discover it isn't the ideal place that we thought it was. We make a commitment, but then comes the opportunity of a lifetime. We discover we married the wrong person. We bring a child into the world, and the child is a problem child.

Some commitments are simply hard to keep.

2. [Human faithfulness is rooted in the faithfulness of God.] In the middle of a conversation about travel plans, Paul starts explaining what *amen* means. It is our response to the faithfulness of God. As a matter of fact, God is faithful. God keeps his promises. When we say "Amen," we are acknowledging the faithfulness of God. It is a commitment to that kind of God.

This commitment determines what kind of people we are. We who worship a God who keeps his promises do not take our commitments lightly. Even little commitments mean something. When we make friends, we are implicitly making a promise to be a friend. We become part of an accountability group with friends, and we are saying that we will be faithful to the commitment to the group. Faculty and students enter into a covenant. At the beginning of the semester, we renew a covenant to educate and be educated, to take our task seriously.

Larger commitments are also promises. We plant a church. We make a promise that this community of believers will be a part of us.

We pledge ourselves to a congregation of believers. They have good times and bad times, but we know that we have made a promise.

3. [In not keeping his promises, Paul appeals to another theological foundation: the sacrifice of Christ for us.] Now I must admit that Paul didn't keep his promise. But there was a higher reason. It was for their sake. There is another story that forms our character. The one who gave his life for others. It is not opportunism that makes our decisions, but our selfless concern for others. This is the beginning of the semester. We recall our story, and it shapes the little decisions we make.

Amen.

Jesus Christ as Lord (2 Cor. 4:1–6)

Theological preaching responds to oversimplifications and bad ideas that redirect the mission of the congregation. In 2 Corinthians 4:1–6, Paul is defending a ministry that is under attack. His opponents point to the ineffectiveness of Paul's work. Here I attempt to follow the logic of the passage. The introductory illustration is intended to focus the issue of discouragement, which Paul is facing. It places the issue within the narrative of our own experience and provides a starting point for discussing our own discouragement. The sermon follows the sequence of Paul's thought.

Churchill's words "we shall never give up" were spoken in England's darkest hour. Of course, his words suggested that giving up must have been raised as a distinct possibility. Why should the lonely nation continue in a lost cause? This lonely island nation seemed to be overwhelmed by the forces arrayed against it.

We also wonder if our Christian faith is a lost cause. What are the prospects for the people of faith? What are the prospects for this church? The reports on the status of religious faith are not encouraging.

1. **[We face discouragement of all kinds.]** The reports never were encouraging. When Paul says repeatedly "We do not lose heart," I am sure that he protests a bit much. The results did not match his claims. We understand his discouragement. He says it in 4:1. He repeats it in 4:16. In fact, the whole discussion is in the context of discouragement.

> We identify with the experience. Why is the church aging? Lesslie Newbigin describes the Western world as the new mission field. The church has lost its place of prominence in the local community.

2. **[Perhaps it is time for us to rethink the message we have been communicating.]** Our disappointments suggest that we can determine the results. Why not do some market research? Perhaps, if we listen to focus groups and recognize what ideas are gaining, we could discover the answer to our declining numbers. They might tell us what we should offer in order to appeal to the greatest numbers. Why not use some ingenuity and program our results?

Paul's church undoubtedly was asking why he was not more effective. Couldn't he "tamper with God's word a bit"? While Paul's ministry languished, others adapted their Christian faith to the prevailing culture, and they appeared to be successful.

3. **[We preach not ourselves, but Jesus Christ as Lord.]** Paul saw the problem when he was faced with opponents who were more successful than he was. The problem is that we know that we have been called into being by the simple message that "Jesus Christ is Lord." Will it succeed? God calls us to be faithful, not successful.

We know that this message transformed our lives. In Paul's words, "It is the god who said, 'Let light shine out of darkness,' who has shone in our hearts to give the light of the knowledge of the glory of God in the face of Christ."

4. **[No, we don't lose heart.]** It is God, not our ingenuity, that determines the ultimate outcome.

A New World (2 Cor. 5:11–20)

Paul's listeners are caught between two perspectives on the ministry: that of the opponents and that of Paul. The opponents offer a case for ministry that is distinguished by power and rhetorical persuasiveness, leaving Paul to commend a ministry that is characterized by weakness and apparent failure. By normal standards of measurement, the opponents have a good case. Paul's task is to win back his opponents to an understanding of ministry that appears on the surface to have little to commend it. The sermon follows the logic of Paul's argument for a "new world" outlook on ministry. Hermeneutical orientation: We, like the Corinthians, are caught between different models of being church.

The text has a chiastic structure that can be utilized. At the beginning and end of the pericope, Paul explains his mission. At the center of the discussion, he defends his mission with a description of the "new world" that determines his ministry. The beginning and end reflect on the ministry. In the center is the reflection on the new creation, which defines Paul's ministry.

Dilbert, the cartoon character who inhabits his cubicle, spoke deeply to the staff in my office recently when his boss demanded that he stop whatever he was doing and prepare a mission statement, complete with his goals and his means of measuring his goals. This demand for accountability has left no institution unaffected. Some of us may work in situations where we spend more time writing mission statements and explaining our activities than we do in performing our actual tasks! No longer can institutions go on with business as usual without establishing a mission statement that is the basis for all of their activities.

1. **[There comes a moment when we must explain ourselves.]** Not even the church is immune from the demand for accountability. With all of the competing visions of church, we

cannot avoid thinking once more about our mission and the ways that we will successfully fulfill our ministry.

How do we measure the success of a church? And what are we trying to accomplish? If we have learned anything in recent years, we have learned to measure the attainment of our goals. We can measure the growth in membership and budget; we can measure the value of the church's property. Whenever we plan our budgets, ordain ministers, build facilities, or make decisions of any kind, we make statements about our mission. But we have questions about the mission of the church. Sometimes our questions boil over into tension as we define our mission in different ways. It was the same way when Paul wrote 2 Corinthians. If we overhear the conversation between Paul and the Corinthians, we are likely to overhear a conversation that sounds like our own. At some moment we must stop and ask if we are fulfilling our mission. Think of the potential directions we can go.

Paul's opposition apparently made much sense. They backed him into a corner and required that he explain himself. The results were meager, and he had little to show for his exhausting work. His detractors demanded accountability, so he offered it.

2. **[Our story determines our mission: "One has died for all."]** He explains his whole ministry with the simple words "One has died for all." Imagine that! In the heat of the discussion about the church's mission, Paul says, "One has died for all." Imagine a church involved in discussing next year's budget or the construction of a family-life center, and someone says, "Remember, Christ died for us." What does this basic creed have to do with our decision about opening a daycare center or building a family-life center or initiating a seeker service? When Paul is asked to explain himself, he says, "One has died for all." Couldn't he have come up with a better answer than that? Or left the words in the hymns where they belonged?

3. **[This is a "new world" way of looking at things.]** "One has died for all." Those are the words we recite each week. One cannot find a more succinct way of summarizing the Christian faith. But have we ever noticed that they are more than words to recall? They define our own being. "One has died for all; therefore all have died. And he died for all, so that those who live might live no longer for themselves, but for him who died and was raised." That is, "If anyone is in Christ, there is a new world."

I know that the translations sometimes read "If anyone is in Christ, he is a new creature." But the appropriate translation here is "If anyone is in Christ, there is a new world." We are the people who have entered a new world. Things that once made no sense to us now make sense. Dying to ourselves makes no sense in a culture of narcissism. Dying to ourselves hardly fits our culture of competition and ambition. "One died for all; therefore all died." Imagine that!

There is a "new world" quality that continues to break through to us. I know it doesn't make sense. A woman spends her life in the slums of Calcutta when she could have made something of herself. A church decides to face the reality of remaining in a changed neighborhood when all of the financial calculations suggest it doesn't make sense. A family decides to lower its standard of living and its professional commitments in order to have time for aged parents.

There is a "new world" of how we define who we are.

4. **[This strange world is from God, who reconciled the world to himself and committed to us the word of reconciliation.]** It is strange, I know, but it is from God. That is, "In Christ God was reconciling the world to himself." The same God has given us the word of reconciliation. And he gave us a ministry of reconciliation. Thus our mission is to speak for God. Perhaps our plans and ministries, if we have heard that story, will not make any sense. We can only say, "Be reconciled to God," even when we don't know our prospects of being heard. Let us remember the story we tell. It will determine the kind of church we want to be.

God's Unfinished Business (Rom. 6:1–11)

In making the case for the inclusion of Jews and Gentiles in the people of God, Paul has appealed to the righteousness of God, which precludes all human works. In Romans 6–8, he anticipates the objections to this doctrine. In 6:1–11, he confronts the claim that the righteousness of God undermines ethical responsibility. His challenge is to demonstrate how this doctrine includes a call for ethical behavior. Hermeneutical orientation: North American Christians have been influenced by a popularized version of Paul's doctrine of grace. Some of the listeners may come with wariness to this doctrine of grace, sharing the ancient objection that this view undermines ethics. Many of the listeners will have discovered grace, turning it into cheap grace.

I have always been bothered by stories with happy endings. When I see all of the pieces come together at the end of the movie, I am suspicious. I want to know what will happen tomorrow. I have always liked the musical *Into the Woods* because it dares to ask that question. It takes all of those stories in which the characters supposedly "lived happily ever after"—"Jack and the Beanstalk," "Little Red Riding Hood," "Cinderella"—and dares to imagine their continued existence. It is not a pretty sight. We cannot freeze the happy moment because life goes on.

I love the happy scenes in scripture where stories come to an end with celebration over God's grace. A prodigal son is welcomed with a party he doesn't deserve. Laborers who worked only one hour are paid for work they didn't do. This is grace. But I must ask what will happen tomorrow. What happens to Christians who have discovered God's grace? This is the question Paul answers in Romans.

1. **[The doctrine of God's grace creates problems.]** Many of us recall our first discovery of Romans. To read that it was not our righteousness, but God's righteousness that effects salvation was the release from a burden. This is release from trying to measure up to God's standards when we know we will fail.

> But the doctrine is also dangerous. It is not even fair. This doctrine of God's grace can create a mentality that comes to expect forgiveness. Elizabeth Achtemeier tells about a father who called his adult daughter to announce that he was leaving her mother for another woman. The father said, "Do you forgive me?" After all, forgiveness is supposed to come easily. "Shall we continue in sin that grace may abound?" It makes sense, doesn't it?[1]

2. **[We died to sin.]** Yes, it makes sense—unless we recall what our baptism means. Paul says, "Do you not know that all of us who have been baptized into Christ Jesus were baptized into his death? Therefore, we have been buried with him by baptism into death, so

---

1. Elizabeth Achtemeier, *Preaching as Theology and as Art* (Nashville: Abingdon, 1984), 28.

that, just as Christ was raised from the dead by the glory of the Father, we too might walk in newness of life." The grace of God is not an invitation to come at the eleventh hour, but a call to leave an entire life behind.

> There are moments in our lives that determine our existence forever. Moments we do not want to forget. We get married, and we can never undo that moment. We remember the date and mark it periodically because it is a part of who we are. We bring a child into the world, and our life is changed forever. Refugees leave behind a war-torn country and build a new life. They do not want to return.

Paul describes baptism as the moment of crossing over from one existence into another. When we have been rescued from disaster, we don't want to go back.

3. **[We are God's unfinished business.]** The righteousness of God or the grace of God is such a dangerous message, I think, because we delude ourselves into thinking that this good news is the end of the story. We like stories with happy endings. The book of Acts has wonderful, dramatic stories that conclude with the new life of converts. Thousands are converted in the opening days, and we never hear from them again. The Ethiopian eunuch is converted and then rides off into the sunset. Here the story ends. Cornelius and his family overcome obstacles to their conversion, but in the final scene they are all converted. Here the story ends.

But God's righteousness is not the end of the story. God hasn't finished with us yet. God's righteousness is the power that enlists us for service. We can tell when we have understood the grace of God. It is when we have opened our lives to God's power, when we place ourselves in his service.

When Nothing Makes Sense (Romans 9–11)

Romans 9–11 is a dense theological argument in which Paul elaborates on the significance of the righteousness of God, answering potential objections to the argument of Romans 1–4. In the original context, Paul's argument has raised questions about God's faithfulness to Israel. He moves from anguish over Israel to celebration over Israel's salvation and doxology over God's mysterious ways. Hermeneutical orientation: We hear Paul's argument for God's mysterious ways in the context of our own questions. I do not wish to burden the congregation with extensive explanation, but I have attempted to follow the major point of Paul's argument. My arrangement follows the sequence of Paul's argument.

In the novel *Roger's Version*, John Updike tells the story of the brilliant young physics student who came to his professor and proudly proclaimed that he had worked out a computer model that had taken him where physics had never gone before. He was confident that his calculations had taken him all the way to the mind of God. "God cannot hide any more," he announced. He had gone back to the beginning of creation; he had come to understand how the universe had come into existence and how it worked. Now through his scientific mind he had come to understand the mind of God. He had taken away the mystery of God.

Wouldn't we like to take away this mystery and unlock the secrets of what God is doing in the world? To tell the truth, many of us have questions about our faith. For example, if God is at work in the world, why can't I track the progress? If God is at work to redeem the world, why can't I see it?

1. **[We face the problem that the results do not match our claims.]** Imagine Paul. All that he saw in front of him seemed to contradict the grand vision of what God is doing in the world. He asked in Romans 8, "What then are we to say about these things? If God is for us, who is against us? . . . Who will separate us from the love of Christ?" Almost in the next breath he says, "I have great sorrow and unceasing anguish in my heart. For I could wish that I myself were accursed and cut off from Christ for the sake of my own people, my kindred according to the flesh." We can identify with his sentiment, can't we? Isn't the world getting bigger while the people of faith are getting smaller? Things don't make sense. Our natural response, especially in our time of confidence in human know-how, is to do something.

2. **[God has always worked in strange ways.]** But what can we do? The fact is that God has always worked in strange ways. As Paul says, God chose Isaac, not Ishmael; Jacob, not Esau. He could even harden Pharaoh's heart. Don't ask me why. No computer model could ever have tracked God's ways. As a matter of fact, even Elijah thought he was the only one left, and no one could have tracked what God was doing in the world. Our faith has looked like

a lost cause for a long time. The biblical faith is a mystery beyond our calculations.

3. **[If God's ways are a mystery, the future is beyond our calculation.]** Now it is really a mystery when Paul says, "And all Israel will be saved." He began this part of the conversation in anguish over Israel. And now he says, "And so all Israel will be saved." Again, don't ask me how or when. We are not sure what "all Israel" actually means. Scholars will debate that question for a long time. The fact is, God's ways are beyond our calculation. In our anguish over a lost cause, we have forgotten one thing. We have forgotten that God's ways are a mystery.

4. **[Reflection on God's ways leads to doxology.]** What can we say to this affirmation of God's mystery? We can only say, "O the depth of the riches and wisdom and knowledge of God." In the midst of our despair over understanding the ways of God, we say with Paul, "How unsearchable are his judgments." Even in the midst of our discouragement, we say, "For from him and through him and to him are all things."

Index of Names

Achtemeier, Elizabeth   39, 162
Achtemeier, Paul   28, 34
Allen, Ronald J.   100, 786
Anderson, R. Dean, Jr.   33, 35, 62, 73
Arzt, Peter   65
Aune, David   34

Bahr, Gordon J.   28
Bailey, Raymond   15, 33
Balch, David   67
Barclay, John M. G.   46
Barclay, William   28
Bartels, K. H.   132
Barth, Gerhard   42, 43
Barth, Karl   6
Bartlett, David   15, 26, 27, 29
Bassler, Jouette   13, 46
Beaudean, John   53
Becker, Jürgen   113, 114
Beker, J. Christiaan   36, 110
Bellah, Robert   10, 98
Berger, Klaus   23, 65, 81
Berger, Peter   106
Betz, Hans Dieter   67
Black, C. Clifton   47
Blaisdell, Barbara Shires   7
Bohren, Rudolf   124
Bormann, Lukas   24
Bornkamm, Günther   42, 136
Botha, Peter   29, 31
Brilioth, Y.   143
Broadus, John   2
Browning, Don   32
Brueggemann, Walter   10, 96, 124, 131
Bultmann, Rudolph   23, 33, 74

Buttrick, David   2, 5, 6, 7, 8
Byrne, Harry M.   85

Callen, Barry   92
Cameron, Averil   8
Campbell, Charles L.   9, 12, 14, 92
Canzik, H.   66
Churchill, Winston   158
Classen, J.   35
Cobin, Martin   30
Collins, Raymond F.   29, 81
Cousar, Charles   15, 116
Cox, Claude   30
Craddock, Fred   3, 4, 5, 7, 8, 9, 12, 14,
   15, 27, 39, 123, 124, 127, 140, 141
Cullmann, Oscar   133

Dahl, Niels   132, 133, 139
Davis, Casey Wayne   27, 33, 34, 72
Davis, H. Grady   4
Dawn, Marva   98, 121
Deissmann, Adolph   64, 65
Del Tredici, Kelly   24
De Vries, Peter   152
Dibelius, Martin   22, 23
Dodd, C. H.   22, 38, 46, 59
Donfried, Karl   22, 136
Doty, William G.   63
Dunn, James   131, 132, 133, 134

Ellingsen, Mark   12
Elliott, Neal   136, 137
Eltester, W.   82
Eriksson, Anders   75, 77, 78
Eslinger, Rick   2, 3

Fant, Clyde   123
Farley, Edward   125
Farmer, W. R.   29
Farris, Stephen   6
Fee, Gordon   116
Ferguson, Everett   67
Fiore, Benjamin   68
Ford, David F.   42
Fosdick, Harry Emerson   87, 108
Frede, Dorothea   23
Frei, Hans   6, 7
Fridrichsen, A.   33
Frye, Northrup   13
Funk, Robert   29
Furnish, Victor   115, 116

Gasque, W. Ward   28
Georgi, Dieter   24
Grabner-Haider, Anton   55
Grant, Robert   62
Greenhaw, David M.   2, 13

Haenchen, E.   82
Hafemann, Scott   42
Harvey, John D.   28, 33
Hawthorne, Gerald   44
Hawthorne, Nathaniel   150
Hay, David M.   13, 40, 115, 116
Hays, Richard   13, 40, 46, 91, 100, 101, 106
Heath, Malcolm   62
Hemingway, Ernest   153
Hendricks, William   121
Higgins, A. J. B.   133
Hofius, O.   52
Holtz, Traugott   32
Hübner, Hans   33
Hughes, Frank W.   35, 86
Hughes, Robert G.   107, 108
Hunter, James Davison   10

Jacobsen, David Schnasa   6
Jensen, Richard   2, 107
Jewett, Robert   14, 82
Johnson, Elizabeth   13, 40
Johnston, Scott Black   7
Jones, Ilion T.   2
Junod, Éric   23

Käsemann, Ernst   131
Keck, Leander   8, 32, 137
Kelber, Werner   33
Kennedy, George   34, 35, 62, 76, 78
Kettler, F. H.   82
Kim, Seyon   41
Koskenniemi, Heikki   63
Kraftchik, Steven J.   120
Kysar, Robert   107, 108

Lasch, Christopher   10, 152
Lausberg, Heinrich   62, 70, 71
Lawrence, D. H.   127
Lentz, Tony   23
Lindbeck, George   99, 105
Lischer, Richard   12, 96, 100, 124, 125
Litfin, Duane   26, 112
Long, Thomas   3, 11, 27, 86, 88, 92
Longenecker, Richard   32
Lowry, Eugene   4, 5, 8, 12
Luckmann, Thomas   106
Lührmann, D.   42
Lyons, George   68

Malherbe, Abraham J.   30, 34, 65, 118
Marrow, Stanley   55, 57
Marshall, Peter   112, 116, 118
Martin, R. P.   28, 44
Martyn, J. Louis   32
McDonald, James I. H.   135
McGowen, Alec   130
McGrath, Alister E.   12
McGuire, Martin   30
Meeks, Wayne   67
Middleton, J. Richard   7
Mitchell, Margaret   67, 68, 70, 72, 77
Möller, Christian   55, 85, 88
Moule, C. F. D.   29
Mounce, R. H.   44
Mudge, Lewis S.   4
Muhlenberg, H.   23
Müller, Peter   24, 25, 27
Mullins, Terence Y.   81
Munck, J.   51
Murphy-O'Connor, Jerome   15

Neufeld, Vernon H.   51
Newbigin, Lesslie   59, 158

Newman, Carey C. ix, 41
Nichols, J. Randall 39
Niebuhr, R. R. 29
Niebuhr, Reinhold 128
Norden, Eduard 67
Norris, Frederick 30

O'Day, Gail R. 3, 27
Olbrechts-Tyteca, L. 78
Olbricht, Thomas 29, 35, 66, 79, 144
Old, Hughes Oliphant 23, 85, 101
Ong, Walter 29, 31, 33, 34
Oort, J. van 23
Orton, David 62
Osmer, Richard 52
Otto, Michel 131

Patte, Daniel 13
Perelman, C. 78
Perkins, Eli ix
Perkins, Pheme 13
Petersen, Norman 13
Petzke, G. 51
Pogoloff, Stephen 112
Porter, Stanley 29, 35, 62, 66, 73, 74
Postman, Neil 61

Ramsey, Ian 108
Read, David H. C. 39
Reck, Reinhold 26, 59, 80
Reed, Jeffrey 35
Reicke, Bo 33
Reid, Daniel 44
Resner, André 69, 146
Richards, E. Randolph 28, 65
Ricoeur, Paul 4, 13, 16
Robinson, James M. 82
Rowe, Galen O. 62
Ruane, Edward 85
Runia, K. 50, 54, 144
Runkel, Hal ix

Sanders, E. P. 28, 29
Sandness, K. O. 41
Schoebel, W. R. 62
Schrage, W. 41
Sellin, Gerhard 23
Sensing, Timothy ix

Siburt, Charles ix
Siegert, F. 23
Siegfried, Regina 85
Smit, J. 67
Standhartinger, Angela 24
Steimle, Edmund 11
Stirewalt, M. Luther, Jr. 32, 33
Stowers, Stanley 35, 65, 74
Stratman, Gary E. 87
Strecker, G. 42
Stuhlmacher, Peter 56

Thomas, Duane 155
Thomas, J. 55
Thompson, Carolyn ix
Thompson, James W. 10, 30
Thompson, M. B. 135
Troeger, Thomas 3, 7

Updike, John 164

Valery, Paul 124
Van Seters, Arthur 12, 96, 97
Vouga, François 23

Wallace, Mark I. 4
Walsh, Brian J. 7
Ward, Richard 30, 31
Wardlaw, Donald 3
Watson, Duane 34
Wells, David 108
White, John 64
Wilckens, Ulrich 131
Wilder, Amos 24, 61
Wilken, R. L. 62
Willi-Plein, Ina 25
Willimon, William 39, 59, 97, 99, 100, 130
Wills, Lawrence 47
Wilson, Paul Scott 3
Witherington, Ben 40, 112, 121
Wolter, Michael 94
Wright, N. T. 10, 13, 44, 46, 49
Wuellner, Wilhelm 62, 73

Yarbrough, O. Larry 102, 111
Young, Frances 42, 69

Zink-Sawyer, Beverly 6

Index of Scripture

Old Testament

Genesis
9:26   82
14:20   82
15:6   138
24:27   82

Exodus
3:11   41
4:10ff   41
18:10   82

Numbers
6:24   81

Deuteronomy
7:6–7   93
32:5   93

Ruth
2:20   82

1 Samuel
25:32   82
25:39   82

2 Samuel
18:28   82

1 Kings
1:48   82
5:7   82

1 Esdras
4:40   82
4:60   82
8:25   82

2 Esdras
7:27   82

Tobit
3:11   82
8:5   82
8:15   82
8:16   82
9:6   82
11:14   82
11:17   82
13:18   82

Psalms
17:46   82
28:6   82
40:13   82
65:20   82
67:19   82
71:18   82
88:52   82
105:48   82
118:12   82
123:6   82
134:21   82
143:1   82

Isaiah
28:16   42
40–55   44

40:8   144
49:1   41
49:6   41
52:7   44, 145
55:11   144
66:22   122

Jeremiah
1:5f   41
1:10   91
20:7–8   41
20:9   41
36   25

Ezekiel
3:17f   41

Amos
3:8   41

Jonah
1:2ff   41

Habakkuk
2:4   138

New Testament

Matthew
12:41   43

Mark
1:14   25
16:8   132

Luke

1:1–4	132
8:13	51
11:32	43

Acts

8:14	51
11:1	51
13:15	47
13:16–37	47
13:16–41	47
13:38–39	47
13:40–41	47
14:12	37
17:2–3	51
17:11	51
17:22–23	47
17:29	47
18:1–18	111

Romans 17

1–4	163
1:2	138
1:3–4	44, 138
1:7	80, 93
1:11–15	71
1:15	135, 136, 137
1:16	25, 49, 52, 136, 137, 147
1:16–17	137
1:17	136, 137, 138
1:18–32	99, 102, 103, 138
1:18–3:20	137
1:24ff	139
3:9–20	138
3:21	44, 138
3:21–26	137
3:27–5:11	138
4:25	44
5:3	73
5:8	45
5:12–21	138
6–8	138, 161
6:1–11	161
6:3	139
6:4	139
6:9	139

6:12–7:25	103
6:16	139
6:17	82, 139
6:18	139
7:25	82
8	164
8:1–11	139
8:18–39	139
8:31	139
8:33	93
9–11	39, 139, 163
9:6	144
9:9	144
10:13	42
10:14	42
10:14–15	42
10:15	42
10:17	25, 42, 48
11:26	139
12–15	140
12:2	92
12:3	106, 140
12:14	134
12:16	140
13:9	134, 144
15:3	45
15:3–4	45
15:6	136, 138, 140
15:14	131
15:14–29	72
15:15	130, 136
15:19	42
15:20	37, 42
15:25–29	42
16:1–2	40
16:2	93
16:15	93
16:19	134
16:22	28
16:25	43

1 Corinthians 18, 72

1–4	112, 114
1:1	76
1:2	93
1:3	80
1:4–9	72
1:8	92

1:10	71, 72, 76
1:10–17	71, 112, 114, 116
1:11–17	72
1:12	112
1:17	25, 43, 62, 66, 147
1:18	94, 114, 115
1:18–25	48, 50, 78, 114
1:18–32	99
1:18–2:4	50
1:18–2:16	114, 122
1:18–4:21	72
1:21	43, 143
1:22	47
1:22–23	48
1:23	45, 114, 115
1:26	115
1:26–28	115
2:1–5	45, 69, 115
2:3	69
2:3–4	147
2:4	43, 49, 52, 62, 76, 120
2:5	66
2:6	76
2:6–16	76, 115
2:7	76, 124
2:10	76
3:1–5	112, 116
3:5	76
3:6	45
3:6–9	91
3:10	45, 148
3:10–17	91, 147
3:13–15	91
3:16	91, 94
3:16–17	88
3:18	112
4:1	77, 145
4:6–13	69
4:8–12	146
4:10	69
4:14	77
4:14–15	56
4:14–21	76, 88
4:15	45
4:17	31, 135
4:21	77, 80

5–16	112	11:23	113	1:15ff	118
5:1–11:1	72, 99	11:23–25	77, 135	1:17	119
5:3	29, 77	11:23–26	70	1:18–2:13	71
5:6	77	12–14	154	1:19	143
5:6b	77	12:1–31	73	1:20	119
5:7	77, 116	12:2	47, 77	1:23	78, 119
5:9	26, 77, 111	12:6	53	2:1	117
5:9–13	111	12:11	53	2:1–4	26
5:11	77	12:13	48	2:4	117
5:12	94	13	73, 153, 154	2:14	42, 69,
5:13	94	13:2	134		82, 119,
6:1–11	113	14:3	56		121, 144
6:2	77	14:3–5	91	2:14–17	78
6:3	77	14:17	91	2:14–33	42
6:7–9	117	14:21	77	2:14–3:6	42
6:9	77	14:33	93	2:14–4:6	119
6:9–11	101	14:33b	135	2:15	94
6:12	70, 93, 116	14:34	77	2:16	78
6:12–7:40	103, 111	15	72, 135	2:17	43, 48, 119
6:15	77	15:1	32, 43, 45	3:1–3	117
6:15–17	116	15:1–3	70	3:1–6	119
6:16	77	15:1–58	117	3:5	78
6:19	134	15:3	50, 113	3:6	78
7:1	103	15:3–4	45, 113, 135	3:14	120
7:10	134	15:3–5	145	3:15	120
7:25	70	15:11	48	3:18	92, 119
8:1	91	15:12	113, 116, 117	4:1	120, 158
8:1–13	73, 113	15:14	43	4:1–6	157
8:3	93	15:51	77	4:2	43, 48, 120
8:6	70, 77	15:54	144	4:3–4	147
8:11	117	15:57	82	4:4	43, 48, 50, 120
9	73	16:1	32	4:5	43, 120
9:1–23	41	16:8–10	40	4:6	42, 120
9:4	134	16:15	93	4:7	120
9:10	77	16:21	28	4:10	69, 146
9:14	134	16:23	81	4:10–11	69
9:16	41, 43, 144			4:12	53
9:18	43	**2 Corinthians**	**18, 160**	4:16	120, 158
10:1–22	73	1.1	76, 93	5:7	120
10:11	77	1:1–2:13	119	5:11	120
10:14	80	1:2	80	5:11–12	120
10:23	70, 91, 116	1:3–7	55	5:11–20	159
10:23–11:1	73, 113	1:6	53	5:11–6:2	119, 144
10:33	70	1:12–2:13	69	5:12	120
11:2	77, 96, 135	1:12–14	71, 119	5:12–21	120
11:2–14:40	72	1:13	26	5:13	121
11:16	135	1:14	80, 90, 120	5:14	122, 145
11:17–34	113, 117	1:15–23	155	5:14b–15	121

5:16	44, 122	12:14	80	6:11	28
5:17	122, 124	12:14–15	76	6:11–17	72
5:18	122	12:14–21	70		
5:18–6:2	122	12:19	80	**Ephesians**	
5:19	43, 54, 122	12:20–21	101	1:2	80
5:19–20	54	13:2	32, 78	6:21	31
5:20	50, 123,	13:4	119		
	144, 147	13:10	78	**Philippians**	75
6:1–2	123, 144	13:12	93	1:1	93
6:3	146	13:14	81	1:2	80
6:3–10	146			1:12–26	69
6:11–12	70	**Galatians**	**39**	1:14	144
7:1	80	1:3	80	1:27	56, 57, 111,
7:3	32	1:8	43		144, 147
7:5–16	69	1:8–9	43	1:29	146
7:6b	55	1:9	31	2:1	56
7:7	55	1:10–2:14	71	2:5	111
7:12ff	55	1:10–2:21	41, 69	2:6–11	110
8:9	145	1:11	43	2:12	80
8:10	70	1:11–24	12	2:13	53
9:15	82	1:15	41	2:15	93
10–13	70, 72, 118	1:16	41	2:16	90, 147
10:2	118	2:2	43	2:19–30	40
10:3	118	2:5	43	3:2–16	41
10:4	78, 79, 118	2:8	53	3:9	137
10:4–5	118	2:14	43	3:20	94
10:8	78	2:15–21	71	4:1	80
10:10	29, 37, 118	2:16–21	137	4:2–3	111
10:10–11	26, 62	2:21	110	4:9	134
10:12–18	117	3:2	25	4:21–22	93
10:16	43	3:5	53		
11:1	93	3:6	110	**Colossians**	
11:1–4	70, 147	3:21	110	1:2	80
11:2	92	3:27	48	1:23	43
11:4	43, 48	4:3	47		
11:5	78	4:8	47	**1 Thessalonians**	**17,**
11:6	37	4:9	93		**18, 36, 49**
11:7	43	4:13	43, 45, 50	1:1	79, 80, 93, 109
11:7–11	118	4:19	70, 79, 89, 147	1:2–3	50, 94
11:16–12:10	73	4:20	25	1:3	53, 101, 103, 133
11:21	119	5:5	110	1:4	50, 93, 98, 103,
11:23–29	146	5:11	48		109
11:28	90	5:14	144	1:4–2:12	50
11:29	119	5:19	134	1:5	50, 120, 133, 147
11:30	119	5:19–26	101	1:5–10	94
12:1	70	5:21	32	1:5–2:12	50
12:5	119	5:23–24	81, 82	1:6	50, 51, 53, 146
12:10	119	5:23–28	81	1:6–10	52, 53

1:7	94	3:7	103	5:23–24	81
1:8	50, 53	3:11	82	5:23–28	81
1:9	47, 50, 51, 53, 94,	3:12	101, 103	5:24	93
	105, 146	3:12–13	82	5:25	103
1:9–10	48, 51, 53, 95,	3:13	57, 91, 98, 100,	5:27	29
	109, 134		109		
1:10	46, 51, 91, 98	4–5	53	**2 Thessalonians**	**75**
2:1	50, 53, 54, 103,	4:1	76, 103, 133	2:5	32
	133	4:1–2	26, 54, 58, 71,	2:15	134
2:1–2	94		89, 101, 133	2:16–17	82
2:1–12	89, 94, 95	4:1–8	111	3:5	82
2:1–13	53	4:2	133	3:6	134
2:1–3:10	71	4:3	91, 98, 109, 149	3:16	82
2:2	54, 146	4:3–5:11	134		
2:3	54, 56, 95	4:3–8	134, 149	**2 Timothy**	
2:3–8	55	4:4	102	1:6	132
2:3–12	54	4:5	47, 94, 102	4:17	43
2:4	50, 55	4:6	26, 95		
2:4–5	51	4:7	95, 98, 109	**Titus**	
2:5	50, 54, 95, 133	4:8	91, 100, 149	1:3	43
2:7	56, 95	4:9	26, 134	3:1	132
2:8	55	4:9–12	95, 103		
2:9	26, 43, 50, 53, 54,	4:10	103	**Philemon**	**75**
	55, 103	4:13	47, 94, 103, 104	3	80
2:11	80, 133	4:13–5:11	89, 91,	7	80
2:11–12	56, 76, 89,		103, 109	8	76
	90, 147	4:14	50, 51, 95,	8–9	76
2:12	56, 57, 63, 93,		134, 145	10	45, 50
	95, 100, 147	4:17	104	19	28
2:13	25, 50, 51, 53, 92,	4:18	91	20	80
	120, 144, 147	5:1	26, 103, 133	22	40
2:13–3:10	95	5:1–2	134		
2:14	103	5:1ff	133	**James**	
2:17	80, 90, 94, 103	5:1–11	104, 151	1:21	51
2:19	94, 98, 147	5:4	103		
2:20	80, 90, 94	5:6	94	**2 Peter**	
3:1–5	94	5:8	101	1:12	132
3:2	89, 90	5:10	50, 145		
3:2–3	90	5:12	76, 103	**2 John**	
3:3	54, 57, 133, 146	5:12–13	104	12	24
3:4	26, 32, 133	5:14	76, 103, 104		
3:5	90	5:23	82, 91, 98, 100,	**Jude**	
3:6	89, 95, 101		105, 109	5	132

Index of Greek and Latin Sources

Aristotle — 61, 67, 71
Rhet. 1.2.5 — 70
Rhet. 1.2.13 — 70
Rhet. 1.3, 1358b, 22 — 70
Rhet. 2.1.2–3 — 68
Rhet. 3.13 — 71
Top. 1.1.100b — 78

Augustine
Doctr. chr. 4 — 67, 73

Cicero — 27
De or. 1.31.142 — 62
De or. 2.80 — 71
Her. 1.2.3 — 62
Inv. 1.7.9 — 62

Demosthenes — 27
Ep. 2 — 69
Ep. 3.35 — 35

Dio Chrysostom
Disc. 14.13–14 — 116

Epictetus
Diss. 4.16.14 — 118

Epicurus — 65

Ignatius — 34
Eph. 9.2 — 34
Magn. 1.1 — 34

Isocrates — 27, 35
Ep. 1–2 — 24

Justin
Apol. 1.67 — 22

Origen — 23

Philo
Conf. 128–31 — 118
Prob. 15 — 118

Plato — 65
Phaedr. 276a — 23
Resp. 602b–c — 24

Plutarch
Rom. xxv.4–xxxiv — 42
Vit. Ant. xxvi — 42

Quintilian — 27, 61
Inst. 1.11.2–14 — 30
Inst. 1.11.12 — 30
Inst. 2.5.8 — 30
Inst. 3.3.1 — 62
Inst. 3.8.22 — 70
Inst. 3.8.33 — 70
Inst. 5.11.1 — 70
Inst. 10.3.3 — 27

Seneca — 66